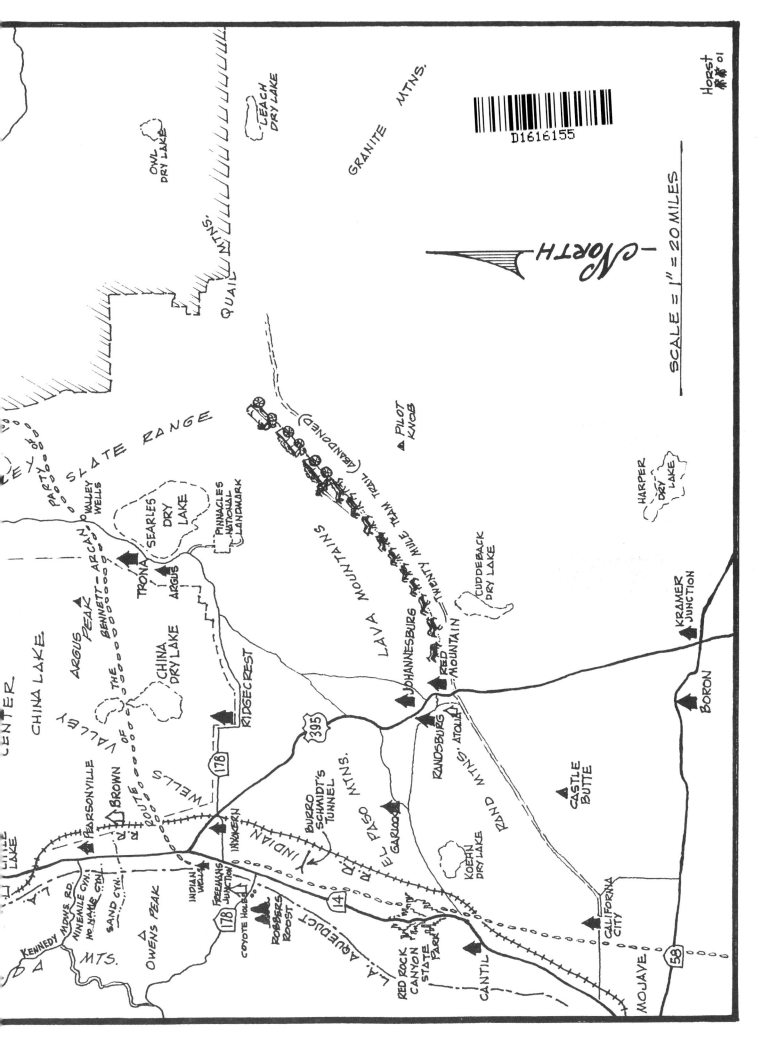

Desert Country

Desert Country

by Bob Powers

With a foreword by
Rod Middleworth

THE ARTHUR H. CLARK COMPANY
Spokane, Washington
2002

Library of Congress Card Number 2002025713
ISBN 0-87062-317-6

Library of Congress Cataloging-in-Publication Data

Powers, Bob, 1924–
    Desert country / by Bob Powers with a foreword by Rod Middleworth.
      p. cm.
    ISBN 0-87062-317-6
      1. Deserts—California, Southern—History. 2. California, Southern—Description and
travel. 3. California, Southern—History. 4. Death Valley (Calif. and Nev.)—Description
and travel. I. Title.

    F867 .P76 2002
    979.4′9—dc21   2002025713

This book is dedicated to

HENRY (HANK) SCHUETTE
and all the Early Timers
of the Indian Wells Valley

Contents

Acknowledgements

Without the help of many people this book would have never been published. I am deeply grateful to each one of you for your part in bringing this book to completion.

My gratitude goes to Hank Schuette for all his help and inspiration, Bill Horst for the great maps, Rod Middleworth for his proof reading and writing the foreword, Larry Holochwost for his proof reading, Juanita Kitchel for typing the captions for the pictures and Roberta Watson for the title page and cover lettering.

Many people were helpful with information and some checked the manuscript to insure the information was correct. Some of these people were: Mark Faull Supervising Ranger Red Rock Canyon State Park, Angelo and Joyce Nefos, Tonie Seger, Arzell Hale IMC Chemicals Trona, Marcia Wynn for the use of photos and text from Desert Bonanza, Winifred Hurst for information of goats on the Mojave Desert, John DiPol for his help with the Los Angeles Aqueduct, Claudine Ives McAlexander, The Maturango Museum and Historical Society of the Upper Mojave, Tom Chapman, Margaret Brush, the Ramsey Family, Liz Babcock and the *News Review* of Ridgecrest.

Foreword

There is no one more qualified to capture the written and pictorial account of the eastern California Desert, than this book's author, Bob Powers. Son of a 7th generation Kern County family, Bob lived, went to school, worked and traveled extensively throughout the vicinity covered in this, his ninth book.

If you drive Highways 14 and 395 between Mojave/Red Rock Canyon and Lone Pine/Owens Lake, or you drive east on Highway 190 to Death Valley, you pass through a land that is rich in history and filled with the nostalgia of forgotten times. In Desert Country Bob brings to life the eastern portion of this high desert and goes down to the depths of Death Valley. On the inside pages you will meet the pioneers and settlers of times past. Through words and pictures you will get to know the folks that built towns, pioneered the land and faced the hardships of those early days. You will even meet a few of the "characters", who added spice to the melting pot of desert settlers. Bob's easy style of storytelling grabs your interest and his pictures add a special flavor to the history of this arid land.

We think that when you are through and this book lies on your coffee table, you will find your mind wandering back to this land of high desert where you'll relive the experiences written by Bob and visualize how it once was and can never be again. You will have been captured by the essence of Desert Country.

Death Valley — Death Valley Borax

DEATH VALLEY—Just the name gives some people an uneasy feeling. Death Valley is remote from civilization, has a scarcity of water, and extreme summer temperatures. It is the deepest, driest, most hostile desert and here death can become a reality. However many people love this desert with its beautiful sunrises and sunsets, exotic desert animals, years when there are bountiful wild flowers, and strange mirages.

In 1849 the people who crossed the untracked wilderness of Death Valley understood what it was to face death. Two members of this group undertook one of the greatest acts of heroism that ever took place in the West.

On November 4, 1849, in Salt Lake City, Utah, a party of one hundred or so men, women and children left the Hunt party which had been traveling from Wisconsin and were headed to the gold fields of California. They struck off on their own because winter would soon be upon them and they had been told of a short cut to California, which would bypass the snowy passes. This short cut was the Old Spanish Trail. It wasn't long before this large group deserted their guide and broke up into seven smaller parties. Each took their own route through country they knew almost nothing about except that they would probably not have snow to contend with.

Although the number cannot be confirmed it is thought that as few as four or as many as thirteen left their bones bleached in the arid plains and mountains surrounding Death Valley during

'49. Most of the men that took the short cut trail lost as much as 100 pounds during their trip to California.

The party, which the most has been written about, was the Bennett-Arcan party. Those in this party were; Asabel Bennett, his wife Sarah, George who was eight years old, Melissa who was five and Martha who was one, Jean Baptiste Arcan, his wife Abigail, and Charles who was three. There were also two Earhart brothers, and a grown son, three unmarried men, 24-year old John Rogers, 29-year old Lewis Manly and 48-year old Captain Culverwell. Mr. Wade, his wife and three children did not mingle with this party, but usually camped a little distance off, following their trail, but shunning their company. It was Lewis Manly's book Death Valley in 49 that gave the most accurate record of the four months suffered by the 49ers in this desert. The book tells of the time spent trying to get from Salt Lake City to Los Angeles.

The plight of the Bennett-Arcan party had become desperate. They were running out of food with only a few small pieces of dry bread left. This was kept for the children, giving them a little now and then. The only other food was the oxen, and if they died, and after they were eaten, they knew they might starve. The party had a meeting to decide what course they were going to take.

The following excerpts are from Manly's book, Death Valley in 49:

Mr. Bennett said, "Now I will make you a

proposition. I propose that we select two of our youngest, strongest men and ask them to take some food and to go ahead on foot to try to seek a settlement, and food. We will go back to the good spring (Tule Spring near Furnace Creek) we have just left and wait for their return. It will surely not take them more than ten days for the trip, and when they get back we shall know all about the road and its character and how long it will take us to travel it. They can secure some other kind of food that will make us feel better, and when the oxen have rested a little at the spring we can get out with our wagons and animals and be safe. I think this is the best and safest way."

After a little discussion all seemed to agree that this was the best, and now it remained to find the men to go. No one offered to accept the position of advance messengers. Finally Mr. Bennett said he knew one man well enough to know that he would come back if he lived, and he was sure he would push his way through. "I will take (pick) Lewis Manly, if he will consent to go." I consented, though I knew it was a hazardous journey, exposed to all sorts of things, Indians, climate and probable lack of water, but I thought I could do it and would not refuse. John Rogers, a large strong Tennessee man, was then chosen as the other one and he consented also.

Now preparations began, Mr. Arcan killed the ox which had so nearly failed, and all the men went to drying and preparing the meat. Others made us some new moccasins out of rawhide, and the women made us each a knapsack.

Our meat was closely packed, and one can form an idea how poor our cattle were from the fact that John and I actually packed seven-eights of all the flesh of an ox into our knapsacks and carried it away. They put in a couple of spoonfuls of rice and about as much tea. This seemed like robbery to the children, but the good women said that in case of sickness even that little bit might save our lives. I wore no coat or vest, but took half of a light blanket, while Rogers wore a thin summer coat and took no blanket. We each had a small tin cup and a small camp kettle holding a quart. Bennett had me take his seven-shooter rifle, and Rogers had a good double-barreled shotgun. We each had a sheath knife, and our hats were small brimmed, drab affairs fitting close to the head and not very conspicuous to an enemy as we might rise up from behind a hill into possible view.

We tried on our packs and fitted the straps a little so they would carry easy. They collected all the money there was in camp and gave it to us. Mr. Arcan had about $30 and others threw in small amounts of money from forty cents upward. We received all sorts of advice. Mr. Bennett had known Lewis (Manly) as a hunter for many long years, and knew that if he went over a place in the daytime he could find his way back at night every time. Others cautioned us about the Indians and told us how to manage. Others told us not to get caught in deep snow, which we might find on the mountains.

This advice we received in all the kindness in which it was given, and then we bade them all good bye. Some turned away, too much affected to approach us and others shook our hands with deep feeling, grasping them firmly and heartily hoping we would be successful and be able to pilot them out of this dreary place into a better land. Every one felt that a little food to make a change from the poor dried meat would be acceptable. Mr. and Mrs. Bennett and J. B. Arcan and wife were the last to remain when the others had turned away. They had the most faith in the plan and felt deeply. Mrs. Bennett was the last, and she asked God to bless us and bring some food to her starving children.

We were so much affected that we could not speak and silently turned away and took our course again up the canyon we had descended the night before. After a while we looked back and when they saw us turn around, all the hats and bonnets waved us a final parting.

By night we were far up the mountain, near the perpendicular rough peak, and far above us on a slope we could see some bunches of grass and sage brush. We went to this and found some small water holes. No water ran from them, they were so small. Here we stayed all night. It did not seem very far to the snowy peak to the north of us. Just higher peaks and the rocks looked as if they were too steep to be got over.

Through this gap came a cold breeze, and we had to look round to get a sheltered place in which to sleep. We lay down close together, spoon fashion, and made the little blanket do as cover for the both of us. In the morning we filled our canteens, which we had made by binding two powder cans together with strips of cloth, and started for the summit near by. From this was the grandest sight we ever beheld. Looking east we could see the country we had been crawling over since November 4th! "Just look at the cursed country we have come over!" said Rogers as he pointed over it. To the north was the biggest mountain we ever saw (Telescope Peak) with snow covering the peaks, which was apparently everlasting.

This mountain seemed to have very few trees

on it and in extent, as it reached away to the north, seemed interminable. South was a nearly level plain, and to the west I thought I could dimly see a range of mountains that held a little snow upon their summit. [The Sierra Nevada]. It seemed to me the dim snowy mountains must be as far as 200 miles away, but of course I could not judge accurately. We asked each other what we supposed the people we left behind would think to see mountains so far ahead.

We saw at once to go over all these mountains and return within the limits of fifteen days which had been agreed upon between us, would probably be impossible, but we must try as best we could, so down the rocky steep we clambered and hurried on our way. In one place we found a little water and filled our canteens, besides drinking a good present supply.

Near by and a short distance north was a lake of water and when we reached the valley we crossed a clear stream of water flowing toward the lake. Being in need of water, we rushed eagerly to it and prepared to take a big drink, but the tempting fluid was as salt as brine and made our thirst all the more intolerable. Nothing grew on the bank of this stream and the bed was of hard clay, which glistened in the sun.

We now began the ascent of the next ridge, keeping a westerly course, and walked as fast as we could up the rough mountainside. We crossed the head of a canyon near the summit about dark, and here we found a trail, which from indications we knew to be that of the Jayhawkers (an abolitionist guerrilla group from Missouri and Kansas in Civil War days). They had camped here and had dug holes in the sand in search of water. We stayed all night here and dug around in some other places in the bottom of the canyon. In the hope to have better luck than they did, but we got no water anywhere.

We seemed almost perishing for want of water, the hard exercise made us perspire so freely. In the morning we started on and near the summit we came to the dead body of Mr. Fish, laying in the hot sun, as there was no material near here with which his friends could cover the remains. This Mr. Fish was the man who left camp some two weeks before in the company with another.

As we came in sight of the next valley (Searles Lake Valley) we could see a lake of water some distance south. This valley we now crossed seemed to come to an end about ten miles to the north of us. To the south it widened out. This valley was very sandy and hard to walk over. When about halfway across we saw

some ox tracks leading toward the lake, and in the hope we might find the water drinkable we turned off at right angles to our course and went that way also. Long before we reached the water of the lake, the bottom became a thin slimy mud, which was very hard on our moccasins. When we reached the water we found it to be of a wine color, and so strongly alkaline as to feel slippery to the touch, and under our feet. This side trip had cost us much exertion and made us feel thirstier than ever.

We now headed west again, making for a canyon (Argus Range northwest of Trona) up which we passed in the hope we should at some turn find a little basin or rain water in some rock. We traveled in it miles and miles, and our mouths became so dry we had to put a bullet or a small smooth stone in and chew it and turn it around with the tongue to induce a flow of saliva. If we saw a spear of green grass on the north side of a rock, it was quickly pulled and eaten to obtain the little moisture it contained. We traveled along for hours, never speaking, for we found it much better for our thirst to keep our mouths closed as much as possible, and prevent the evaporation. Thirst began to be something terrible to endure, and in the warm weather and hard walking we had secured only two drinks since leaving camp.

We were so nearly worn out that we tried to eat a little meat, but after chewing a long time, the mouth would not moisten it enough so we could swallow, and we had to reject it. It seemed as if we were going to die with plenty of food in our hand, because we could not eat it.

We tried to sleep but could not, but after a little rest we noticed a bright star two hours above the horizon and from the course of the moon we saw the star must be pretty truly west of us. We talked a little, and the burden of it was a fear that we could not endure the terrible thirst a while longer. The thought of the women and children waiting for our return made us feel more desperate than if we were the only ones concerned. We thought we could fight to the death over a water hole if we could only secure a little of the precious fluid. No one who has ever felt the extreme of thirst can imagine the distress, the despair, which it brings, I can find no words, no way to express it so others can understand.

The moon gave us so much light that we decided we would start on our course, and get as far as we could before the hot sun came out, and so we went on slowly and carefully in the partial darkness. The only hope left to us being that our strength would hold out till we could get to the shining snow on the great mountain before us. We reached the foot of the range we were descending about sunrise.

We had no idea we could not find any water till we at least got very near the snow, and as the best way to reach it we turned up the wash although the course was nearly to the north. In order to not miss a possible bit of water we separated and agreed upon a general course and that if either one found water he should fire his gun as a signal. After about a mile or so had been gone out I heard Roger's gun and went in his direction. He had found a little ice that had frozen under the clear sky. It was not thicker than window glass. After putting a piece in our mouths we gathered all we could and put it into the little quart camp kettle to melt. We gathered just a kettle full, besides what we ate as we were gathering, and kindled a little fire and melted it.

I can but think how providential it was that we started in the night for in an hour after the sun had risen that little sheet of ice would have melted and the water sank into the sand. Having quenched our thirst we could now eat, and found that we were nearly starved also. In making this meal we used up all our little store of water, but we felt refreshed and our lives renewed so that we had better courage to go on.

All the way had been up hill and very tiresome walking. We were still several miles from the base of this largest of the largest mountain. As the sun got further down we could see a small smoke curling up near the base of the mountain. We thought it must be some signal made by the Indians, as we had often seen them signal in that way, but we stopped and talked the matter over. As we were yet a long way from the bluff which, had been our objective point, we concluded we would investigate the smoke signal a little closer. So we set off toward it in the dusk and darkness and when within about a mile we found we were in a tract that had been somewhat beaten. Feeling with my fingers I was quite sure I could distinguish ox tracks, and then was quite sure that we had overtaken the Jayhawkers, or at least were on their trail. And then I thought perhaps they had fallen among the Indians, who now might be feasting on their oxen and it became clear to us to use great caution in approaching the little smoke. (This did turn out to be the Jayhawkers who were hopeless and desperate. They asked Manly and Rogers to let their families know that they had died there in the desert. This happened at what is now Indian Wells on Highway 395 about five miles northwest of Inyokern.)

As we went down the canyon there was a spring of good water and some good grass growing around. This was pretty good evidence that some one had been here before. We took a good drink and filled our canteens anew, for we did not expect to get another drink for two or three days at least. (This was Desert Spring near the present Cantil.)

We took the trail again and hurried on as the good water made us feel quite fresh. After a few miles we began to find the bones of animals, some badly decayed and some well preserved. All the heads were those of horses and it puzzled us to know where they came from. As we passed along we noticed the trail was on a slight up grade and somewhat crooked. If we stepped off from it the foot sank in about two inches of dirt finer than the finest flour. The bones were scattered all along, sometimes the bones of several animals together. Was it the long drive, poison water, or what? It was evident they had not been killed but had dropped along the way. (While crossing the desert, these animals had died before they reached water) It was a dreary trail at best, and these evidences of death did not help to brighten it in the least. We were yet in the desert and if we kept our due west course we must cross some of the snow before us which if steep gave us some doubts whether we could get through or not. We did not know exactly what the people left behind would do if we were gone longer than we intended. If they started on it was quite plain to us they would be lost, and as seven days had already passed we were in serious trouble for fear we could not complete the trip in the time allotted to us.

As this low ground was quite wide we lost our trail in crossing it, and we separated as we went along, looking to find it again, till nearly dark when we looked for a camping place. Fortunately we found a little pond of rain water, and some strange trees (Joshua trees) that were dead gave us good material for a fire, so that we were very comfortable indeed, having both drink and fire.

Starting on again our course was now ascending slightly, and we came across more and more of the trees, and larger ones than at first. The bayonet shaped leaves seemed to fall off when old and the stalk looked so much like an old overgrown cabbage stump that we named them "Cabbage trees."

So we pushed on, still keeping a distance apart to look our for the trail. Before night in the rolling hills, we saw here and there faint traces of it, which grew plainer as we went along. About sundown we reached some water holes and from some old skulls of oxen lying around the ground showing that it had at some previous time been a camping ground. We found some good large sagebrush, which made a pretty good fire. But our poor meat was pretty dry food. However it kept us alive, and we curled up together and slept, for the night was cool, and we had to make the little blanket do its best.

In the morning the trail led us toward the snow, and as we went along, a brave old crow surprised us by lighting on a bush near the trail. We surprised him by killing him with a charge of shot. "Here's your fresh meat," said Rogers as he put it into his knapsack to cook for supper. We crossed over several miles of hard snow, it moistened up our moccasins and made them soft and uncomfortable. After we had turned down the western slope we killed a small hawk. "Here's your meat," said I, as the poor thin fellow was stowed away for future grub, to cook with the crow.

We followed down a ravine for many miles and when this came out into a larger one, we were greatly pleased at the prospect. For down the latter came a beautiful running brook of clear pure water, singing as it danced over the stones, a happy song and telling us to drink and drink again. You may be sure we did drink, for it had been months and months since we had had such water, pure, sweet, free from the terrible alkali and stagnant taste that had been in almost every drop we had seen. Rogers leveled his shotgun at some birds and killed a beautiful one with a topknot on his head, and colors bright all down his neck. It was a California quail.

We dressed our three birds and got them boiling in the camp kettle, and while they were cooking talked over the outlook which was so flattering that our tongues got loose and we rattled away in strange contrast to the ominous silence of a week ago. As to these birds, the quail was a superb morsel as ever a man did eat; the hawk was pretty fair and quite good eating; but that abominable crow! His flesh was about as black as his feathers and full of tough and bony sinews. We concluded we did not want any more of that kind of bird, and ever since that day, when I have heard people talk of "eating crow" as a bitter pill, I think I know all about it from experience.

There seemed to be no other way for us but to push on in the morning and try to obtain some relief for the poor women and children and then get back to them as fast as ever we could. We shouldered our packs and went down the canyon as fast as we could. About 10

o'clock I felt a sudden pain in my left knee, keen and sharp, and as we went along it kept growing worse. I had to stop often to rest and it was quite plain that if this increased or continued I was sure enough disabled, and would be kept from helping those whom we had left. I hobbled along as well as I could but soon had to say to Rogers that he had better go on ahead and get help and let me come on as fast as I could. For every moment of delay there was a danger of death to our party who trusted us to get them help. Rogers refused to do this, he said he would stay with me and see me out, and that he could not do much alone, and had better wait till I got better. I endured the pain all day, and we must have advanced quite a little distance in spite of my lameness, but I was glad when night came and we camped in the dark brushy canyon, having a fire which made me quite comfortable all night. I felt a little better in the morning and after eating some of our poor dried meat, which was about as poor as crow but a little worse, we continued on our way.

The hope was that my lameness might not continue to retard our progress in getting back to the place of our starting. And, that the poor waiting people might begin to get out of the terrible country they were in and enjoy as we had done, the beautiful running stream on this side of the mountain. If I did not get better the chances were that they would perish, for they never could come through alone, as the distance had proved much greater than we had anticipated, and long dry stretches of desert were more than they would be prepared for. As it was we feared greatly that we had consumed so much time they would get impatient and start out and be lost.

I continued to hobble along down the barren valley as well as I could and here and there some tracks of animals were discovered, but we could not make out whether they were those of domestic cattle or elk. Before us now was a spur from the hills that reached nearly across our little valley we climbed up over it to shorten the distance. When the summit was reached a most pleasing sight filled our sick hearts with a most indescribable joy. I shall never have the ability to describe the beauty of the scene as it appeared to us. So long as I live that landscape will be impressed upon the canvas of my memory as the most cheering in the world. There before us was a beautiful meadow of a thousand acres, green as a thick carpet of grass could make it, and shaded with oaks. Over the broad acres of luxuriant grass was a herd of cattle numbering many hundreds, if not thousands.

Such a scene of abundance and rich plenty and comfort bursting thus upon our eyes which for months had seen only the desolation and sadness of the desert, was like getting a glimpse of Paradise, and tears of joy ran down our faces. This was suddenly opened to us on that bright day which was either one of the very last of December 1849 or the first of January 1850. I am inclined to think it was the very day of the New Year, but in our troubles, the accuracy of the calendar was among the least of our troubles.

Down by a gully, cut by the rains, a yearling steer was feeding and I took the rifle and crawled down near him and put first one ball through him and then another, before he fell dead. We quickly got some good meat and had it roasted and eaten almost quicker than can be told.

We hardly realized how near starved we were till we were satisfied for once and till we had plenty before us again. We ate till we were satisfied for the first time in many long dreary weeks. We kindled a fire and commenced drying the meat, one sleeping while the other kept the fire, and changing off every four hours. What a rest that was! One who has never been nearly worn out and starved, down nearly to the point of death, can never know what it is to rest in comfort. How we felt the strength come back to us with that food and the long draughts of pure clear water. I was still very lame and as we started along the walking seemed to make it worse again, so that it was all I could do to follow John on the trail down the valley.

A house on higher ground soon appeared in sight. (This was the del Valle home one-half mile south of Newhall Ranch Service Station at the junction of Ventura Highway 126 and Highway 5) As we came near the house no person was seen, but a mule tied to a post told us there was someone about, and a man soon made an appearance. As we came near we saluted him, bidding him good morning, and he in turn touched his hat politely, saying something in reply, which we were not able to understand. I showed him that I was lame, and taking out some money pointed to the mule, but he only shook his head and said something I could not comprehend. Rogers now began looking around the house, which was built of sun dried bricks about one by two feet in size, and one end was used as a storehouse. As he looked in, a man came to him and wanted a black, patent leather belt, which Rogers wore, having a watch-pocket attached to it. He offered a quart or more of coarse corn meal, and Rogers made the trade.

We tried to inquire where we were or where we ought to go, but could get no satisfactory answer from the man. So we concluded to go on a little way at least, and I hobbled off in the direction he pointed. As we passed on a mile or two we stopped on a big patch of sand to rest. Rogers wet up a part of his meal with water and put it to bake on the cover of his camp kettle. There was a fair sized cake for each of us, and it was the first bread of any kind we had eaten in months. Being a very acceptable change from an exclusively meat diet.

Looking up the valley we could see a cloud of dust thick and high, and soon several men on horseback who came at a rushing gallop. I told Rogers they were after us, and believed them to be a murderous set that might make trouble for us. I hastily buried our little store of money in the sand, telling him that if they got us, they would not get our money. Putting our guns across our laps in an easy position we had them cocked and ready for business, and our knives where we could get them handy, and awaited their arrival.

They came on with a rush until within a short distance and halted for consultation just across the creek. One of them advanced toward us and as he came near us we could see he was a white man, who wished us good evening in our own language. We answered him rather coolly, still sitting in the sand. He asked us where we were from and we told him our circumstances and condition and that we would like to secure some means of relief for the people we had left in the desert, but our means were very limited and we wanted to do the best we could. He said we were about 500 miles from San Francisco, not far from 100 miles from the coast and thirty miles from Los Angeles. He told us to go across the valley to a large oak tree, which he pointed out, and said we would find an American there, and we should wait there till morning. He said he would go back and stay at the house we had passed, and would do what he could to assist us to go to Los Angeles where we could get some supplies. We saw no way but to follow the directions of our newfound friend.

The time for our return was almost up and there was no way of getting back in fifteen days as we had agreed upon, so there was great danger to our people yet. It seemed very likely to take us twenty-four or thirty days at best, and while they probably had oxen enough to provide them with food for so long a time they might take a notion to move on, which would be fatal.

At the big oak tree we found an American camped, who was on his way to the gold mines.

As soon as were alone (after the camper had gone to sleep) Rogers mixed up some more of the meal which we baked in our friend's frying pan, and we baked and ate and baked and ate again, for our appetites were ravenous, and the demand of our stomachs got the better of the judgment of our brains.

It was hard to find time to sleep, we were so full of the plans about the way, which we must manage to get relief for the people. We had many doubts if animals could ever come over the route we had come over. Our sleep was troubled from another cause. Being so long unaccustomed to vegetable food and helped on no doubt by our poor judgment in gauging the quantity of our food, we were attacked by severe pains in the stomach and bowels, from which we suffered intensely. We arose very early and with a light breakfast, for the sickness admonished us, we started back for the house we had first passed, at which our friend on horseback, said he would spend the night and where we were to meet him this morning. He said he could talk Spanish all right and would do all he could to help us.

Our suffering and trouble caused us to move very slowly, so that it was nine or ten o'clock before we reached the house, and we found they had two horses all ready for us to go to Los Angeles. There were no saddles for us, but we thought this would be a good way to cure my lameness. We mounted, having our packs on our backs, and our guns before us, and with a friendly parting to the people who did not go, all four of us started on a trip of thirty miles to the town of Los Angeles. When we reached the foot of the mountain there appeared to be one quite large house in sight, and not far off, which the man told us was the Mission of San Fernando, a Roman Catholic Church and residence for priests and followers. We would dismount and let our leaders get half a mile or so ahead of us and then mount and put our horses to a gallop till we overtook them again. We had walked so long that riding was very tiresome to us, and for comfort alone we would have preferred the way on foot, but we could get along a little faster, and the frequent dismounting kept us from becoming too lame from riding.

About noon we met a man on horseback who lived up to the north about a hundred miles. His name was French and he had a cattle range at a place called Tejon. He said Los Angeles was so clear of emigrants that he did not think we could get any help there at the present time. Now, said Mr. French, "You boys can't talk Spanish and it is not very likely you will be able to get any help. Now I say, you boys turn back and go with me and I will give you the best I have, I will let you have a yoke of gentle oxen, or more if you need them, and plenty of beans, which are good food for I live on them. Besides this I can give you an Indian guide to help you back. Will that do?" After a moment we said we doubted if oxen could be gotten over the road. We wanted to get something for the women and children to ride, for we knew we must abandon the wagons, and could not walk so far over that dry, rough country.

"Well," said Mr. French, "I will stop at the place you were this morning, I know them well, and they are good folks, and I am sure when I tell them what you want they will help you if they possible can." This looks to me to be the most sensible course. For us to go clear back to his range would take up so much valuable time that we were almost afraid of the delay which might mean destruction to our friends. French said he had a packsaddle with him, and we could put it on one of our horses.

When night came we were again at the Mission we had passed on the way down. We were kindly treated here. They gave us good dried meat to eat and let us sleep in the big house on the floor, which was as hard as granite. We offered to pay them, but they would take nothing from us, and we left leading our horses over the steep mountain, and reaching the house again late in the day.

We were very tired and sat down by the side of the house and rested. A dark woman came out and gave each of us a piece of cooked squash. We were given a place to sleep in the house, in a storeroom on a floor, which was not soft. This was the second house we had slept in since leaving Wisconsin, and it seemed rather pent-up to us.

In the morning we were shown a kind of mill like a coffee mill, and by putting in a handful of wheat from a pile and giving the mill a few turns we were given to understand we should grind some flour for ourselves. After a little while our dark woman came and gave us each a pancake and piece of meat and also another piece of roasted squash. This we thought, was the best meal we had ever eaten. The lady tried to talk to us but we could not understand the words, and I could convey ideas to her better by the sign language than any other way. She pointed out the way, from which we came and wanted to know how many day's travel it might be away. I answered by putting my hand to my head and closing my eyes, which was repeated as many times as there had been nights on our journey, at which she was much surprised that the folks were so far away. She then placed her hand upon her breast and then held it up, to ask how many women there were, and I answered by holding up three fingers, at which she shrugged her shoulders and shook her head. Then pointing to a child by her side and in the same way asked how many children. I answered by holding up four fingers, and she almost cried, opening her mouth in great surprise, and turned. I shall never forget the kindness of those original Californians.

The provisions we prepared were, a sack of small yellow beans; a small sack of wheat, a quantity of good dried meat, and some of the coarse, unbolted flour we had made at the mill. They showed us how to properly pack the horse, which was a kind of work we had not been used to, and we were soon ready for a start. I took what money we had and put it on a block, making signs for them to take what the things were worth. They took $30 and we were quite surprised to get two horses, provisions, packsaddles and ropes, some of the latter made of rawhide and some of hair, so cheaply. To make it easy for us they had also fixed our knapsacks on the horses.

The good lady with the child, came out with four oranges and pointed to her own child and then to the East, put them in the pack meaning we should carry them to the children. With a hearty good bye from them and a polite lifting of our hats to them we started on our return.

Toward night we came to a wagon road crossing the valley. We kept on the road for a few miles and overtook a wagon in their camp and camped with them over night. We told them we considered our outfit entirely too small for the purpose intended, which was to bring two women and four children out of the desert, but that being the best we could get. One man offered to sell us a poor little one-eyed mule, its back all bare of covering from the effect of a great saddle sore that had very recently healed. He had picked it up somewhere in Arizona where it had been turned out to die. The beast became mine at the price of $15 and the people expressed great sympathy with us and the dear friends we were going to try to save.

Another man offered a little snow-white mare, as fat as butter, for $15, which I paid, though it took the last cent of money I had. This little beauty of a beast was broken to lead at a halter, but had not been broken in any other way. Rogers said he would ride her where he could, and before she got to the wagons she would be as gentle as a lamb. He got a bridle

and tried her at once, and then there was a scene of rearing, jumping, and kicking that would have made a good Buffalo Bill circus in these days. No use, the man could not be thrown off, and the crowd cheered and shouted to Rogers to "Hold her level."

After some bucking and backing on the part of the mare and a good deal of whipping and kicking on the part of the man, and a good many furious dashes in lively, but very awkward ways, the little beast yielded the point, and carried her load without further trouble.

The people gave us a good supper and breakfast, and one man came and presented us with 25 pounds of unbolted wheat flour. They were of great assistance to us in showing us how to pack and sack our load. This gave me a horse to ride and a mule to lead, while Rogers rode his milk-white steed and led the other horse. Thus we went along and following the trail soon reached the summit from which we could see off to the east a wonderful distance, probably 200 miles, of the dry and barren desert of hill and desolate valley over which we had come. We turned due east and soon came to a lake (Elizabeth Lake). Here we watered our animals and filled our canteens."

(They then steered a little southeast where they found the Jayhawkers trail, which they took, down a brushy canyon to a rain water hole. Getting water here they went back to the trail. They then went on to Desert Spring, one half-mile east of the present Cantil, where there was good water. The Jayhawker's oxen had eaten all the grass, so their animals had little feed. The next day they went by the water holes at Indian Wells. These holes held about two pails of water each. The horses wanted water so badly they drank by putting their heads in up to their eyes and drank ravenously. It was thirty miles to the next water and night overtook them and they made a dry camp. The horses began to walk with drooping heads and slow, tired steps, so they divided the load among them all and walked to a site northeast of the present China Lake. The water here was so salty the horses would not drink it.)

The white animal left the trail and walked with full force, head first, against the solid rock. She seemed to be blind, and though we went quickly to her and took off the load she carried, she had stopped breathing by the time we had it done. Not knowing how far it was to water, nor how soon some of our other horses might fall, we did not tarry, but pushed on as well as we could, finding no water. We reached the summit and turned down a ravine, following the trail, and about dark came to the water they had told us about. (Indian Joe's Spring, near the north end of Searles Lake Valley.) There was water enough for us, but no grass. It seemed as if the horses were not strong enough to carry a load, and as we wanted them to get through if possible, we concluded to bury the wheat and get it on our return. Next morning the little mule carried all the remaining load, the horses bearing only their saddles, and they seemed hardly strong enough for that.

An important question was to be decided, and that was whether we should continue to follow the Jayhawker's trail which led far to the north or to cross the mountain so steep that it seemed as if a dog could hardly climb it. (Panamint Range) Our wagons were nearly due east from this point over the range, not more than fifty miles away. While to go around to the north was fully a hundred miles and would take us four or five days to make. The horses must have food and water by night or we must leave them to die. All things considered it seemed to be the quickest way to camp to try and get up a rough looking canyon, which was nearly opposite us on the other side. So we loaded the mule and left the Jayhawker's trail, taking our course south and went directly to the mouth of the canyon we had decided to take. The horses now had to be urged along constantly to keep them moving and they held their heads low down as they crept along seemingly so discouraged that they would much rather lie down and rest forever than take another step. We knew they would do this soon in spite of all our urging, if we could not get water for them. The canyon was rough enough where we entered it and a heavy up grade too. This grew more and more difficult as we advanced. The little mule skipped over as nimble as a well-fed goat, and rather seemed to enjoy a little variety in the proceedings. After some coaxing and urging the horses took courage to try the extra step and succeeded all right. A small pile of lone rocks enabled the mule to go over all right but all our efforts were not enough to get the horses along another foot. We had to leave the horses and go on. We removed the saddles and placed them on a rock, and after a few moments hesitation, we left the poor animals to their fate and moved along. Just as we were passing out of sight the poor creatures neighed pitifully after us. We both burst into tears, but it was no use to try to save them we must run the danger of sacrificing ourselves, and the little party we were trying so hard to save.

We found the little mule stopped by a still higher precipice rise of fully ten feet. Our hearts sank. The little mule looked around to us and then up the steep rocks before her with such knowing, intelligent look of confidence, that it gave us new courage. We decided to try to get the confident little mule over this obstruction. Gathering all the loose rocks we could we piled them up against the south wall, beginning some distance below. We built a sort of inclined plane along the walls gradually rising till we were nearly as high as the crest of the fall. It was all I could do to cross the space, and there was no foundation to enable us to widen it. We unpacked the mule and getting all our ropes together, made a leading line. We fastened the leading line to her and with one above and one below we thought we could help her to keep her balance. Without a moments hesitation she tried the pass. Carefully and steadily she went along, selecting a place before putting down a foot, and when she came to the narrow ledge leaned gently on the rope, never making a sudden start or jump, moving slowly along. There was now no turning back for her. She must cross this narrow place over which I had to creep on hands and knees, or be dashed down fifty feet to a certain death.

I tell you, friends, it was a trying moment. It seemed to be weighed down with all the trials and hardships of many months. It seemed to be the time when helpless women and innocent children hung on the trembling balance between life and death. Our own lives we could save by going back and sometimes it seemed as if we would perhaps save ourselves the additional sorrow of finding them all dead to do so at once. I was so nearly in despair that I could not help bursting in tears, and I was not ashamed of the weakness. Finally Rogers said, "Come Lewis" and I gently pulled the rope, calling the little animal, to make a trial. She smelled all around and looked over every inch of the strong ledge, then took one careful step after another over the dangerous place. The mule had no shoes and it was wonderful how her little hoofs clung to the smooth rock. We felt relieved. We would push on and carry food to the people, and we would save them all.

Around behind some rocks only a little distance beyond this place we found a small willow bush and enough good water for a camp. We had walked two days without water, and we were wonderfully refreshed. The way up this canyon was very rough and the bed full of sharp broken rocks cut through the bottoms of our moccasins and left us with bare feet. I took off one of my buckskin leggings and gave it to

Rogers, and with the other one for myself we fixed the moccasins with them as well as we could. But I think if our feet had been shod with steel, those sharp rocks would have cut through.

Starting early we made the summit about noon, and from here we could see the place where we found a water hole and camped the first night after we left the wagons. Down the steep canyon we turned, and over the sharp broken pieces of volcanic rock we hobbled along with sore and tender feet. At last we got down and camped on the same spot where we had set out twenty-five days before to seek the settlements.

From this place we had a wagon road to follow, but not a sign of a human footstep could we see. We were some seven or eight miles along the road when I stopped to fix my moccasin while Rogers went slowly along. When I had started up again I saw Rogers ahead leaning on his gun and waiting for me, apparently looking at something on the ground. As I came near enough to speak I asked what he had found and he said, "Here is Captain Culverwell, dead." He did not look much like a dead man. He lay upon his back with arms extended wide, and his little canteen, made of two powder flasks, lying by his side. This looked indeed as if some of our saddest foreboding were coming true. How many more bodies would we find? Or would we find the camp deserted, and never find a trace of the former occupants?

We marched toward camp like two Indians, silent and alert, looking out for dead bodies and live Indians. About noon, we came in sight of the wagons, still a long way off. Half a mile was the distance between the camp and us before we could see very plainly as they were in a little depression. We surely left seven wagons. Now we could see only four and nowhere the sign of an ox. No sign of life were anywhere about, and the thought of our hard struggles between life and death to go out and return with the fruitless results that now seemed apparent was almost more than human heart could bear.

We kept as low and as much out of sight as possible, trusting very much to the little mule that was ahead, for we watched her closely to see how she acted. She slowly walked along looking for food, and we followed a little way behind. We became more and more convinced that they had taken the trail of the Jayhawkers, and we had missed them on the road, or they had perished before reaching the place where we turned from their trail.

One hundred yards now to the wagons, and still no sign of life, no positive sign of death, though we looked carefully for both. Finally Rogers suggested that he had two charges in his shot gun and I seven in the Colt's rifle, and that I fire one of the shots and await results before we ventured any nearer. And now both closely watching the wagons I fired the shot. Still as death and not a move for a moment, and then as if by magic a man came out from under a wagon and stood up looking all around, for he did not see us. Then he threw up his arms high over his head and shouted, "The boys have come! The boys have come!" Then other bare heads appeared, and Mr. Bennett and wife and Mr. Arcan came toward us as fast as ever they could. The great suspense was over and our hearts were first in our mouths, and then the blood all went away and left us almost fainting as we stood and tried to step. Bennett and Arcan caught us in their arms and embraced us with all their strength. Mrs. Bennett when she came fell down on her knees and clung to me like a maniac in the great emotion that came to her, and not a word was spoken. They stopped two or three times, (walking back to camp) to speak but there was too much feeling for words, convulsive weeping would choke the voice.

Bennett soon found voice to say, "I know you have found some place, for you have a mule." Mrs. Bennett through her tears, looked staringly at us as she could hardly believe our coming back was a reality, and then exclaimed, "Good boys! O, you have saved us all! God bless you forever! Such boys should never die!" It was some time before they could talk without weeping. Hope had almost died within them.

We told them it must be 250 miles yet to any part of California where we could live. Then came the question, "Can we take our wagons?" You will have to walk was our answer, for no wagons could go over that unbroken road that we had traveled. As rapidly and carefully as we could we told them of our journey and the long distance between the water holes, and that we lost no time and yet had been twenty-six days on the road. For long distances the country was about as dry and desolate as the region we had crossed east of this camp. We told them of the scarcity of grass, and all the reasons that had kept us so long away from them.

It would be very difficult for anyone who has never been through the terrible suffering this little band of 49ers went through, to fully appreciate their feelings. As the men, women and children left their camp at Tule Springs, it is reported that almost to the last person they called out, "Good by Death Valley."

Although he tried, Manly could not find the adjectives to describe the feelings of the little band as they left Death Valley (north of where the Furnace Creek settlement is now) and started on the grinding journey back across the three separate mountain ranges to Rancho San Francisquita and the city of Los Angeles. Prospects did not look good. It was approximately 250 miles and by moving right along it had taken them 26 days to make the round trip and they were in better shape than most of the party they were attempting to rescue. They had brought a little flour and beans and some dried meat with fat on it. They still had the mule with them, but told the party they would have to abandon the wagons, as they could not make it over the route they had chosen. The canvases that had covered the wagons were used to make harnesses and packsacks, of a sort, for the oxen they had left. They made shoulder straps, hip straps, breasts straps and breaching to complete the harness. The only way they could fasten the bands around the animal was for one person to get on each side of the animal and pull it as tight as possible, then tie a knot, as they had no buckles or rings for their harness.

For the ox they called Old Crump, they took two strong Hickory shirts and by turning the sleeves inside out and sewing the necks up and sewing the two tales together it made two pockets that could be placed over Old Crump's back and would hold the two smallest children. Two bands were also tied around his body for two other children to hold on to.

One of the oxen carried two kegs of water. The other oxen carried the bedding. They took only a camp skillet in which to make soup, a tin cup each and some knives and spoons. Each one had some sort of canteen for water, which they would fill at every opportunity. They also had a shovel with which to bury Captain Culverwell and to pile up sand below the waterfall (precipice) to break the fall of the oxen in case they fell.

It was a difficult return trip with the women and children. They all arrived back in civilization on March 7th, a little over four months from the time they left Salt Lake City.

It would be very difficult for someone who had never been through the terrible suffering from thirst or hunger to fully appreciate this little party's feelings. The author feels that one of the greatest acts of heroism in history has to be that of Manly and Rogers making the 250 mile trip from Death Valley to civilization and back again. They did this to rescue the men, women and children with whom they had no family ties, but they had given their word and felt they had to carry out their promise or die trying.

DEATH VALLEY BORAX

When other 49ers crossed Death Valley they found, in several places, ore bearing large amounts of silver and gold. Stories of these finds brought many miners back into Death Valley as early as 1861. In the long run it wasn't gold or silver, but borax that paid the largest dividends. Although the 49ers had seen hundreds of acres of the glistening crystals on the dry lakebeds they didn't realize it could be made into borax or of its potential value. Borax was used for laundry, making jewelry, pottery making, preserving meat and scores of other uses. It was to become an American icon. It appeared in almost every home in America.

In 1872 borax sold for $700 per ton, but even after discovering this vast supply it was passed up because of the seemingly insurmountable job of hauling it to the railroad. Finally in the fall of 1881 Aaron Williams filed on a number of claims and then sold them to William T. Coleman and Francis M. Smith who created a monopoly on the distribution of most of American borax. Williams received $20,000 for his claims and was pleased, thinking he made a good deal. In all Coleman and Smith filed on 27 claims, totaling nearly 4,000 acres. In 1882 Phil Lee and two companions discovered a whole mountain of white salt just south of Furnace Creek wash, which they named Mountain Blanca. It was from this salt that borax was extracted. Coleman and Smith bought this discovery for a mere $4,000.

Soon, Coleman set up a plant near Furnace Creek called the Harmony Borax Works. Rudolph Neuchwander, a 45-year-old Swiss immigrant, was hired as superintendent. Three quarters of the forty men crew they hired were Chinese from San Francisco. They worked seven days a week, ten hours a day. Their pay was $1.50 a day for gathering the salt. Much of their pay came back to Coleman over the counter of his store for staples such as tea, rice and dried cuttlefish. It was hot, dusty backbreaking work out on the flats, scraping the salt into windrows, shoveling it into hand-

Harmony Borax works
at Furnace Creek

carts and then into wagons to be hauled to the works. At the works the job wasn't much more inviting, even though it paid 50 cents a day more. These men had to shovel the salt into two tanks, one that held 3,000 gallons and the other holding 2,000 gallons where it had to be stirred while it boiled. Some of the men also had to gather greasewood to fire the boilers. After the salt was boiled it became borax. Few of these workers ever returned for another year.

The Harmony Borax Mining Company was producing about 2 million pounds of borax per year from the Death Valley and Amargosa deposits and in 1886 the company started shipping a comparable amount of coleminite from deposits discovered near Calico. Coleminite is a mineral in the same group as borax and was named after its discover, William H. Coleman. Coleminite was shipped to San Francisco to be used in the manufacturing of glass. The problem was how to transport all those many tons to the Atlantic Pacific Railroad at Daggett. Charles Bennett hauled all of Coleman's material out. First Bennett hauled to the Daggett railroad station, but later found a better route by leaving his old road at Granite Wells and heading straight for Mojave which also had a railroad. Coleman hired a man by the name of J.S.W. Perry to build

ten giant wagons to carry the borax from the Harmony Works and the coleminite from the Calico Mountains.

Mr. Perry knew the following facts. There were only three watering places between Mojave and Death Valley. It was a little over 50 miles from Mojave to the first spring, called Black Water. It was six and one-half miles to the next watering spot at Granite Springs. The final spring was Lone Willow, 26 miles away. He also knew that a team hauling a heavy load could travel only about 15 miles a day. That meant long stretches without a watering place and there was no food for either men or animals along the way. Perry made a thorough study of all types of large wagons used by freighters. He obtained dimensions of these vehicles and the weight they could carry. The wagons were built in the town of Mojave, not on a contract job, but by work performed by the day.

Perry's blueprints called for wagons with rear wheels seven feet high and front wheels five feet high, each with steel tires eight inches wide, and one inch thick. The hubs were 18 inches in diameter and 22 inches in length. The spokes of split oak, measured five and one half inches wide at the hub and four inches wide at the point. The axletrees were solid steel bars, three and one half

DESERT COUNTRY

Right: Death Valley Borax

Below: On the return trip the wagons hauled hay and grain for all the overnight stops, going and coming.

inches square. The wagon beds measured sixteen feet long, four feet wide and six feet deep. Each empty wagon totaled 7,800 pounds. Loaded with borax it weighed 31,800 pounds. Two loaded wagons, plus the water tank, an additional 9,600 pounds, made a total load of 73,200 pounds or 31-1/2 tons. The cost of each wagon was approximately $900. They were so well constructed that after five years of constant use there had never been a failure.

While the ten wagons were being constructed, trip plans were scheduled through 165 miles of desert road so there would be stopping places at the end of a good day's journey. The surveyors realized that in certain steep places the time element would be different for the teams than when they were moving on flat areas. Perry realized that on returning to the valley the wagons would be much lighter and schedules were arranged taking this into consideration.

Ten stations were established at intervals for the heavily laden wagons heading for Mojave. Other stations cared for the wagons on the return trip. Where watering places were not available, dry camps were established. Iron tanks with a 500-gallon capacity were filled at springs and pulled behind the wagons, then refilled at the next spring when empty. At all stations feed boxes were built for hay and barley using the same alternating plan used for supplying water. Springs were developed, and others not on the direct wagon trail were made use of by connecting pipes, which brought water to the tank wagons. Black smithing equipment for emergencies was also provided at each camp.

It was soon discovered that twenty mules could pull more weight per mule than an eight or ten mule team could. Perry bought ten twenty-mule teams to pull his wagons. In each 20-mule team the "wheelers" were a pair of draft horses from the strongest and finest stock available the rest of the team were mules. The horses were hooked up to the singletree immediately in front of the wagon. A chain was attached to the breast strap on the lower part of the collar of each wheeler. This chain supported the wagon tongue. Horses were usually heavier and their weight made it easier for them to handle the wagon tongue when it whipped over rough ground and on sharp turns. It was much easier to call them a twenty-mule team instead of a two horse and eighteen-mule team. The lead pair of this historic string of animals was mules, harnessed 100 feet in front of the wagon and controlled by a cotton jerk line. A steel chain stretched from the front axle to the front team of mules, equipped at intervals with spreaders and singletrees for the other nine pair of mules. The lead pair was trained to take a position at the head of this long chain, and the other mules would then fall into place. Each mule knew its own place in the "string." In front of the wheelers were placed the pointers who worked on the end of the tongue, while ahead of them were the "sixes," the "eighths," the "tens," and on to the leaders. Thus the "20 mule team!" The driver's

Borax wagons hauling between Mojave and Death Valley, 1884

DESERT COUNTRY

Borax team leaving
Death Valley in 1884

whip had a six-foot handle and a 22-foot lash. He also carried a long braided leather whip, called a "blacksnake."

The real guiding power for the team was the jerk line. This line, a round cotton rope about a half inch thick, was attached to the bridle of the nigh (left) leader and ran the length of the team, through rings on the harness of each mule, back to the driver. This was the only means for the driver to communicate with the lead animals; a steady pull on the line indicated a left turn; a series of sharp jerks, a right turn. The mules instinctively followed the leaders.

There was a danger of pulling the wagons off the road on the sharp curves because of the tremendous power exerted as the animals turned. To counteract this, the pointers and sixes were trained to jump over the chain and pull furiously at an angle to the rest of the team until the wagons had safely reached the point of the turn. This was a very difficult maneuver, but one that was made several times each trip, and made safely.

The teamster had the job of inspecting each piece of harness as he harnessed and hooked-up the animals. The teamster then rode on the left 'wheeler' and handled the brake of the lead wagon. A swamper who had many duties assisted each driver. He rode on the rear wagon and took care of the brake on the downhill

grades. The swamper also had charge of camp, gathering the fuel for fires, cooking and washing the dishes. Not the least of his duties was keeping a supply of rocks on hand to throw at the mules to keep them moving on the upgrades. Profanity, too, is said to have become a master art with the swampers.

The drivers and swampers had to be skilled in ways other than driving and urging the animals onward. They had to know how to care for a sick animal, and how to shoe one, (especially a high-kicking mule). They had to endure heat and exposure to sun and cold winds. There is no doubt, they and the drivers were special men.

Teamsters earned from $100 to $120 per month, when wages for most jobs were about $30 a month, but they were worth every penny. The round trip from Death Valley to Mojave, which was 330 miles, took 20 days and ran like clockwork. They were paid at Mojave at the end of each trip and had only one afternoon and evening for a fling till they would start out again. These teams ran for nine months each year from mid September to mid June and they never lost a wagon or an animal. Larger teams have been used at various times in the West but it was the teams of Pacific Coast Borax Company that would later immortalize its advertising campaign for "Twenty Mule Team Borax"

Although the twenty-mule teams only oper-

Left: "Old Dinah" Burned one and a half ton of coal per day. She was used for one year

Below: "Old Dinah" on display in 2002 at Furnace Creek Ranch in Death Valley

ated from 1884 until 1889 the trademark of the Twenty-Mule Team Borax became the most recognized trademark in America.

By 1887, because there was so much borax being produced, the price had fallen to $120 a ton in San Francisco from a high of nearly $300 a ton just four years before. In 1886 Coleman, then in his early sixties, turned his business over to his two junior partners, Carlton, his youngest son and Frank S. Johnson. First the partners tried to take over the Pacific canned salmon industry and also the raisin market. They lost over one million on raisins in just one year. Coleman started negotiating the sale of the Death Valley Borax operation to bail them out. He was just about to close the sale with an Englishman for two million dollars when Congressman Roger Q. Mills of Texas introduced a tariff reform bill to remove the duty on a number of commodities, including borax. With the possibility of foreign competition, Coleman's buyer backed out; the creditors demanded payments and Coleman's empire collapsed on May 7, 1899.

The Harmony Borax Mining was promptly shut down, never to resume. Death Valley mule teams days were over and the great wagons and teams dispersed. Sixteen years after the teams stopped hauling in Death Valley the famous wagons were sent on a tour of the United States as an advertisement for U.S. Borax. They appeared at the St. Louis World's Fair and many State Expositions and rumbled along in city parades. The tourist who rode on the wagons had a taste of the Old West. In 1917 they appeared in the Tournament of Roses Parade in

Pasadena, where they won first place. In 1937 they were at the opening of the Oakland Bay Bridge. This same year, fifty-two years after they were built, a 20-mule team drew two of the wagons over the original route from Death Valley to Mojave with no break down.

When the California Centennial celebration was held in Death Valley in 1949 they made a spectacular appearance. In 1998 the president of the Tournament of Roses requested they take part in the parade again, and this was to be their last appearance. However, in 1999 they showed up for the first time in fifty years for the Death Valley 49ers Encampment at Furnace Creek in Death Valley.

"Death Valley Days" started as a radio show with the Old Ranger Stanley Andrews, telling true stories about Death Valley. The Twenty-Mule Team Borax was their trademark. Then in 1952 the show switched to television and the twenty-mule team was seen on every episode. This show ran for eighteen years and was one of the most successful shows of its time. Western history came alive to the audience. There were five hosts during its run starting with Stanley Andrews and including the young Ronald Reagan.

While Francis Smith was head of the combined borax companies of the desert he felt there should be some other method of hauling more modern than the mule outfit. He purchased a traction engine (which the miners called "Old Dinah") together with two ore wagons. The engine burned a tremendous amount of coal—a ton and a half daily—for the trip between the borax mines in the Calico Mountains and the railroad at Daggett. The engine went about three and a half miles an hour on hard, level ground, but did not do so well in the soft sand stretches. The crew, consisting of an engineer, a fireman and a brakeman, claimed she went upgrade like climbing a bar of soap, slipping and sliding with the wheels out in front rearing up like a bucking mule. It took a mechanic's service all night, after each day's run, to put it in shape for the next day's run. At the end of the first year the engine was abandoned and the mules were back on the job. "Old Dinah" stands today as a museum piece on the grounds at Furnace Creek Ranch in Death Valley along with one of the original 20 mule team borax wagons—both of them a mute tribute to the days of long ago when strong, rugged men were trying to 'tame' Death Valley.

The first camp in Randsburg. left to right Burcham, Singleton and Mooers, locating the now famous Yellow Aster Mine. Unidentified miner at far right,.

The Rand Mining District
Randsburg, Garlock, Johannesburg, Atolia, Red Mountain

RANDSBURG

In the southern end of Kern County in the early 1890s there was quite a bit of gold mining activity in an area that was called the New Summit Dry Diggings. There were several small groups of miners working the gulches and washes. As there was no water in the area, they used the dry wash method for placer mining. They would use small machines that were hand operated. By turning a crank to power a fan they blew away the light material, it would save the heavier material that contained the gold. They would later have to pan this out using a small amount of water to separate the gold from the black sand that was almost as heavy as the gold.

Most of these miners only received about one and a half to two dollars a day for their efforts. There were no businesses in the area and supplies had to be hauled from Goler, which was ten miles north of Randsburg. Working together in this area in the early days of 1895 were three miners, John Singleton, Frederic M. Mooers and Charles A. Burcham. Burcham's wife, Rose La Monte Burcham, a physician in San Bernardino, had financed their prospecting venture. They were about ready to leave because they had run out of cash when Frederic Mooers found a piece of float (a piece of rock that has washed down off a ledge) that had specks of gold in it. This changed their minds and they wanted to stay in this area long enough to prospect, because this

area had not been covered by other prospectors up to this time.

Burcham went back to his wife and got another grubstake which she told him would be the last. They set up their camp on the side of a hill and started looking for promising outcroppings. Singleton knocked off a chunk of rock from an outcropping that looked different from other rocks in the area. He stared in disbelief and let out a yell! This was on April 25, 1895. They started to dig a shaft. Because the gold ore they found resembled the rich strike in the Rand District of South Africa they called the mining district Rand. Their camp was also called Rand. Later when it became a town, it was named Randsburg.

Being careful not to disclose their discovery and after staking out their claims and recording them, Burcham headed for San Bernardino to get the financing for more supplies needed to develop their work. Mooers and Singleton stayed at the spot.

Doctor Rose Burcham finally agreed to finance them, but told them again that this was the last time she would give them any money. When Burcham arrived back at their claims he found that in his absence his partners had started financing on their own. They had been offered $10,000 to put up a mill for half interest in the claims and a six-month option to buy the property for $500,000. Mooers and Singleton were eager to sign the papers because after being down to their last cent this sounded like a mar-

Discoverers of the Yellow Aster: Charles Austin Burcham, John Singleton, and Frederic M. Mooers

velous deal. Burcham couldn't sign without the consent of his wife because to get the last financing he had signed over fifty percent of his interest to her. He wrote to her and explained what he thought was too good a deal to pass up. Rose was leery of jumping into anything this quick. She wrote to her husband to meet her in Mojave and packed her bags.

After a long, slow trip by train to Mojave, her husband met her with a team and light wagon. They still had 50 miles to travel in the desert's July heat before arriving at their camp. It was dark by the time they reached Garlock so they decided to camp there for the night. This way they would leave the long climb to the camp for the next morning when the team would be rested.

Nothing that Rose Burcham's husband had told her could have prepared her for the camp. There were just a few tents perched on the side of the mountain beside a small shallow exploratory shaft. The partners probably thought Rose would head back to San Bernardino when she saw the primitive conditions she would be living under, but they were wrong! By the time they arrived at the camp she had a pretty good idea of the sort of country in which she'd bought an interest. She climbed down stiffly from the unrelentingly hard seat of Burcham's wagon. It had been like riding a wooden saddle on a sawhorse, those hot, dusty fifty miles from Mojave. She didn't complain, nor was she too tired from her traveling to take a quick look around. She noted there were only a few miners, whose numbers she calculated by the tents, scat-

tered on the slopes of the mountain. This surprised her. She had concluded from the excitement the discovery had created that there would be many more men. However she was unable to see that many miners were living off in little depressions in the hills, many of them burrowed into the sides of ravines.

She could not have known that not long after the three partners started developing their gold claims, other prospectors started moving in. They set up their tents and staked claims in the nearby washes and on the steep hillsides. Later in the day when so many appeared out of nowhere to greet their newest fellow citizen she was very surprised.

The three discoverers had established their own camp further up the mountain than the other miners, nearer the original discovery rock. When the doctor arrived at the upper camp it consisted of just two tents. This comprised all the shade there was in the owners' camp. That first summer the doctor took up her cooking and mining duties on the brown, dry slopes of Rand Mountain.

There were very few real conveniences. However, one they did have was the ever present, burlap-covered cooler of the desert dweller. These simple yet effective coolers were built out of various types of boxes, including old divided apple crates. Across the open face was hinged a screen door, and as a rule the backside was knocked out and covered with screen. Then the box was covered with several thicknesses of burlap. The burlap was kept wet by the cloth

The Baltic Mine with ten-stamp mill and cabins in the background. Placer operations in the foreground.

wick that trailed over it from a pan of water kept on the top of the cooler. In the dry atmosphere of the sage country these burlap coolers were most effective.

There was still another, simpler device of cooling in the camp. The men put their precious bottles of beer, after a trip to the stores in Goler, into their "horning" tub. This was a regular old-fashioned wash tub, the same type that was used for bathing and washing clothes. No matter how scarce water was, the men couldn't work without their "horning" water, which was used in testing pulverized ore as well as placer ground.

The doctor wore the long, sweeping skirts of the Gay Nineties, and high-necked shirtwaist, with long mutton-let sleeves and pinched-in, heavily corseted waist. But being a practical minded woman and remembering what her husband had told her of desert walking and camp

conditions, she had brought along some good stout walking shoes. And she came prepared to work, if that was what was necessary to win and hold a mine. She later would wear khaki clothes at the mine. It could, conceivably, be no tougher going than struggling against what she had encountered as a woman practicing medicine in a field that was traditionally masculine at that time. For a time she did the cooking for the four of them while the men dry-washed their placer and crushed by hand in small mortars the high-grade ore from their richest stringers. They did everything they could to bring in a few dollars for the first development work.

The doctor, having a practical mind, was nevertheless a woman. She couldn't resist tidying up the camp and adding a few feminine touches, one being the oilcloth she placed on the ground floor of the cook tent. She kept her hand in all the business matters, making sure her money wasn't wasted. The doctor went completely feminine and greenhorn when a big king snake sought the inviting shade of the cook tent one hot afternoon, and startled her nearly out of her high-buttoned shoes. She had just finished stirring up a batch of miners' biscuits, and as the unwelcome visitor slithered across the oilcloth floor, she instinctively aimed and threw the heavy mixing bowl at the intruder's head. Too late, she realized he was perfectly harmless and was as startled as she was. She might better have saved her biscuits!

Within the next few months Rose Burcham had a thorough course in roughing it. It might not be to her fancy, but the fact that she was camped on a mountain of treasure, of which she owned a share, made life easier to handle. What she lacked in mining experience she made up in business know how. She mistrusted all outside offers of financial assistance, realizing that to pursue such an easy course of developing the mine would eventually lose them control of the property. The men left much of the detail work of the business end in her hands. They were still pick and shovel

Dr. Rose LaMonte Burcham,
part owner of the Yellow Aster Mine

The young Rand Camp, January 1896

DESERT COUNTRY

A tent saloon in Rand Camp - 1895 with gambling tables.

miners; wheelbarrow engineers. Doctor Burcham was cook, bookkeeper and secretary.

She adjusted quickly to living in a tent and working for three men, washing with little water, keeping the records and she soon proved she had the ability to quickly recognize a shady deal. Her business abilities were such that the mine developed into a million-dollar business. When the book, *Men of Achievement in the Great Southwest* was published in 1904, Doctor Rose Burcham was the only woman to appear in its pages.

The first five and one half tons of ore milled from what would be the famous Yellow Aster Mine had to be hauled ten miles down the steep mountain side to Garlock. That first milling in September of 1895 brought the partners eight hundred and fifty dollars.

One man in particular wished the doctor had stuck to delivering babies in San Bernardino. This was the well-known Pat Reddy, a lawyer of early Inyo days. He went to Mojave by train and demanded the most comfortable rig in town to ride to the new discovery on the side of Rand Mountain. "Aut" Smith, who once drove stage for Rice and Shippey to Garlock, Goler and Randsburg said, "Rice told me I'd have to drive Reddy to the Yellow Aster that day." Pat would

have nothing but a surrey, preferring its shading top and side curtains to open riding in a wagon. Pat also insisted on a couch being wedged in, so he could take it easy across the sage. All the way to Rand Mountain he was in high hopes of being able to buy or bargain for some of the Yellow Aster holdings. But when he arrived the doctor turned down all his propositions with a mighty firm "No!" Aut said that Pat returned to Mojave and that all the way back to town he traveled under the darkest clouds of despair, greatly sorrowing that a mere woman should stand in the way of a man's enterprise. He was just plain mad, through and through, and swore he would never have anything to do with a woman again!

But he must have relented as time passed. Reddy did gain a partial interest in the mine, through legal services. It took a long court fight before the owners were able to settle the issue, pay off the lawyer for his share and regain control. Even before the area proved its worth as a legitimate gold producing area the saloons and girls came in to give the miners recreation after their long hours of digging in the ground and to relieve them of a portion of what hard work had rewarded them.

Other businesses started cropping up in this tent city. It was said that every other new business was a saloon and almost every saloon had a gambling table. There wasn't any system to the town layout. The tents, and eventually the wooden structures, were placed along curves in wagon roads and many stood at odd angles to each other. Even though there were miles of desert to build on, the camp was huddled in one small draw leading up to where the mine diggings were.

Randsburg is unique because very few typical, early day mining towns in California's southern desert survived the years. But this one has! Starting out with gold discovery and in succeeding years silver and tungsten were discovered. Following the end of the big tungsten boom at the close of World War I, the town was on its way out. But still it hung on. Randsburg lies in a range of sagebrush mountains, just off the Searles Lake borax road leading toward Death

Valley from the town of Mojave. It is less than a hundred and fifty miles north of Los Angeles. At an altitude close to four thousand feet the winters are cold and the summers are hot. Very early in the town's development there was an invisible line that separated the different sections. That line was between the miner's tents, the dugouts along Fiddlers Gulch, the saloons and the red light district. There was a small segment of the population that started pushing for churches, schools and forms of entertainment that would compete with the saloons.

Life was rough in the Rand Camp. The first winter the old timers told of camping out under wagons with a canvas draped over the side to keep the snow from blowing in and of trying to boil coffee with a fire made with wet sagebrush. Many of the prospectors had arrived thinking because it was a desert the climate would be

The first school in Randsburg opened for classes early in 1897

DESERT COUNTRY

Prospectors leaving Randsburg
for a trip into the desert hills

mild and they didn't bring adequate clothes or bedding. However, this was the high desert and the climate was anything but mild in the winter. In the winter the streets were muddy and in the summer they were dusty. The living and working conditions left much to be desired, but not many complained.

Without TV to keep the children occupied, they made up their own form of entertainment. They all loved to ride the burros that roamed around town and the boys tried their hand at setting off dynamite. There was always some dynamite handy that wouldn't be missed and with all the blasting going on at the nearby mines nobody took notice of one more blast. Mojave was the jumping off point for the miners and passengers who left the train and boarded the stagecoach for Garlock and Rand Camp. The stage was pulled by four to six horses and gave the passengers a hot bumpy ride in summer or a very cold ride in winter. Some packed food with them, but for those who did not, they could get a meal at the way stations where horses were changed.

According to reports they were usually served tough beef, beans, and boiled potatoes topped off with a dish made of dried fruit. The trip from Mojave to the mines was $3.75 and there was never an empty seat. Fortunes were made and lost in the Rand area almost over night. A good example of this was the discovery of the Big Butte Mine by two men, one with the last name of Ramie and another man named Sommers. They discovered their claim in 1896 and after very little development sold it for a profit of $17,000 each. The story goes that Sommers took off his work clothes, dressed up and swore he would never work another day in his life. He never left Randsburg, but three months later he was back working at the Big Butte Mine for three dollars a day.

Fire was a big factor in the early mining towns. The two main things that made fire such a hazard was the lack of water and no organized fire department. Randsburg had its first recorded fire on December 23, 1897. It didn't amount to much, but less than a month later, a big fire destroyed much of the town. The *Los Angeles Times* ran the following story:

> Rand Street is in ashes. Every building is burned between Broadway and Staley Avenue on the east side, and on the west side taking down to the Elite Theatre, down below Nelson's real-estate office. On Broadway four buildings were burned on the north side, stopping at Wagner's Saloon. The buildings on the south side of Broadway and on the north side of Butte Avenue opposite were scorched and were many times on fire, but were saved through the heroic efforts of the firemen and others present.

The alarm was sounded a little after midnight, the fire being first discovered in the rear end of the Mojave Saloon on Rand Street. It soon got beyond control and the adjacent buildings were wrapped in flames. The night was perfectly still, but the dry wooden buildings burned like tinder and the flames and smoke, mounted hundreds of feet skyward, made a grand but awful sight. Men, women and children filled the streets, everybody near the fire being intent on saving their homes and furniture. Part of the contents and furniture were removed from most of the buildings, except in the St. Elmo Hotel, where everything was lost, the guests escaping with their clothing only. The post office was burned with all fixtures, but the mail was saved, being hastily thrown into bags and carried to a place of safety.

For two long hours the suspense was terrible, there being no certainty that any part of the town would be saved. Many people remained up all night watching the fires or protecting their goods scattered everywhere about the burned district. Today many are making preparations to rebuild, and the people, notwithstanding their losses are cheerful and hopeful. Other buildings are being moved onto the vacant lots and some firms will resume business tomorrow.

The primary firms burned out are: Hammond's Grocery, Post Office, Wilson's General Merchandise Store, Southern Pacific office, St. Elmo Hotel, Elite Theatre, White Fawn Saloon, Crawford's Saloon, Hooper's Merchandising Store, Postal Telegraph office, Homestead's Drug Store and numerous real estate and assayer's offices, small stores, saloons and bakery.

After just five short months another fire destroyed the town again. This time the town was leveled. The *Los Angeles Times* reported again on May 6, 1898: "Another terrible fire in Randsburg wiped out all the remaining part of the town and not a building is left from the corner of Staley Avenue up Butte Avenue to the Russ House on the other side, and but four buildings are left on the south side of Broadway and three on the north.

The fire started in George Glitter's residence on Butte Avenue about 3 PM and was well underway before the alarm was given. A strong wind was blowing from the west up the street. In an incredibly short time it spread both ways, crossing the street and taking the Express and Telegraph office, together with the bank, which only moved in yesterday.

Several persons were hurt, Miss Griffin was severely burned and her life is doubtful. Her clothing caught fire and she was terribly burned about the face. The business loss is enormous. But one general store is left in the place, and there is a general feeling of despondency. The loss cannot be estimated but it is very great. Thirty or forty dwelling places have burned and tonight every unburned house in town is crowded. Many men have given up their bed tonight to accommodate women and children.

The fire was finally stopped by the free use of dynamite, blowing up all small buildings. Men are on guard to save the remains of the town. The Orpheus Theater reopened tonight in the Skating Rink, and many if not all the business houses will be rebuilt. The Miner's Newspaper office was three times on fire, but heroic work saved the building and contents with but little damage. The fire reached Wagner's Saloon and stopped. The peculiarity of this is the fact that the last fire came as far as this building at the other side and stopped, leaving the saloon as it has this time.

Early in 1897 the Gordon brothers arrived in Rand Camp and started a livery stable. They had 35 horses and a number of burros. They rented out a team and buggy for $10.00 a day.

In later years a fourth of July parade was held in the sister town of Johannesburg. The next big social event was a New Years' celebration in Randsburg. People came from miles away to Rand Camp for a New Years' dinner and dance. The amount of liquor consumed built tempers, and although there were many fights, there is no record of anyone being killed or even seriously injured, only black eyes.

Marcia Wynn, in her book *Desert Bonanza* tells the following story about one of Randsburg's early doctors: "Like all early mining camps of any size, Randsburg had its share of tribulations. There were litigation, fires and serious epidemics. The most serious epidemic was when smallpox appeared in town during the winter of 1901-02 right at Christmas time.

Doctor Baxter, a young dentist, had opened an office near the office of Doctor Macdonald's. It was the day before Christmas when Doctor Baxter found a man outside the door waiting for the dentist to open his office. When the man sat down in the chair it was found he had a badly

The Randsburg fire of May 6, 1898

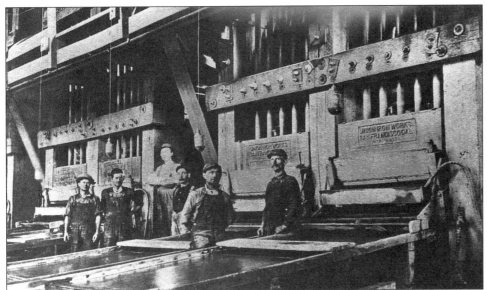

Left: The Yellow Aster 30-stamp mill

Below: Dry washers in the Stringer district, 1898

THE RAND MINING DISTRICT

Butte Avenue in Rand Camp, November 1897

infected tooth. Dr. Baxter noticed blisters on his face. He had never seen a smallpox case before but he suspected he was seeing one now. He pulled the tooth anyway and excused himself on some pretext. While the patient waited, he rushed around to Dr. Macdonald's house waking the doctor who was catching up on some much-needed sleep. He told him of his suspicions. The doctor swore and leaped out of bed, "If that's what it is, we're in for it. This camp can't take care of an epidemic." The doctor grabbed his pants and rushed to the dentist office while still struggling to get his shirt tails into his pants. As he went through the door of the office he gave the sick man a searching look. "Your right man, why did you pull his tooth? Now I'll have to quarantine you too unless you've had smallpox." Baxter said he was a total stranger to the disease.

They questioned the visitor and found he had come over from Arizona and had come from Mojave by stage several days before. He had been unable to find a room in town so had spent the night in the Steam Beer Saloon and other places of recreation. The first thing Dr. Macdonald did was to fumigate the office and vaccinate the dentist. He then notified the medical authorities in Bakersfield and told them they had better get a man over there to appraise the situation. There was nothing more they

Dr. Reginal E. MacDonald in his Randsburg Office

DESERT COUNTRY

could do at this time but to sit tight and hope for the best.

The night before Christmas a big dance was being held. People were coming from miles around and the Doctor felt he couldn't very well say it couldn't be held because everybody felt hail and hardy. Later most of those who attended the dance came down with smallpox.

Dr. Macdonald wired Bakersfield and he was given authority over the district to take what measures he thought necessary no matter how drastic. Before the epidemic was over it was estimated that over 500 cases of smallpox made their appearance within the Randsburg vicinity.

The small hospital could take care of only a few, so a large tent was erected. It was winter and bitterly cold, especially at night or when the wind blew. There were only two doctors in town and several nurses. Dr. Macdonald depended mostly on volunteer help. Even with the lack of facilities and the cold there were very few deaths.

One of the emergencies the doctor had to deal with was that some of the mild cases tried to leave town instead of being quarantined to their cabins or be placed in what they called the "pest tent". To prevent the would be travelers from taking smallpox to Los Angeles and other areas, the doctor posted the following notice in large letters. "Notice to all public carriers, conductors of trains, ticket agents and drivers of stage coaches. You are notified that all persons intending to leave Randsburg or Johannesburg either by coach or train must have a certificate of health, signed either by the health officer or Dr. Macdonald, the physician, who has charge of the health district. The railroad and stage companies will be held to a strict accountability for violation of this rule. Signed, E.M. Skillings, Department Health Officer, Kern County, Bakersfield, California."

Each evening the doctor added to his already strenuous duties the task of examining all departing train passengers. He would drive a fast horse over to Johannesburg, a total of five miles, board the train, walk down the aisle of the single coach, and peer closely at each face to see if the traveler looked the bit flushed or if

View of the Yellow Aster Mining Operations showing Randsburg in the background

THE RAND MINING DISTRICT

there were any signs of blisters. The ladies invariably tried to escape detection by means of the then popular veils. They didn't know that the doctor paid special attention to those wearing face coverings. Those who had an indication of smallpox were taken back to Randsburg via the Black Maria, a light delivery wagon that had been covered with black canvas and placed under quarantine.

A number of serious situations arose. Some of the first cases were among the red light women, some of whom were quarantined in the big "tent pest" house. The first thing the doctor knew, some of these camp women were receiving visits after dark from some of the townsmen. The doctor who had been up night after night, and with no time to forestall any more of these visits, stationed a couple of family men he could trust at the entrance of the quarantine tent during the evenings.

Randsburg survived this epidemic and continued to be a magnet for rough and tough miners looking for riches.

Following the death of Charles Burcham in 1913 and John Singleton in 1914, the Yellow Aster's affairs had gotten into a turbulent state. Lawsuits between the heirs over control of this famous old producer made many headlines for southern California newspapers as personal

grievances, charges and counter-charges, flew thick and fast. Eventually the various issues were settled and in time the mine came into control of Albert Ancker and Arthur Asher. Dr. Rose Burcham, the only one left of the original owners, still held many of the shares and remained on the company's board of directors. Edwin D. Mooers, son of one of the three original discoverers had been, for a time, vice president of the company. The Ancker and Asher families had long been associated with desert interests, especially in Tehachapi and Mojave.

With prices for machinery and labor going up during the war, the mine had not been paying dividends as before. With the hostilities in Europe and the lack of manpower, the mine ceased to be worked. However, one matter of importance had been settled for the Yellow Aster, and that was the calling off of one of the longest labor strikes on record. The secretary of the local union announced the end of this strike, begun sixteen years earlier, in May of 1918.

During the several years previous to this time the Yellow Aster had been, on several occasions, obligated to cut some close corners financially. In shaving one such corner, Dr. Rose Burcham had gone to Randsburg and temporarily laid off all but two men. She confided in Max Hess, one of

Early saloon and first billiard hall of Rand Camp

Witt Children in Randsburg. Front Row *left to right*: Wade, James and Hiram. On car: Tim and Mary. On top, middle: Margaret and Sue, Mike in front of Margaret, Albert on head light and Robert on hood.

her old employees, that she needed some grub cash. She asked if he knew of any good ore on top of the ground that could easily be gotten together for a short mill run. Max said he happened to know of some extra rich high-grade, which had been found under an old haystack when cleaning up around the mine barn. It was probably an accumulation of specimen pieces or the secret hoard of an educated packrat, who placed it there to exchange for currency later. Max gathered all the high grade he could find, added to it whatever was in the bins, and on the dumps, then he and the other miners took up the sand and dirt beneath the mill floor boards, just under the stamps and mill plates. Altogether out of all this they managed to clean up about seven thousand dollars in two cleanups.

One of the families who lived in Randsburg during the 1920s and 30s was the Witt Family. Father, James Newton Witt was a blacksmith from Tennessee. He said he left Tennessee for his health, ten steps ahead of the revenuers. The mother, Nellie Grace Gessell Witt was a teacher from Indiana. James and Nellie raised a family of ten children, Wade, James, Susan, Margaret, Hiram, Timothy, Twins Albert and Robert, Mary and Mike, all born in Randsburg.

Many Witt relatives lived in Randsburg including Hardee, one of James Witt's sons from a previous marriage. Hardee, his wife, Bertha, and their son, Hardee Jr., ran the Ford Garage in Randsburg. James' brother George, his wife Margaret and family operated a rooming house there. Nellie Witt's parents, Ed and Letta Gessell operated a bakeshop. Other family members living here were; Nellie's sister, Mary Grant and husband Hiram, Nellie's brothers Ray and Ralph Duram and their families.

Margaret Witt wrote a book in 1995 titled, *Childhood Memories of Randsburg*, filled with poems and stories. One of her poems that describes their lives was entitled "Love Is":

Nellie Gessel Witt, pioneer school teacher.

Watching ten little children
Running as fast as they can
Down the street to meet their dad
To see who could hold his hand

Our daddy was a blacksmith
In a desert mining town;
Though his heart was weak,
You would never see him frown.

When Daddy played the Jew's harp
Mama sang a pretty song
Our house would rock with laughter
As we tried to sing along.

Dad was in a lot of pain
When he first had his teeth out,
But he made ugly faces
Just to hear his young-uns shout.

We each shared a part of him;
He taught us everything he could,
I often feel his presence
As I walk the path he would.

My three year old brother Tim was lost on the Mojave Desert. He walked away from a three family picnic in Red Mountain a small mining town. Volunteers came from miles around to help. Men to aid Dad in the search and their women to prepare food and comfort our mother with the other nine children.

Campfires burned throughout the night, in various locations, hoping to attract the attention of little Tim. We all knew the perils of the desert, so when all seemed hopeless a seven-foot tall Indian tracker and his dogs were called in, out of Bakersfield.

Timmy's footprints carried them over and around many dangerous obstacles. He was found about daylight, curled up beside a mine-shaft, safe but hungry and thirsty.

In the late 1930s the Witt family, minus their father, moved to the Kern River Valley. In 2001 Margaret, James and Sue lived there. At the time World War I was brought to a close, Randsburg's production of both tungsten and gold had sharply diminished. The Yellow Aster was undergoing its first real shutdown since 1895. Many of the old timers had died, including the three original discoverers of the Yellow Aster. A number of families had left for other parts. Mining methods were changing. The population of Randsburg had dropped to a couple of hundred. At this writing there are approximately the same number of people.

GARLOCK

Cow Wells later know as Garlock, was at the foot of the Rand grade. John Kelly and his wife Ida, moved here from the Rand Camp because there was a well. Cow Wells was not as pleasant as Rand Camp as it was hotter and the view wasn't as grand, but they had a well. Cow Wells was nothing but the hot flat desert.

The Kellys put up a tent and went into the feed and grain business, their sole equipment for housekeeping being what they were carrying in the covered wagon. As people started traveling this route to the mines, Ida began serving meals to the miners. She attempted to prepare the meals she had been accustomed to at home. Her meals were very popular with the miners. Making an outdoor fire of creosote (greesewood) brush, she would put the Dutch oven over the coals, place her biscuits, stew or bread inside, then fill the depressed rim of the heavy iron lid with live coals. When the men found time they would haul mesquite wood for her, which made an even better fire.

When John Kelly hauled a cook stove out from Mojave, Ida felt she was living in luxury. Shortly they moved into a one-room cabin, with dirt floor and wall bunks. This was another step up from living in a tent or a covered wagon. On April 10, 1896, Ida Kelly was appointed the first postmistress of Cow Wells or Garlock, as it was then known.

In the fall of 1895, Eugene Garlock hauled an eight-stamp mill from Tehachapi and set it up on the flats. They set the mill up here because they had the use of the water for milling, (at least most of the time) which they didn't have at Rand Camp. It was after the arrival of Garlock and his mill that the watering place discarded its old name and was to be known as Garlock.

The Yellow Aster had its first local milling at the mill of Eugene Garlock. The owners sent their ore down to this little custom mill in large creaking, dust-raising ore wagons. The larger mines in the area were the Kelly, Smith, Henry, McKernan and the Visalia. When Garlock began to receive more custom ore than he could handle, other mills were built nearby. The early mills of Garlock were considered inefficient because they left so much gold in the tailings. Later when buyers approached the mill owners and desired to purchase the tailings for reprocessing, the owners refused to sell, wishing to keep this rich "waste" in their own backyard for future reclamation.

At this time there was no Wells Fargo office or other agency to take over the shipping of the gold. Mojave had been the bullion shipping point for years, so it was up to the mine's owners to transport the gold to the railroad town.

When the cluster of tents, frame and adobe houses increased and more business came to Garlock the town felt it needed a constable. John Kelly was given the job. When Mrs. Kelly gave up her duties as postmistress she and her husband moved to Randsburg, and he was made constable there.

Saloons, stores, hotels, and a school rose up out of the sage flats and Garlock had, for a time, a population of several hundred. They even put up three or four lampposts along the main street. At the top of these posts hung coal oil lanterns, with ladders placed so the lanterns could be refilled and lit each evening.

JOHANNESBURG

Johannesburg, or Joburg as everyone called it, was more of a family town than just a mining camp. Soon after Randsburg had its beginning, Joburg came into being. It was a properly laid out town. The camp had the luxury of having water piped to the doors of the homes. Everyone who wished to could take a bath. Another thing that set this town apart was the Randsburg Railway, a small independent railroad that had its terminus in Johannesburg. Randsburg swore up and down that the tracks would someday continue to its town but that never happened.

This railroad was approximately 28 miles long and connected with the Santa Fe line at Kramer. This railroad arrived in Joburg in the winter of 1897-98, just in time to lift the town out of a temporary business slump. Because the railroad was only about a mile from the Yellow Aster Mine, the mine started moving large shipments of ore to Barstow. At Barstow it was milled at the

The old Johannesburg Hotel - 1898

The Johannesburg Golf Club members. Their "greens" ran almost around the town—no grass.

Barstow Reduction Works. Some of the other mines in the area also started to ship ore to Barstow.

Records revealed that the Yellow Aster shipped about seventy-five tons a day. Most of this ore was from surface working on the side of Rand Mountain. The ore wasn't what miners would call "lousy rich" but was a vast amount of medium grade ore rather than ore of any consistent richness.

Because of the increasing monthly returns of the Yellow Aster, the owners continued to invest more and more money into the mine. The returns ran from fifty to sixty thousand dollars a month, which was equal to all of the other mines in the area. The short railroad that ended at Joburg was busy coming and going, hauling supplies in and ore out.

The train was also an important factor in the social structure of the district. Visitors came in greater numbers and the people of the nearby towns could travel easier and cheaper to the city. The Randsburg stage met the train at Joburg. However the rails did not entirely replace the longer stage lines between Randsburg and Mojave for years. Joburg was also the staging and freighting center for much of the mining country to the east, which were Searles Lake,

Post Office Springs (later Ballarat), Skidoo, Death Valley, and the Slate Mountain Range.

All this activity helped business in Joburg. Ten to twenty-mule teams were a common sight on the roads leading out of town for years. Longer lines of teams were running at least as late as 1911, but by now they were not running as often as in the previous years. The Johannesburg Hotel was the largest building in that section of the desert. A large box shaped building had a veranda that ran on both sides and in front. It had 36 rooms, (some reports say 40 rooms) a bar and billiard room. The hotel also had a 24-foot by 24-foot office and a large ladies parlor with an elegant piano.

Slightly up on the hillside above the town was the Red Dog Mill. It was painted red and the rhythmic pounding of its stamps and the noise from the mill spelled prosperity for the town. Mining towns where the stamp mills were quiet usually meant the town was doomed for ghosthood.

The town had a post office, two general merchandising stores, a variety store, billiard and poolroom, real estate office, two saloons, a music hall, several boarding houses, two laundries, a lunch counter, two lumber yards, two livery stables, a barber shop and more. These were all built in the first year or so of the town's existence. There was a telegraph office with a line to Mojave and also a telephone line to Randsburg and several other smaller mining towns. One thing the town didn't have was a church, but the Methodist minister drove over from Randsburg and held services in the schoolhouse.

One of the social clubs of Joburg was the Laurestina Club. Their members had a comfortable clubhouse, which contained a good billiard table, a piano and all the equipment for card parties, dances and suppers. A number of young couples belonged to this group and often they would put on some very interesting programs. There were a number of pianists, mandolin and guitar players, and group singing was popular. Also started was the "jackrabbit" golf course. It had twelve members, five gentlemen and seven ladies. The links began at the Red-Dog mill and ran clear around the town, crossing the railroad twice, and ended just where it began. There were nine greens. Johannesburg was considered an "up-to-date town."

ATOLIA

Atolia was five miles south of Randsburg. Located at the base of Red Mountain it had the convenience of a railroad already at its door, although water had to be hauled in by tank cars.

Atolia dates back to 1905, and was California's first important tungsten camp. It boomed wildly during World War I, and was still an important source of tungsten in the early 1950's. *The Pacific Mining News* in August 1922 said the unusual name "Atolia" was suggested by Charley Taylor. It was the combination of two names belonging to prominent tungsten miners, Atkins and DeGolia. These two miners put up the first tungsten mill around 1907. When tungsten was first discovered near Randsburg it was worth about $6.00 or less per unit. A unit of tungsten was 20 pounds of ore, and prices quoted referred to ore or concentrates containing 60 per cent or more tungsten.

The following news items from the *Los Angeles Times* on October 25, 1915, will give some idea of how the tungsten prices shot up: "A year ago, a few weeks before the war broke out, Atolia had a population of about sixty souls. At this writing there is a small city, mostly tents, of over 300 inhabitants; storekeepers of Johannesburg and Randsburg are paying as high as $1.25 per pound for high grade float, which is derived in placer form. New outfits are coming every day and the desert is alive with campers who are prospecting in this vicinity."

Six months later the *Times* had still a better report: "And today storekeepers are trading" grubstakes" for 60 per cent ore at $3.50 per pound. 'They have gone crazy over tungsten', a mine superintendent said recently when discussing his difficulty getting miners." Another article in the same paper by Al G. Waddell said: "A few months ago Atolia was a sleepy desert town. Tungsten was worth something like $6.00 per unit and the Atolia Mining Company was supplying all the tungsten needed with a small crew working in the mine and mill. The war produced a great demand for the mineral because of its ability to harden steel. Tungsten ore jumped to $90 per unit. It was then that the population of Atolia jumped to 2,000 souls. When tungsten first jumped there were two automobiles in Randsburg. Today there are 200 cars to be seen on the main street most any evening.

Illingsworth and Dunnell, two local merchants, were taking tungsten ore in exchange for groceries and general merchandise or buy it outright. The firm has taken in $200,000 worth of tungsten since the first of the year." Even before tungsten went up, a man could have highgraded a fortune in a month by bringing up a few "spuds" in his pockets each day. One day a miner stepped out of the skip when coming off shift and tripped over the cable, falling to the ground. He had so much high-grade on him that he could not get up.

When the tungsten discovered around Atolia became so valuable, the miners were watched like the laborers in the South African diamond mines. The Atolia Mining Company would not allow the miners to bring up their own dinner buckets. As soon as the men were through eating a guard would take the buckets and send them to the top of the 900-foot shaft. They were inspected and given to the men when they came up. The miners were even made to change their clothes before and after coming off shift.

At the end of the First World War, with prices and demands down and the cream of the crop picked off the top, tungsten production leveled out around Atolia. By now, tungsten could be shipped in from China as cheap as it could be mined in California and mining slowed.

RED MOUNTAIN

In 1919 there was another mining boom in the Rand Mining District. This time it was a silver strike near Red Mountain. This was one of California's largest and richest silver discoveries up to that time. The discovery became known as the "Rand's Big Silver." Hamp Williams and Jack Nosser made this silver discovery. During the first period of the mine's operation, June 1, 1919 to August 1, 1923, the gross value of production was $7,330,450.91! That figure does not include the returns from the Grady lease, which amounted to $1,599,979.98. Just one carload of ore during the mine's early production ran $54,000.

Hamp Williams was the son of Wade Hampton Williams, known as Hamp Williams Sr. Hamp Sr. had arrived in California in 1849 and discovered some of the richest gold mines in what was later Kern County. His son, Hamp Williams Jr., started his adult life as a cattleman, but lost 1,500 head from his herd during the four-year drought that ended in 1898. He then turned his attention to prospecting for gold as his father had before him.

In August of 1900 he discovered the Cowboy Mine in the Amelia Mining District in Stud Horse Canyon, near Paris Lorraine on Caliente Creek near Walker Basin. This mine eventually produced about $200,000. He sold a quarter interest in the mine to Doctor Briscen for $5,000. In the same year he discovered the Gold Peak Mine in the same area. He received $9,000 for this claim which produced another $200,000. Another small mine produced $3,000, which he sold for $100.

On April 25, 1903, Hamp Jr. married Estefena Miranda at the ranch of her father, Jesus Miranda, below Weldon in the Kern River Valley. He and his bride moved to Stud Horse Canyon, where he built a house 13 miles from Caliente. In 1914 Hamp Jr. discovered the Pine Tree Mine in Pine Tree Canyon northeast of Mojave. Here, he declared, were some of the richest rock he had ever seen. In 1919 when Hamp Williams and Jack Nosser filed on the "Big Silver," considered then the richest silver mine in California, they named it "The Kelly" after another partner they had taken in. John Kelly, a former Kern County Sheriff and Edith Coons, Kern County Assessor grubstaked the project and she also became a partner in the

Hamp Williams, Jr., discovered the famous Kelly Silver Mine at Red Mountain, California.

mine. Kelly and Coons raised $4,000 for the development of the claim. This mine eventually produced 20 million dollars in silver and gold.

Hamp told this story of the discovery. He and Nosser had walked from Randsburg to the area south of the town of Red Mountain. They went there to check an ochre deposit, a red clay material they might sell for paint pigment. On the way back to Randsburg they became tired and sat down on a rock to rest. Hamp spotted a rock shot through with silver. Samples were taken to Bakersfield to be assayed. The report came back that one sample had assayed $60 gold, 436 ounces silver per ton, the other $36 in gold and 326 ounces silver per ton. Williams, Nosser and Kelly staked out 22 claims before the news could spread.

The first carload of ore they sent to the smelter brought $2,300 and the second carload $4,700. These shipments were all from surface ore. The first shaft they drove to 90 feet brought them over $200,000. Sixty shafts were dug for deeper and richer ore.

The Kelly mine had a very good record for safety, considering the extent of their underground workings and all the men they employed. In all the years of its operation this big mine had only five fatalities. Carl Johnson died in a cave-in May of 1934. In 1935 while testing new dynamite for underground blasting, deadly fumes overcame three men. They were Jack Laird, Bob Warren and William Peterson. In 1941 "Tuffy" Landon, who had worked there many years, was crushed to death when he was caught between some timbers.

In 1939 there was "almost" a mine catastrophe. A number of men were working at the 1,100-foot level. When they were ready to come off their shift they signaled the hoist man a number of times. After receiving no response for a long time they decided to climb the steep dangerous ladder up to the top. One slip would mean death for the whole crew. When they made it to the surface they found that there was no one on duty. The hoist man, Vic Johnson, had had a few too many drinks and had gone home to sleep it off.

There were four large mines named Big Four, Santa Fe, Silver King and Silver Grance. Several smaller operations were striking good silver also. The ore body covered a considerable area.

Alfred Harrell, of Bakersfield, later bought a quarter of Hamp Williams' interest. When the company was incorporated Harrell became president. Soon after the original discovery Hamp moved his family from Stud Horse Canyon to Randsburg.

In 1938 Hamp and his family moved to Los Angeles so his children could attend school there. He then moved to Weldon in the Kern River Valley to help care for his dying mother. In 1941 the family moved to Mojave, with Hamp still doing some prospecting. It has been said that Hamp was 'part South Fork Indian and all prospector.' Hamp liked to recall early memories, like the herd of 50 antelope that he chased on horseback between the Castle Buttes, east of Mojave. He said, "The darn things just flew, and we tried to rope one of them, but couldn't get close enough." He also remembered the tales told of the Indians before the white men came, who used clay from the red clay deposits in the Jawbone Canyon area to cover their bodies to blend into the scenery so they might sneak up on the mountain sheep, which they killed for food. Hamp Jr. died in his little home near Rosamond at the age of 90 in 1961. The first carload of ore taken from The Kelly totaled 45 tons. This ore was shipped by rail from Johannesburg to the American Smelting and Refining Company in Selby, near San Francisco. Williams later sold all his shares, except 80,000, to Ken Sills for $50,000. When it was made public that $50,000 had been paid for a fractional interest in the Kelly Mine, the mining world began to sit up and take an interest. Miners, prospectors, engineers, and businessmen came flocking in.

Living quarters, which were usually at a premium in new mining camps, were not so critical here because empty houses were moved in from the now defunct Atolia. There were also hotels, rooming houses and even a few empty houses in nearby Randsburg and Johannesburg. The nearby

The California Rand Silver Mine

town of Randsburg changed almost over night into a lively metropolis. Businesses boomed in all lines, from knee-top boots, grubstakes, and whiskey to all other necessities for the miners.

There were several settlements nearby. One of these was the Osdick railroad siding where tents and cabins were put up. This area was named for Pete Osdick who had lived over the bonanza without knowing it for many years and loved the desert. Another group of dwellings was called Hampton and one settlement was referred to as Inn City. This name is thought to have been named by a coal delivery man as miners left notes for him saying they were either "in or out." It became quite a joke when each miner tried to outdo the other. Signs read Do Drop In, Come On In, In and Out, Never In, Out Not In, Lives In, Seldom In, and all variations of the word "in". With the coming of saloons, gambling, and other miners activities the settlement was often referred to as Inn City, Sin City or Gin City.

A struggle developed between Pete Osdick and some of the residents. Pete hired one man to paint "Welcome to Osdick" signs and put them up daily. Each night the signs were torn down and a sign that said, "Welcome to Inn City" was put up in its place. The town of Osdick was recognized in 1921 and they opened a post office by that name the next year. Things didn't change just because Pete had managed to get the post office. Mail continued to come to Hampton and Inn City until the Postal Department decided in 1929 to combine the three areas of Hampton, Inn City, and Osdick and they named the town Red Mountain. Pete Osdick, one of the first residents in that area never got over what he felt was an insult, and for the rest of his life he had his mail delivered to Osdick Town c/o Red Mountain Post Office.

Red Mountain became classified as one of the wildest, wide-open, boomtowns in mining history. In what was described as the "Lively Twenties" town, it not only provided entertainment and relaxation for the miners of the Rand mining area, but it was also the center of activity, on their days off, for the men working for The American Potash Company in Trona. The Potash community looked at Red Mountain as a desirable neighbor town that kept the undesirables out of their young community and was just far enough away. Red Mountain also cut their labor turnover by providing entertainment for many of their employees who might otherwise leave the isolated area for the glamour they might find in the cities to the south.

In the 1920s during the prohibition period liquor ran freely in Red Mountain, where the authorities seemed to look the other way. Liquor was considered a necessity of the time and place. Red Mountain was especially lively on Saturday night and some residents of Los Angeles drove 150 miles to enjoy the unbelievable sight of 30 saloons running wide open and to take part in their activities. The post office was the only place in town where you could not buy liquor. All the town's hotels had gambling tables and bars. In the twenties the liveliest spots were the Silver Dollar, Annex, Monkey House, Northern, Little Eva's, The Owl, Pacific, and Red Onion. In the 1940s only the Silver Dollar and the Owl remained and were still going strong.

To draw trade from the competition these places of entertainment tried to get performers. Musicians were always made welcome. Anyone who could squeeze an accordion, blow a mouth harp or play a fiddle could have all the free drinks they wanted. By putting down his hat he was able sometimes to accumulate enough silver to equal a day's pay. Hired musical groups were often employed by the larger places to play on Saturday nights.

One of the entertainers was a square built man they called the "Tungsten Kid." The bar where he performed was sure to have the biggest crowd. He had carried supplies to the Klondike in his earlier days and it seemed the more he drank the better he danced. A group of young men from Los Angeles usually provided the live music for the dance halls and bars. If they piled into their cars early Saturday morning they could arrive in time to play for the night crowd. They would usually receive $15 each plus a place to stay for the night. With the washboard dirt roads and flat tires being an excepted part of the trip, it was slow traveling.

Saddle horses were being rented for $3.00 to $5.00 per day, depending on how far they were to be ridden and burros for $.50 to $1.00 per day. Many miners that hit a good pay streak put every cent back into the operation and in many cases the pay streak pinched out and they went broke.

Red Mountain was once wild, woolly and rich. Today as you pass by the old buildings on Highway 395, you can almost see the ghosts of the miners of days gone by.

Early Stockmen of the Mojave Desert

LANDERS

In the late 1870s William W. Landers, had a ranch on the South Fork of the Kern River, which was west of Indian Wells Valley. At this time he started using the Mojave Desert for his cattle grazing operation. Cattle ranches such as the one operated by Bill Landers from the 1870s through the 1890s were as different from ranches of today as night and day. The main reason for the difference was that Landers ran his herds twelve months of the year on government land. Today those who graze their stock on government land have a limited grazing permit and must own enough land to feed them the rest of the year.

The United States General Land Office was created in 1812 to regulate use of cattle on government land. After California became part of the Union in 1850 this office should have regulated the land on which Landers ran his cattle. However, it wasn't until the early 1900s that much was done about curtailing the number of cattle grazing on government land or issuing permits for these privileges.

The area Landers chose for his range when he moved to the South Fork of the Kern River in 1877 covered the Mojave Desert from Little Lake on the north to Antelope Valley on the south, with some of his cattle drifting as far south as Victorville.

After the Civil War, the United States government transferred 200 million acres to the Union Pacific and Central Pacific Railroads, to assure that they would be able to construct transcontinental railroad lines. Some of these railroad sections were scattered down the Mojave Desert in the area Landers chose for his new range. He filed homesteads on these parcels as well as parcels in Kelso Valley and Kelso Canyon. He purchased or homesteaded other choice parcels of school sections. Many of these parcels of land had the only stock water for miles around, and in this way, he controlled the range by controlling the water. Adjoining the desert land was range at higher elevations, such as Piute and Scodie mountains. Further south, there were also areas of higher elevation where he could move his cattle in the summertime when feed and water dried up on his desert range.

In the South Fork Valley, Landers first purchased what is now known as the Onyx Ranch and used this as his headquarters. He also purchased a choice parcel of land from H. L. Mack. Before the flood of 1868, which changed the course of the Kern River, it used to run through this property. There were, and still are, about 200 acres of choice native pasture. Landers used this large pasture to hold about 2,000 head of big three-year-old steers for three or four weeks until the buyer from Visalia came over to make arrangements to purchase them and to have them delivered to Visalia.

When Landers was working his desert range in the spring, he employed about twenty cowboys. To mount this size crew, he would have to take on the drive with him a seventy or eighty head remuda (horse herd). When the wagon

A group of Landers' cowboys pose for the camera on their wiry Coso mustangs.

wasn't out on the drive, Landers didn't keep many horses on the home ranch. When the spring work was finished, which included branding calves and gathering the beef steers, a big part of the remuda would be taken to the horse range in the Coso Mountains. This range is now the northern part of the Naval Air Weapons Station China Lake. A few of the young horses that had just been started that year would be kept for the men to ride in the winter camps. The rest would all have their shoes pulled off in preparation for spending the rest of the summer and winter on the horse range.

Wild horses have roamed this range since the 1850s. In the 1880s Landers turned eighty registered Morgan mares out with these wild horses. In the spring they would gather the horses. The day before a crew of men would go to Cole Springs and camp with Dave Cole, who lived there with his family year round keeping track of the horses and prospecting a little. The next day, these men would have the wild bunch in the area of a horse trap, which was a dead end canyon. Then a crew would bring some broke horses from the ranch and run the two bunches together. By

taking them together into the trap, it made it much easier to corral the wild bunch. They roped and branded all the colts born since they had last gathered and castrated the male colts. They picked about twenty head of four and five-year-old geldings to break. They didn't break anything younger than that as they felt the younger horses didn't have the stamina for the long hard days of work they would be exposed to.

During the last part of May each year, Landers would gather his crew and get ready to work the range. Besides his foreman, he kept about six men on during the late summer and winter. These men had been staying in line camps out on the range for the past nine months, checking the water and seeing to it that Landers cattle didn't drift too far off their range. The majority of his crew was hired only for the time of spring work. These twenty men were mostly Indians from the South Fork.

The Indians in the Kern River Valley got their first horses from the missions along the coast about 1800 or earlier. They seemed to be naturally born horsemen and made some of the finest cowboys in the West. Jose Perez, a friend of Landers'

DESERT COUNTRY

foreman, John McCray, said, "When I saw John and his boys, I really felt sorry for my old friend. His cowboys were Indians, poorly dressed, and their outfits were shabby. They didn't look smart enough to work cattle. My men were Mexicans and white men who wore good clothes and had fine saddles, bridles, and riatas. But when it came to rounding up the strays and renegade cattle (those that got away time after time), it was the Indian cowboys who brought them in every time. My boys couldn't do the work in the rough mountainous country."

Many of the Indians herded sheep or worked in the fields farming with horse and mule teams. When the time of year rolled around for the Landers wagon to go out they quit whatever job they were working and showed up ready to go to the desert for the spring work.

In the '70s and '80s many of the Indians didn't have a last name, and were listed on the books as Indian Willie, Indian Jack, Indian Henry, Indian Pedro, etcetera. Regardless of what name they went by, the Indian cowboys were hard to beat.

The Indian families of Chico, Andreas, Apalatea and Bencoma each had several generations of cowboys who worked for the Landers Ranch. While they made good hands in all aspects of ranch work, working cattle was their first love. Most of them were exceptional trackers and could tell from looking at a bunch of tracks how many cattle had passed, whether they were cows, calves, yearlings, or bulls, also how long ago they had made the tracks. For the Indians this was a carry-over from the generations of hunting and tracking wild game before the white man came.

There were always three or four young boys working for Landers. Some had to be helped on their horses because they were too short to reach the stirrups. Ad Cross was one of these young lads. He was twelve years old when he came to work for Landers in 1878. Willie Nicoll was only nine years old when he ran away from home and went with the Landers chuck wagon. Willie's dad caught up with them that night and brought him back, but it wasn't long before his parents realized that it did no good to try to discourage him from following the cowboy life. My dad, Marvin Powers, first worked for Landers when he was fifteen, and his brothers, Charlie, Preston, and Jack, all went out with the Landers' chuck wagon at an early age. It seemed as if, from the time the boys on the South Fork were able to climb on their first horse, to ride for Landers was their main ambition.

When the regular hands went to the desert horse range and brought back the remuda, they started shoeing them and getting the wagon ready to leave. The chuck wagon and a bed wagon would head south, camping the first

A group of Landers' cowboys. Left to right: Frank Apalatea who worked for all the owners of this ranch for half a century, Ramon Bencoma, Charlie Andress, Clayton Ripley and Willie Andreas, Sr.

Above left: Marvin Pleasant Powers 1910 when he worked for Landers.

Above right: Claude and Clifford Cross who followed in their father's footsteps. Pictured when they rode for Landers in 1916. Clifford's son Clifford Jr. also rode for this ranch in the 1950s.

Left: Ad Cross started cowboying at the age of twelve for the Landers Ranch in Onyx.

night at Kelso Valley line camp. The twenty or so cowboys rode along with some of the younger hands, driving a herd of 70 to 80 horses. The second night out, they camped on the outskirts of the little railroad town of Mojave. Approximately 20 cowboys turned loose in town overnight usually livened things up considerably. Several times, one or two of the cowboys had to be hauled along in the chuck wagon the next morning until they could operate on their own steam. When the chuck wagon reached the southern part of the range around Antelope Valley, the work would start.

Once work started, the remuda would have to be herded night and day, and this job always fell to one of the youngsters. Ad Cross started his cowboying by watching the horse herd, and his son Clifford told me the following story about

this job his dad was given as horse wrangler. Ad, who was just twelve when he started, got his sleep in short snatches between his job of keeping track of 80 or so horses and keeping the cook supplied with wood. He was given a mule to use each night as he took the horse herd out to graze. He would tie his blankets behind the saddle and after getting his charges settled on good feed, he would tie his mule to a Joshua Tree and roll up in his blankets. He never did have trouble going to sleep. There was just one mare in the bunch, and she had a bell around her neck. The horses, as a rule, would follow this bell mare. If the horses drifted too far away and Ad's mule couldn't hear the bell, he would start pawing, braying, and raising such a ruckus that Ad would wake up, saddle his mule and ride off to find the wandering horses, sometimes in pitch dark. He would find them and bring them back to where they were supposed to be, roll up in his blanket, and go back to sleep. He never had any trouble finding them as the mule would put his nose to the ground and track them like a bloodhound, even on the darkest night.

By the early 1890s Landers had over 20,000

head running on the desert. When work started on the southern range, local cattlemen in the area, such as the Cuddebacks, would throw in with the Landers wagon and also work their cattle. Landers furnished the grub for the whole outfit. Landers, in return, branded all the "Big ears" (calves who had left their mothers) with his "£" brand. These animals, most of them yearlings or older, couldn't really be called calves, but had quit following their mothers and there was no way of knowing who they belonged to.

The chuck wagon cook was a big part of the early cattle business, and his word was law in the vicinity of his cooking fire. Even the cowboss very seldom disputed his word, and the cowhands, especially the younger members of the roundup, walked mighty lightly in the area of his domain.

Once in awhile, someone might remark that the gravy was mighty salty, but would quickly add, "But that's the way I like it!" These cooks had a big job. Often they had a helper, but many times they would feed from fifteen to thirty men twice a day, in addition to moving the wagon every day or so and setting up camp again. Some of the cooks remembered include Shorty Burnett, Phil Seybert, a black cook named Citano and Ed Gessell.

These meals eaten out of a tin pan while sitting on their bedroll by a sagebrush fire, made either favorable or unfavorable impressions on most of the old time cowboys. A cook that was most remembered was Louie Bowers, and here again, different cowboys had different impressions of his culinary skills. Frank Apalatea said, "Louie was the best cook I ever saw, always had hot grub whenever you came in, day or night." Pete Labachotte, on the other hand was not so impressed with Louie. He noted that, "He was the dirtiest cook I ever saw, spit right across the frying pan and didn't make it every time either. You know one time I cut a stink bug right in two in the bread."

At best, the cooking conditions were anything but ideal. The cook had a small table that hooked up to the tailgate of the wagon with a canvas fly or tent over it. The rest of the cooking had to be done on the ground. Different cooks might favor certain types of cooking, but most of them followed the same procedure in setting up their cooking area. Generally, a six-foot long pit was dug about a foot wide and eight inches deep. Greasewood was used mainly for fuel in the desert, and was hard to beat for cooking. When the fire had burned down to a three-inch bed of coals, you had a good, even heat that would last long enough to cook a meal. Some of the cooking

Above: Pete Labachotte

At left: Louie Bowers, the controversial cook on the Landers chuck wagon in his later years

was done on rods laid crossways over the fire pit. However, most cooking was done by driving two iron stakes in the ground vertically. Each stake had a fork at the top, on which another rod was placed horizontally. From this rod cooking vessels would hang with the aid of fire hooks. These were called "short irons" and were crooked in the opposite direction at each end. The cooking equipment numbered four or five frying pans with long handles and as many Dutch ovens, a few kettles, and the ever-present coffeepot. The Dutch oven (a large cast iron pot with a rim on the lid to hold the coals) was the most used of any of the cooking paraphernalia.

Bread was baked for each meal and to the cowboy nothing would measure up to sour-dough bread. The cook had his sourdough keg or crock, which he guarded with his life. This keg usually held about two gallons.

The sourdough batch was started by simply placing in the crock, flour, salt, and enough water to make a medium-thick batter. When this was well stirred, it was put in a warm place for a couple of days to ferment. The good sourdough cooks said that you had to use sourdough at least twice a day to make it work the best.

At each meal the cook would take out enough sourdough starter from the crock to make his bread, then replace more salt, flour and water to always have plenty of working batter. He now added more flour, a little soda, salt, and a gener-ous amount of melted lard to the sourdough starter he had taken from the crock. To make sour dough biscuits, the cook would make sure that the soda and lard were thoroughly mixed in, then he would pinch off pieces the size of an egg. These were then coated with hot grease and placed as close to each other as possible in a pre-heated Dutch oven, as this made them lighter by rising more. The full Dutch oven was then placed beside the fire for about half an hour to rise. The cook put the Dutch oven on the coals at just the right time with a generous supply of coals on the lid, which he had taken out of the fire pit. This would make sure they were fin-ished cooking when the rest of the meal was done, as sourdough biscuits are best eaten hot.

Much of the mystery that surrounds a good sourdough cook came from his knowledge of the right temperature to keep his working batter, and the fact that he used it at least twice a day. The rest was just years of practice. No recipe ever

Willie Nicoll rode for Landers' Ranch.

handed down seemed to get the results that those old boys achieved. Even higher on the cowboy's list of necessities was his coffee, and a three-gal-lon size pot was always on the fire. The cowboy liked his coffee strong, and the usual recipe was a handful of coffee for each cup of water. The sight of the wide bottomed, smoke-blackened coffeepot on the coals, with the brown boiling liquid over-flowing down its sides, was a picture that would make the cowboy's mouth water. Although he drank huge quantities of this potent brew, it never seemed to keep him awake at night.

The first wagons that went out on any cattle drive had on their bill of fare only meat, bread, and coffee; later, beans were added. The usual sight when the meal was being prepared was a black iron pot with cooking beans bubbling in it, over the coals, which would whet the appetite of any man. Years later potatoes were used almost at every meal, and the wagon cook also started using canned goods. Canned tomatoes were the most popular, but some vegetables, such as canned peas and corn were also used.

Plenty of good, desert-raised beef was killed on the spot whenever the supply on hand ran out. Usually a big heifer calf that was still fol-lowing its mother was butchered. They didn't age the beef as they do now, but started eating it the day after it was killed. Much of the beef was fried, but stew got its share. Most often on the menu were plenty of boiled potatoes, although fried potatoes were common. Gravy that was

Landers' Cow Camp in Kelso Valley. Still being used in 2001.

made in the frying pan, by adding canned milk and water after the meat was cooked, accompanied most meals. Occasionally some type of dried fruit was cooked up for dessert. These were the simplest of diets, but they seemed to stick to the ribs. It kept the cowboys going about their daily work, which was anything but light.

As an army marches on its mess kitchens, the cowboy works on his chuck wagon. Sometimes the cook would have a canvas fly or tent hooked to the back of the wagon, but it usually wasn't enough to keep the blazing sun from baking his back and shoulders or the cold rain from soaking him. Regardless of all the drawbacks—wind that blew sand in the food, a shortage of wood, and a limited variety of food stuffs on which to draw—these old boys still left reputations behind them that are hard to top. The type of riding done by the cowboys called for top physical condition, and vittles from the chuck wagon filled the bill. Besides the two regular meals each day, the cook was expected to have something for the crew to eat when they went on duty for night herding (herding was mandatory since there were no fences). The night was divided between two shifts, and all hands took their turn. When the men went on at midnight, a pot of beans or stew

and plenty of coffee was kept warm by the fire so they could fill up before going out.

Each morning just about dawn, the chuck wagon would come alive with activity. The cook had been up for an hour or more working by lantern light, starting breakfast. The following was typical of this colorful scene. The wrangler ran the horses into a rope corral. This consisted of only one rope being held waist high by the cowboys. Each man took his turn entering the corral and roping his horse for the day. The horses were led to an area close to the chuck wagon where they had been unsaddled the day before. As each man saddled his horse, the picture livened up considerably. Things started to happen. Out of twenty or more horses being ridden that day, there were always at least two or three that wanted nothing to do with the saddle. Even after being hobbled, they might tear up half an acre of ground before they could be saddled and made ready to go. Later when the men started to mount and get their broncs lined out for the day's work, what you were apt to see is mirrored in one of Charlie Russell's paintings, "Bronc at Breakfast Time." It pictures a cowboy riding a bucking horse through camp, scattering things right and left. There was a lot of cursing and shouted threats from the cook, but he knew, as everyone else did, that there was no turning or directing a bucking horse. This was the high point of the day for many of the cowboys as they offered shouts of encouragement to the rider, and maybe a hat or two sailed under the bronc to encourage him. If the undetermined route happened to take them through a bunch of Joshua trees, it would get a big laugh from all hands, and several days of discomfort for the unfortunate rider as the punctures ran their course.

As the sun popped over the Superstition Mountains, the cowboys headed off in groups of five or six to where they split up to work the country scheduled for that day. Although everyone knew what was expected, the cow boss still would issue a few brief instructions about who went where.

As the day wore on, cattle started streaming into the predetermined rodeo ground, (an open spot were they could work the cattle) and by late morning all the riders had been accounted for.

Many times, the wrangler would bring the remuda out and fresh horses would be caught for the rest of the day's work. A branding fire was built off to one side. Those calves belonging to the smaller cattlemen would be roped and branded first. When all these were accounted for, the rest of the calves, along with any "big ears", would be branded for Landers. Once in a while, while branding the Landers' calves, one of the men would sing out, "Points up," meaning the points of the "L" brand put on the left hip had to be pointing up or the brand would be upside down. Branding was hot, dusty work; however, it was looked forward to, as it gave the men a chance to show their skill with a reata (a rope made with braided cowhide used for roping).

When all the branded calves had trotted back to their mothers with smarting hides, 'cutting' the beef cattle out of the herd began. Again, a lot of the men would rather cut cattle than eat. As with the branding much of the success in putting on a good show and getting the job done quickly depended a great deal on the horse they were riding. These little mustangs took naturally to cow work and a man had to have a deep seat in the saddle and many times grab the saddlehorn to stay with them as they dodged and turned to cut out the older steers. In many cases, these steers had a horn spread of over five feet and weighed as much or more than the horse. They

had become rolling fat on the desert wild flowers, and the sun glistening off their multicolored hides made these creatures a sight to behold.

With branding and cutting of the beef finished, the main herd was turned loose to scatter onto the range. The "cut," (beef cattle cut from the herd) were driven back to camp and included with those that had been cut during the previous days.

As work progressed, the herd of beef steers continued to grow, meaning each night quite a few men had to take turns standing guard for two or three hours. Also, they had to give the steers a chance to graze enough each day to keep their weight stable. By the time the crew came through Kelso Valley and down to the Mack Ranch Meadow across from the Methodist Church in the South Fork Valley, there would be two to three thousand fat three-year-old steers. When they came into this lush meadow, they would string out for more than two or three miles.

Each summer, as water became scarce and the desert feed dried up, the cattle were "stirred up and started towards the hills." These cows, having run on the same range for years, would travel from thirty to forty miles to the foothills or to their summer range. These included Kelso Valley, the Piutes, the Scodie Mountains in the north end of the range and Tehachapi Mountains farther south. In November or December they would be pushed back out into the desert. This system did not always work. There are quite a few years recorded when, because of lack of rain, there was hardly a blade of grass on either the mountain or desert range. After one four-year drought there was no feed left for the cattle on the desert. In 1898 when John McCray finished the count on Landers' cattle, he found there were only 2,000 head left from the 20,000 head on the range a few years before. Eighteen thousand head of cattle were lost to starvation. This was the original number of cattle he started with in the 1870s. The old timers said it was really a sickening sight. You could ride for miles and never get away from the stench of rotting cattle. Some ask why they did not drive them to feed or ship feed in to them. In those days, a big steer would bring only seven or eight dollars and there was no sale for them in their poor condition. Even if you could find feed, the cost would have been prohibitive. All the cattlemen could do was borrow a little money, if possible, to buy beans and pay their riders for the following year, tighten their belts a couple of notches, and hope the next few years would bring them out of debt.

HUNTER

Several other families in the northeast part of Indian Wells Valley also ran cattle in the early days. In 1967, Lester Reed authored a book entitled Old Timers of Southeastern California. Two of the families he wrote about in this book were the Hunters and the Laceys.

William Lyle Hunter arrived in Inyo County in the early 1870s. He had a string of mules and horses, with which he packed ore out of the Coso Mountains' mines. He sometimes took water in to mining camps when water systems were out of order from freezing or other causes. His stock was also used for road work and hauling mining machinery. As William Hunter added to his pack string and mule teams he had to find a range where he could take the mules at times when he did not have work for them. He finally worked the number of his stock up to 200 head and found feed for them in the Coso hills. In 1875, William Hunter married Carolina Duval. Their old home at the Cerro Gordo Mine was still standing in 1967. Hunter and his wife had four sons and one daughter. One of his sons by the name of Bev, was born in 1882. Bev and his son Roy Hunter are the two Hunters featured in this chapter.

From the time Bev became big enough to sit on a horse, until he was 85, horses and cattle were his life. He told how thoughtful his father was in letting him go on cattle and horse drives when he was very young. He made his first cattle drive from Independence to Mojave at 15 years of age. As he looked back over his life he remembered the interest his father took in asking him questions concerning the cattle and horse drives he made as a boy.

The owner of the cattle on one drive was a man by the name of Hulbert, who would go into the Owens Valley and buy cattle until he had as many as he wanted for a drive. Mr. Hulbert would buy hay from Bev's father to feed to the cattle while holding them until he had enough for the drive. On one of these cattle drives there were some oxen in the herd that were bought from a Rawson's Sawmill. Some of these old steers with plenty of age on them weighed around 1800 or 2000 pounds. They were bought for only ten dollars per head. Bev said Mr. Hulbert was a real good cowman, and remembers that his cowboys were not allowed to yell and shove behind a herd. No extra horses were taken on these cattle drives. He told how these old horses would actually snore when having an opportunity to rest.

The cattle were driven from Olancha to Mojave, making it a 131-mile drive. Watering places for the cattle herds after leaving Olancha were Reese Springs near the south end of the present Haiwee Lake, Little Lake, Grapevine Canyon, Coyote Hole (Raymond's Station), Red

Bev Hunter at his log cabin in Hunter Mountain area. Photo by Lester Reed.

Rock Canyon, and then there was no more water until arriving in Mojave. In Mojave the cattle would be shipped out by train.

Bev also helped to make horse drives from Owens Valley to Los Angeles at a very early age. Here the horses would be shipped to different parts of the nation. The drive with horses to Los Angeles required seven days. The return trip on horseback to Independence was another seven days with the riders earning $1.50 per day. He tells of riding on horseback from Los Angeles to their ranch at Georges Creek south of Independence in 48 hours, stopping only in Mojave to feed and rest his horse. Perhaps we of today would, for a time, want our meals served while standing up if we were to make a ride like that.

As a boy, Bev could always be found where there were either horses or cattle involved. He and the son of W.K. Miller, who owned the stage line between Keeler and Mojave, became great friends. Often, Bev stayed at Indian Wells and from here he and young Miller would ride the stage on the route toward Keeler, or toward Mojave to the south.

One time when a drove of cattle was going through, a big bull gave out about seven miles from Indian Wells. After hauling hay and water to the bull for several days, W.K. Miller decided he would get the bull to Indian Wells where he could take better care of him. Bev went with Mr. Miller, in a light buckboard pulled by two of the stage horses. The idea was that the bull could be tied to the rear of the buckboard, and with one of them driving the team, the other could walk along behind the bull. As usual, the bull was lying down to keep off of his sore feet, so all they had to do was drive right up to the bull, place a rope on his horns and tie it to the rear of the buckboard. However, the moment the rope tightened, the bull made a lunge, breaking the doubletrees, setting the horses back on their haunches, the tongue came out of the neckyoke, and the bull was headed off down the slope at full speed with the buckboard in tow. Wheels and other parts began flying off the buckboard, and after running a mile or more the bull gave out, still tied to what little was left of the vehicle. The bull refused to try to get on his feet again and had to be killed. Mr. Miller laughed until he cried, then each of them mounted a horse bareback and rode back to Indian Wells. Bev would sell horses to the stage line owner on credit, and then he

and other members of the Hunter family would ride out the price of the horses as their fare on the stage line.

Early in life Bev Hunter started on the way to becoming an outstanding wild horse hunter of his time. Over in the Lida area of Nevada where wild horses were numerous, he caught, rounded up and drove many of them into the Owens Valley. He has been referred to as a man who could think like a wild horse. He said, "When a man thinks he is smarter than wild horses, he has not even started to learn about them yet." He tells of how an old stallion will often linger long behind his harem of mares in a manner that will lead the inexperienced to believe he would not be difficult to catch. This cunning animal has plenty of speed to outdo the average good saddle horse. We think of wild horses running in large bands, but it is more likely that a stallion will have a harem somewhere near a dozen. When a stallion is leisurely following his band of mares, and one or more of his band start to go their own way, the stallion will head them off and really work them over with his teeth until they are back in line again. If some of the mares linger too far behind, their master will again go back and give them a working over with his teeth. Bev told about a man from Arizona that made his camp near theirs while he was gathering wild horses in the Lida area. The old fellow had two mares.

Early the following morning the man from Arizona came over to where Bev was and claimed that one of his men had stolen one of his mares. The old boy was carrying a rifle, and Bev, seeing that he was pretty hostile tried to handle him as easily as possible, while trying to explain that most likely one of the wild stallions had stolen his mare. Not knowing the ways of wild horses this was difficult for the man to believe. After the man cooled off, they went with him to see what they could learn about the absence of the mare. Both the mares had been hobbled, so it was not difficult to follow the sign of the one that was gone. After following the signs of the mare, with additional signs of the wild stallion working her over as he headed for his band, they could see the two of them in the distance. The stallion was still trying to hurry her along to get her with his band. When they caught up with them, the stallion ran off a short distance, and of course, the mare was willing to stop as soon as the stallion left. When the man saw how badly the stallion had skinned the mare up, he turned and killed her with his rifle. When they arrived back at camp, the man from Arizona knew more about wild horses than he had known when they had left camp. And he knew who had stolen his mare.

One time, Bev Hunter and Ed Cornell, with other men helping them, gathered about five hundred head of wild horses out of the Lida Valley, Nevada. They did not get them all at one time as the horses ran in small bands and usually it is not practical to try to drive too many in one herd. When Bev and Ed first started to gather them, they made a camp at the Oasis Ranch where hay was cheap and plentiful, so their saddle horses could be kept in good shape. When they sighted a band, they would ride around them at quite some distance so that when the horses started they would be headed for the flat in the vicinity of their camp at the Oasis Ranch. In this way they gathered enough horses together for a drive.

Today the number of wild horses has been greatly reduced partly due to the many that have been gathered. During World War I there were those who would shoot the wild horse just for the hide that was selling at a fair price. This type of man did not appreciate wild horses as a part of the outdoor way of life, nor as an animal that has served the cowboy so well in his everyday work. In the Coso Range there are still the remnant of wild horses and burros that have been there for many years. They originated from animals brought in during some very dry years during the 1870s. These horses and burros were never all captured. Over the years the ones born and raised there are as wild as can be. Over the years being chased many times does not tend to make them tame or gentle, but they are truly wild!

Soon after, the city of Los Angeles began buying out ranches in the Owens Valley with the idea of taking Owens River water to that city. Bev Hunter heard that they wanted to hire some mules for the building of the Tinemaha Dam a few miles south of Big Pine. The dam is mainly a dirt structure extending across the valley, well over half a mile in width. Bev contacted the proper authority and a contract was drawn up and signed to the effect that he was to furnish 45 head of mules. At that time he had two mules broke to work, and the only harness he had was for those two mules. At ten dollars per set he bought enough harness from ranchers who had sold to the city that he could outfit the 45 mules.

He then went to Hunter Ranch, between Saline and Panamint Valleys, to start gathering mules.

The weather was so wet and stormy that there was some delay in getting enough mules together, but through two gatherings he brought 45 head to a ranch in Owens Valley where the breaking of mules to work was soon underway. In a large round corral he prepared a large metal wheel for a drag. He hitched bronco mules to this with one of the mules that was already experienced as a work animal. The mules were started inside the corral, then taken out in the open and driven around until they learned to be guided. When starting on the job, the mules were hitched four abreast to a Fresno Scraper. A man on horseback on each side would have a lead rope on the outside mule. As soon as each team of four mules became used to the noise of the scraper they would be turned over to the teamster. In this manner the 45 mules were soon gentled to their work, and it wasn't long before the teamsters would jump on the back of one of the mules when going to and from the construction camp.

The construction camp was on the eastside of Owens River near the narrow gauge Carson and Colorado Railroad. The track led south to Keeler, a little desert mining town near the north shore of Owens Lake. Bev decided the mules were doing well enough that he could leave, and so he did.

When vacation time came, some of the construction men, thinking the mules were broke to ride because of riding them to and from work, decided to use some of them for a riding and pack trip. The mules appeared so gentle on the job that they decided to put packs on some of them and ride others into the high country. Of course this was completely out of line with their everyday routine, so riders and packs were scattered in all directions and it was thoroughly demonstrated they were not yet broken as saddle and pack animals.

About 1901, Bev Hunter joined the 101 Rodeo Show at Bliss, Oklahoma, and went with them from there to Birmingham, Alabama, where the state fair was going on. The show advertised that Bev would ride anything they would bring in as a saddle bronc. He said he was fool enough to try to back up the advertising. He said some of the old grain-fed horses were really rough to ride on the hard ground that was always chosen for putting on the show. Instead of riding eight seconds as is the rule in rodeos today, they were required to ride the horse until it quit bucking. The posters also advertised him as an expert steer roper.

When Bev told of traveling with the 101 Rodeo Show, he talked about "cowboys" who wore high heeled boots, big hats, and a line of talk that did not at all belong to the life of a working cowboy, or a cowboy that could really ride or rope.

Tom Mix was traveling with the show at this time and also the original Annie Oakley. Annie later joined the Buffalo Bill Show when Bev was with them, and he said she could really shoot.

Lester Reed, who worked with Bev said, "Bev is a type of old-timer that is very difficult to find any more. If a horse was mean to buck, he harbored no thought, only to ride him if he could, and experience had taught him that he was well mounted if he kept such horses between his knees."

One of the old-timers in the early days of Inyo County and the Cerro Gordo area was a Portuguese man by the name of Manuel Silva. He owned some cows from which he furnished milk to the residents of Cerro Gordo during the booming days. When the price of silver dropped causing the smelters to close down and the boom days were over, Manuel took his cows down into Owens Valley and started in the cattle business. From his milk cows he built the herd up to several hundred head and held a grazing permit for them in the Mulky Meadow area of the Sierra Nevada. When the cattle were to be brought out of the high country they were started out by way of Diaz Meadow to what is still known as The Portuguese Slide. There, Silva with the aid of his three dogs shoved the cattle down the slide to come out in Cottonwood Canyon. When he took the cattle into the mountains they were driven up Cottonwood Canyon trail, for the Portuguese Slide was too steep for them to climb up.

Silva was often seen working his cattle when there was no one helping but his three dogs. If he were cutting out some of the cattle, two dogs would be holding up the main herd, while the third dog would be holding up the ones he had cut out. Most likely all the cowboys in the country could not have shoved the cattle over the Slide as did this man with his three dogs. Nor could the cowboys have held the cattle up as well while they were being worked either. The cattle were use to the ways of the dogs, and Manuel's way of handling them. This man never petted his dogs. They always stayed back some

distance from him, and when time came to feed them, a hunk of beef would be thrown to where each one was waiting his turn. One time a man was trying to get one of the dogs to come up to him and Manuel caught him and made it clear that the dogs must not be petted.

Manuel had no cabin at Mulky Meadow, nor did he have any horse pasture. He depended on the dogs to keep the cattle off the grass near camp so his horses would stay around close on the better grass. Manuel lived in a tent, his horse was very shabby and slow, and what Manuel and the slow horse could not do was left up to these wonderfully trained dogs. And a good job they did.

LACEY

Another old time rancher who ran cattle on the same range as the Hunters was Mark Lacey. Mark was truly a native son of California. He was born November 25, 1888 at Fort Independence in Owens Valley. Mark's father was John W. Lacey. Lacey came out west in 1873 from Madison County, Missouri traveling by train to Elko, Nevada where the line ended. From there he traveled by stagecoach to the Owens Valley. Mark's mother was Anna Marie Meyer who came from Denmark in 1873. John and Anna Marie were married in June 1886.

John and Anna Marie lived on a 160-acre ranch at Fort Independence until after their four children were born. The sale of a mine John had acquired in Nevada on his way west had paid for their ranch. When they finally sold their ranch, they moved to Georges Creek where John became a partner in the cattle business with Hans Meyer until Meyer's death.

Georges Creek received its name when John Kispert located on the creek and named it for a Piute Indian from whom he bought the claim. The Indian was known to old-timers as Indian George, and the creek still bears the name.

The first Forest Service permit for the grazing of cattle in the Monache Meadow was issued to John W. Lacey, Hans Meyer, and Edward Walker in December 1903. The Secretary of the Interior decided to allow the grazing of cattle and horses in the South Division of the Sierra Forest Reserve (now the U.S. Forest Service) during the season of 1904. The letter stated that not more than 500 head of cattle could be grazed under the permit of any one person.

Mark Lacey and Jack Fitzpatrick

In 1913 it became necessary to build a drift fence near the lower end of Monache Meadow to keep the cattle from Owens Valley separate from the cattle from the South Fork Valley on the Kern River. This drift fence would benefit John Lacey, August Walker, Frank Butler, Charles Summers, Albert Lubken, Arthur Lubken and John W. Lubken. All of these men were from the Owens Valley. On the South Fork side of the fence were the cattle of Thomas S. Smith, Warren A. Rankin, Leroy Rankin, Charles Powers and Johnny Johnson.

When Mark Lacey was 17 years old he took his first train ride with eight carloads of cattle to San Francisco. The cattle were driven from their ranch on Georges Creek to Kearsarge, north of Owens Lake, and put on the narrow-gauge railroad known as the Carson and Colorado. To reach San Francisco the cattle were shipped by way of Reno, Carson City, Truckee, Sacramento, and finally San Francisco.

Before going on the trip to San Francisco with the cattle, young Mark had sold a horse to have spending money while on the trip. When he was at the Big Pine Hotel he wrote a letter to his father. The letter was dated November 25, 1905, and reads:

"I sold my gray horse to Mr. Colton for twenty dollars. Let him take the horse when he comes. We will start for San Francisco tomorrow. I have gained five pounds. I have been to Bishop and to

Laws, but I did not see Miss Burke. Tell mama that I am all right. Your loving Son, Mark Lacey. P.S. I have the money for my horse."

When World War I started, Mark went into the service where he served his country in France. Mark was proud of his military service and belonged to the American Legion.

When the Laceys sold the ranch on Georges Creek, they moved to Long Beach where Mark became very unhappy and longed for the cattleman's life in Owens Valley. In 1929 he went back to Olancha near the southern end of Owens Lake and bought a ranch from the estate of August Walker. He wintered his cattle on the desert range of the Coso Hills, and took part of them to the High Sierra for the summer. It was then that he met an Olancha schoolteacher by the name of Elizabeth Lindsay. On August 21, 1937, another cowboy fell from the bachelor ranks. Approximately one year later their only child, John William, was born.

In his book *Old Timers of Southeastern California*, Lester Reed said:

About the first of May 1945, when my brother Gib and I were camping at the Lacey Ranch in Olancha, Mark came over to our camp and wanted me to go to work for him. Wanting to stay away from cattle work for awhile, I told him that I would rather not. He said there was another man he might get. A few mornings later Mark came over to our camp and said, 'You've gotta go to work for me.' Feeling that he really meant it, I promised to work until the following November.

The first work was to gather the cattle off the desert range in the Coso Hills where I saw the best desert range I have ever ridden over. The desert flowers were good, and the browse was what I called the very best. The watering places that had been prepared under the program of the CC camps were what I thought the best I had seen. To attest to the range and watering conditions, the cattle were in the very best of order.

The first gathering we made was of the cattle watering at the Junction Ranch, a piece of land and good watering place owned by Mark Lacey. I learned that the place had been a way station in the early days for the stagecoaches. Mark had acquired rights to the range from Summers and Butler, and before them the rights had belonged to Domingo Dominique. There were still joints of pipe in a number of places where this man had piped water to save the cattle from as much extra travel as possible.

On our second gathering of the cattle off the desert, we camped at Cole Spring, and there we butchered an unbranded yearling heifer still nursing the mother and what fine meat that was. The heifer was as fine and fat as any I have ever seen when still getting the milk of the mother and grazing of the desert flowers and the desert brush. No antibiotics had been injected into its flesh, and at that time I had never ridden over a range were there was so little sign of livestock losses. Knowing we had not found all the cattle we started for the ranch at Olancha.

On this second drive the old-timer Bev Hunter and his son Roy were both along. These two cowboys realized that cattle not wanting to leave the desert must not be permitted to spread out. Upon arrival at the Olancha Ranch the cattle were rested for a few days, then the calves were branded, vaccinated for blackleg, ear-marked and castrated. This was planned so they would have time to heal before going into the Sierras for the summer. At that time Mark had just begun to drive his cattle into the mountains by way of the trail between Sage Flat and Monache Meadow. Before this time the cattle had been driven to the high country over the Cottonwood Creek trail. They were not use to the steep Monache trail, so they did not want to travel, and it was quite a chore to get them to Summit Meadow.

Lester along with his brother "Gib" went to brand the calves, which had been left on the desert. In addition to branding up the unmarked cattle, they counted the wild horses that they found and did so with reasonable accuracy. They didn't count the droppings of the horses, as the "experts" do when counting deer. They felt that should some good cowboys start gathering the horses, the number would fall far short of the "pellet" count. They counted what they actually saw until they felt they would be likely to count the same ones more than once. The wild horses they actually saw were 180 head, hence they felt it would be perfectly safe to estimate there were 300 or more horses in the area.

My first horse came from the wild horses on the Coso Range. An Indian named Andy Chico caught him in 1934 and sold him to my Dad, Marvin Powers. I claimed him right away. He turned out to be a great little horse, but he didn't look like much. He was what we called a flea bitten gray (gray with small black spots). He had hard feet and we never had to shoe him. Having learned to run with the wild bunch he could lope for miles and would not even be breathing hard. However, he had one bad habit: he always wanted to get back to his home range. When we moved loose horses from camp in the canyons of Indian Wells Valley, he was always trying to get away. He did get away twice and went back with the wild bunch. Both times Mark Lacey, who was running cattle in the Coso range, caught him and took him to Olancha. He would call our ranch on the South Fork and say, "Tell Bob I have his horse. He can come and get him." When he became too old to work cattle anymore I sold him to a man at the Walker Pass Lodge. I told him that whatever he did, never turn him loose or he would end up on his old range.

By 1900 the Smith and Powers families from the Kern River Valley were using the canyons on the west side of Indian Wells Valley as their winter and spring range, taking the cattle up Nine-Mine Canyon in June to the Sierra Nevada range for the summer.

GOATS ON THE MOJAVE DESERT

Not only were there cattle and sheep grazing on the Mojave Desert but in the late 1800s and early 1900s there were as many as 5,000 Angora goats being grazed on this desert from Haiwee, near Lone Pine, to Mojave to the south.

I didn't know much about goats on the desert

until I had started this book. One of my elementary school classmates, Winifred Hand Hurst, asked me if I had ever seen the letters her father and uncle, Phil and Charlie Hand, had written to their mother while herding goats for their Uncle Bart. Winifred's father, Phil Hand, sent the first letter from Haiwee on August 29, 1899. He told about his trip from Mojave to Haiwee on the stage, which had two horses that were driven almost at a run where the roads were good. The line was 120 miles long and they changed horses five times.

When he arrived in Haiwee there were 15 almost full-blood Angora goats in the field which were tame enough to eat out of a fellow's hand. Nearly five thousand goats were on the range about sixteen miles from there in Little Lake Canyon.

On September 15th while camped in Nine Mile Canyon Phil wrote a letter. The following are excerpts from it:

We only hear from the world about two or three times a month because our camp is away off from the ranch. Fred comes to it only to bring eatables and to move the camp to another canyon when the feed is all gone. I went to work the first of September and haven't done anything yet except run around over the mountains and have a good time in general, though it is rather lonesome at times.

When I came up on the stage I saw lots and lots of skeletons of horses, colts, cows, calves, sheep and lambs along the road. The driver said that about two years ago a lot of men started to drive their stock up to the mountains above here and it was so hot and the feed and water was so scarce that they died by the hundreds all along the route.

We don't eat but two meals a day up here and the less we have to carry the better it is for us, so we don't carry either lunch nor canteen. Sometime we go all day long without a drop of water and we are pretty nearly empty at night when we get into camp, I can tell you.

We get up here in the morning a little after sun up and as we haven't any lantern we go to bed as soon as the stars begin to shine. Each fellow takes his blankets and his dog and lies down on one side of the band of goats at night so the dogs will keep the coyotes and wild cats away. There are lots of coyotes and wild cats and thousands and tens of thousands of little striped chipmunks running over the rocks with their tails curved up over their backs.

These coyotes up here have more gall than a government mule. The way they try to lift a kid under our very noses in broad daylight. I wish I had a rifle, I'll bet I'd scare them mighty well even if I couldn't hit them. I haven't the slightest idea I could for I never did hit anything I shot at, excepting once and that was purely accidental.

You needn't send any books up here because they will only get spoiled and I won't get a chance to read them at Haiwee. I won't be there more than once or twice a year, and out here we go with the goats as soon as we swallow our breakfast and don't get back to camp until after sundown. If Charles comes up here this winter, he wants to bring good heavy under clothes and socks and gloves or mittens. It gets cold as can be up here in the winter. Henry said when he was herding up here one winter he wore three coats and other clothes in proportion and nearly froze in them.

On September 17, 1899 Phil wrote,

I am in considerable misery just now on account of this old Indian has just returned from Haiwee with two burro loads of grub including watermelons, apples and grapes, wherefore my stomach aches.

These little kids up here are the darndest, most aggravating little cusses on the face of the earth, I do believe. Sometimes when we are a little late about getting into camp at night, and of course in a great hurry, the little brats poke along as if they didn't want to get home until morning. When we start a little ahead to turn the leaders the right way and then stop to wait for the kids, they come tagging along at a snail's pace over the top of some little rise until I think the last one is in sight. I start on my way rejoicing, when ba-a-a-a from away above me, and I see some little white or black head peeping over the hill. Perhaps half a dozen others follow it and I will perhaps get to the bottom of the hill with these few and begin to congratulate myself upon being nearly to camp and ba-a-a-a comes from some other little varmint at the top of the hill. I often go back determined to 'knock the natural stuffin out of him', but they look up in such a funny way as if to say, 'Now what in time does this big galoot want to come howling around here for?' Then I have to laugh at them instead of giving them the whaling they need.

Sometimes my dog won't work and I give him a scolding or throw a rock at him and he starts for camp on the trot. Pretty soon, back he comes with abject apologies suspended from

Phil Hand in 1900 after he had quit herding goats on the Mojave Desert. He had been to town, had his hair cut and put on new clothes.

every hair on his most abjectly wagging tail and then he does pretty well for a while.

On November 9, 1899 he continued,

I put a patch on the knee of my overalls the other day and it is really quite a creditable job. A fellow is obliged to be an all around man up here, cook, tailor, goat-herder and butcher as we kill our own meat. You ought to have seen the loaf of bread I made the other day, it was a dandy, I tell you. I think it weighed about forty pounds. We managed to wash it down by putting lots of gravy on it and sending coffee down after each bite, but it would have been tempting providence to have gone swimming after a meal. The failure wasn't so much my fault as that of the sourdough spoiling by putting it too close to the fire so that it cooked a little before we used it. We have fresh meat all the time and its mighty hard to beat, fried or boiled. Here is our average bill of fare: Breakfast; fried meat, fried beans, gravy, bread and coffee. Supper; boiled meat, boiled cabbage, rice or macaroni, occasionally stewed raisins, bread, gravy, and tea. One of us comes into camp about an hour before time to bring the goats in, and has supper ready by the time the others get in.

We killed a big fat goat last night before supper and he will probably last us a week or maybe ten days, you see our appetites aren't at all delicate. Charlie is getting fat and I'll be 21 years old Monday.

On November 27, 1899 Phil continued,

Charlie went to (Coso) Hot Springs this morning leaving Ginger (an Indian herder) and me to follow our own noses, likewise the goats. Ginger is going over tomorrow and I guess I'll go the day after as they are only about nine miles from here and it's too good a chance to miss as we may not be so near them again in a year or more. Fred says there are a couple of bathhouses and a little stone house built there for the benefit of rheumatic people who care to go there.

Over in the last place we camped there was a lot of Loco Weed and the goats were eating it pretty lively. We moved Saturday but it was like jumping from the frying pan into the fire as the Loco is as bad or worse here. We haven't been camped in a canyon since Charles came out here and I'm getting homesick for a nice one again though it isn't quite such difficult work herding on level ground as the goats can't get out of sight so easily.

I burned my shoes so badly when I tried to dry them after the rain that they broke all to pieces and I had to get a new pair though I hadn't had those a month. They cost $3.50 a pair and this is my third pair since I've been here. They weigh four pounds a pair and they tired my legs pretty considerable when I first began to wear them and I expect when I get back into my light shoes again I'll be stepping high like a purebred horse until I get use to them.

We are just starting for a place abut fifty miles south of here called Sage Canyon and we expect to be until the first of February in getting there, stopping for three or four days at different canyons, according to the quality and quantity of feed in each.

We have been having a spell of about as beastly weather as it has ever been my luck to be out in, rain, snow, sleet and wind. The last named blowing at an average velocity of fifty billion miles an hour. We herded in a snowstorm all day a few days ago and as there happened to be no wind that day it was surprisingly warm and pleasant. There is a deep wash right next to the camp and at night when the wind blew so hard as to make our heads feel rather wobbly on our shoulders, we went down there and made an elegant fire under an oak tree. We were really quite comfortable except when an unusually big gust came whirling down the gulch and filled our eyes with smoke so that our tears irrigated a large area and caused the grass to flourish in a way wonderful to behold.

From Red Rock Canyon Phil wrote:

I didn't get to Mojave even long enough to get my hair cut and I am beginning to look a great deal after the Buffalo Bill order, with my waving black curls catching every breeze which comes. That is saying a good deal as the wind has been blowing great guns for two weeks with hardly a pause for breath and it doesn't go down with the sun either.

We got the goats sheared in Cameron, a little place about ten miles west of Mojave. As there was no feed there we have been obliged to take our back tracks and a hard time we had of it too. It was bright moon light and dreadfully windy so that the pesky goats didn't want to stay in camp at night so we had to guard them all night long by relays. We were all completely tired out with a long day's drive from sunup until sunset without a stop.

The foreman has to go back to Cameron and get a couple of hundred goats we left there because the little baby kids were too young to travel. We didn't have a big enough wagon to haul them in. He forgot to bring out milk buckets so we have to milk our little 'cows' into a granite basin. He only brought three cups so that one of us has to use a baking powder can to drink our coffee out of and he only brought three forks and he left a couple of donkeys on the road somewhere because he was too lazy to hunt them up. He hauled the camp things up in the wagon and he had about fifty little kids in it too before we got up here and they felt awfully bad without their mothers and kept things lively with their chin music.

Last night was the first full night's sleep I have had for some time so I don't feel quite so ornery today as usual. Even the fool goats get so tired and sleepy with their night running that when they camp in the middle of the day for a rest, as they almost always do, some of them will go to sleep and sleep so soundly that I have to go and wake them up after the rest of the band starts out or they will get lost and they haven't sense enough to come to camp at night without being driven.

The goats chewed my hat one night so I was obliged to go very nearly bare headed for a week or more until Fred could bring my other one from Haiwee. We have to haul our water in kegs in the wagon or pack it on burros so that we are as saving of water as possible. We generally make it a point to wash our hands and faces at least once a week, whether they need it or not, and then we give the dogs the water.

I have a few over two thousand in my band and in the band that Charlie, Mr. Bellows and Fred take care of there are about two hundred and fifty old nannies and two hundred and seventy little kids. Fred and Charlie get the same wages that I do and Mr. Bellows has their supper all ready for them when they come in at night. I have to cook mine after I come in at dark. How is that for fairness? Don't you think I have a right to register a pretty strong kick? Charlie took my band out one day so that I could get a chance to take a bath and he was so tired that night that he went to bed as soon as he had eaten his supper.

It is almost like being at home again to get back into the mountains after being so long down on the hot, dusty desert. If you could see some of the beauty spots I herd in every day you wouldn't wonder that I like the hills the best. Some of the slopes are as yellow as gold with poppies, dandelions, daisies and butter-cups. Perhaps the very next sandy slope will be as blue as the last was yellow with baby blue eyes, larkspur and two or three other varieties that I don't know the names of and never saw anywhere else. The willows in the creek in the bottom of the canyons are all leafed out and there is a little shrub that grows among them with blossoms on, almost exactly like peach blossoms.

From where I am sitting now I can see old Kaiwa's little ranch in the bottom of the canyon and the ditches he dug for irrigation. There used to be three or four old shacks on the ranch but the Indians got into trouble with some of the white people at South Fork, over the other side of this range. The sheriff with two deputies came over to arrest a couple of the young bucks and they shot the sheriff (Constable Johnny Powers), and one of the deputies (Oliver McCoy). They would have shot the other deputy (Sam Gann) if he hadn't run too almighty fast that a bullet couldn't catch him. The two that were shot killed three Indians before they died and then some of Powers relations came over and cleaned out the whole out-fit and burned down the houses so that all there is left is the stone fireplace and chimney of one of them. One of the Indians (Wampei Jiggens) was sent to San Quentin and he died there in a very short time. An Indian can't stand confinement for very long.

The goats behaved themselves so well yesterday that I wasn't any more tired when I got to camp last night than I was when I left it in the morning. You see, when I have them in the hills if they start to running too fast I simply turn them up a sandy slope and the climbing soon takes the vinegar out of their legs and puts it into their appetites. Just now they are on a big pile of rocks and are chasing each other back and forth over them and having more fun than half a dozen Sunday School picnics. They are not at home on the plains and don't know how to behave themselves any more than a fish out of water.

The goats are away over at the other side of the canyon now and the bells sound fine coming from so far. There are thirteen different toned bells in the bands and when they are all ringing at once it sounds almost like music. One would hardly believe that any animal could be fool enough to run through feed six inches high day after day until they would get so poor that they couldn't run any more. But that is just exactly what these fools do and the better the feed the faster they go until I get so disgusted with them that I never want to see another goat or have anything to do with them.

I don't much fancy the long hot drive to Mojave but I guess it won't hurt us much as we have made the trip twice already. After we leave Sage Canyon on the down trip there comes a drive of about 35 miles across the desert and there isn't a bit of water for the goats. We have to pack water in kegs on the burros for our own use. It will take ten days or two weeks to make the trip and I expect it will be hotter than the skillets the whole way down there.

It seems almost a pity to have to give it up now after staying with it all through the winter and just as the goats are getting fat and lazy so that they don't care to move around very fast and we are beginning to enjoy ourselves a little more. I wish I had a hundred dollars to spent so I could get a pass clear through to Chicago (on the train with the goats that were sold in Mojave) and return but my purse doesn't show more than $75 and I'll hang on to that until I get another place to work.

These letters give just a little flavor of the lesser-known art of goat herding, and to visualize their lives during this time. These men were strong, tough, innovating individuals. They helped build the West.

The Owens River – Los Angeles Aqueduct

The story of the Owens River-Los Angeles Aqueduct is the story of a great city (Los Angeles) built on a desert that one day awoke to the very serious fact that it must stop growing or find more water for its use. The city did not wish to stop growing, but it needed more water. It had to utilize to the utmost limit every drop in every stream to which it had a right.

When the Mission San Gabriel was founded in 1771 and the pueblo of Los Angeles was founded ten years later, there was very little water anywhere between Tehachapi and San Diego. Although there are a number of riverbeds through this section of country, during most of the year they are dry streaks of dust. The pueblo of Los Angeles obtained most of its water from the Los Angeles River, which has a considerable underground flow, although there is very little water visible. At that time there was sufficient water. But as the "gringos" crowded into the village, a shortage soon developed. For a while engineers had succeeded in obtaining additional supplies of water by drilling wells, which were sufficient to meet the growth of population until 1904. However, a series of dry years greatly diminished the supply from the rivers and caused the underground level to lower. The necessity for an additional water supply was impressed on the water commissioners in 1904, when for ten days in July the daily consumption exceeded the inflow into the reservoirs by four million gallons. Temporary measures of conservation were used and meters checked excessive consumption.

The population of Los Angeles in 1905 was 200,000 and experts estimated that by 1925 the city would have a population of 400,000 and be tragically short of water. The city administration sent out engineers in all directions in a quest for more, but they reported there was no water to be had south of Tehachapi or west of the Colorado River.

According to some authorities, Fred Eaton, an entrepreneur, engineer and later the mayor of Los Angeles, had an interest in the Owens River as a potential source of water for Los Angeles, as early as the 1890s. Knowing the city needed the water so badly, his thinking became more focused after the turn of the century. Eaton's plan was to acquire ownership rights to the Owens' water and for Los Angeles to build an aqueduct and purchase the water from him. On his trips to Los Angeles from Owens Valley, Mr. Eaton, with the eyes of an engineer, had naturally been interested in the physical characteristics of the country. After going over the possible route which an aqueduct would have to take, he decided that it would be possible to carry water from the Owens River to the city of Los Angeles. He was fearful lest the city government would not approve such an enormous project. He made plans to carry out the project by a private organization should his proposals be refused.

The newly formed U.S. Reclamation Service was investigating the feasibility of initiating reclamation projects in several sites in the southwestern United States. The Owens Valley was one of the sites. The purpose of these projects was to develop water resources in arid areas to promote agricultural expansion and production by irrigation. In 1903 the Service had a small staff of engineers under the supervision of Joseph Lippincott. Lippincott had been a resident of Los Angeles since 1891. He was an experienced and highly respected hydraulic engineer.

In the summer of 1904 Eaton, Lippincott and others took a pack trip, later advertised as a "vacation," into Owens Valley and the Sierra in Long Valley. Lippincott shared with Eaton information obtained from the Service's field studies, about the location of a dam site on the Owens River at the southern end of Long Valley. Eaton shared some of his thoughts about a possible aqueduct to Los Angeles. Lippincott would later deny this.

William Mulholland was a self-made, self-taught man who rose from a simple water tender to become the driving head of the entire water works of Los Angeles. He was superintendent of the water system when the city purchased the system from the private company in 1902. Mulholland continued as superintendent.

In September 1904 Eaton briefed Mulholland regarding his concept of an aqueduct and sparked Mulholland's interest. Quickly, Eaton and Mulholland embarked on a trip to Owens and Long Valley where they spent several weeks conducting their own studies. At the end of that time Mulholland was convinced that the project of an all-gravity flow aqueduct was feasible. He returned to Los Angeles to make his report. Mulholland recommended the project to the Board of Water Commissioners, with a cost estimate of $25,000,000.

All were in agreement to keep their actions secret. They feared speculation, increasing costs for acquisition of lands and water rights for any aqueduct project. Events began to move rapidly. In November 1904 Mulholland met with Lippincott and F.H. Newall, Chief of the Reclamation Service. Newall agreed to provide the City with all the data, reports, surveys, etc. gathered by the Service. In late 1904 and early 1905 Eaton began to buy up options for land and water rights in the lower Owens Valley.

When Eaton first started buying land and water rights Lippincott asked him, as a favor, if he could look up some certain hydroelectric site filings located in Independence. Lippincott gave Eaton an authorization letter to this effect. When he showed this letter at the Land Office, they concluded that he was an agent for the Reclamation Service and that all the land/water options he was taking up were on behalf of the Reclamation Service. Many landowners were gladly giving options on their water rights for the benefit of the supposed Reclamation project,

William Mulholland

and not charging exorbitant prices. Later, Eaton claimed that he had never said that he was an agent for the Service, but he apparently never dissuaded people from that impression.

After the engineers, the Water Board, Mayor McAleer, and City Attorney Matthews had made their reports, Eaton and Mulholland made another trip into the Valley to inspect the proposed project. Mr. Eaton had obtained as many water rights, options and contracts for the proposed sale of lands along the proposed route as possible. These he was willing to sell and turn over to the city. The Water Board approved the plan and agreed to buy Eaton's rights.

When it came time for the city to purchase all of Eaton's holdings there was an agreement for the Rickey Ranch holdings in Long Valley for $450,000. However, Eaton limited the easement for reservoir land to only the land covered by a 100-foot dam. For the 140-foot to 160-foot dam

Electric tunnel train, showing rocker dump muck cans

that Mulholland wanted, and ultimately needed, Eaton wanted an extra one million dollars. Mulholland refused to pay that price. A bitter enmity arose between the two men and they never spoke to each other for 30 years. This is why a large capacity reservoir was not built at the beginning; an omission that Mulholland was bitterly criticized for, and the lack of which might have been the cause of the terrible controversies between Los Angeles and the Owens Valley in the 1920s.

In July 1905 the project was first made public in the *Los Angeles Times*. The announcement created a great sensation with the whole population. Here was the solution to the water problem, which had confined the growth of the city. Now as far as the water supply was concerned there was no limit to the city growth. The engineers had estimated this water supply sufficient for a city with a population of two million. The aqueduct, with a drainage area of twenty-eight hundred square miles, would bring 260,000,000 gallons of water daily or 290,000 acre-feet annually, to the city.

On June 7, 1907, a bond issue for $23,000,000 was submitted to the voters and was approved by a vote of ten to one. Superintendent Mulholland was now also assigned as the Chief Engineer for the construction of the aqueduct within the Department of Public Works.

The real construction did not begin until October 1, 1908, although work on the Elizabeth Tunnel under the San Fernando Mountains began in October 1907. This tunnel was one of the most difficult obstacles to overcome. It was 26,780 feet in length and ten by twelve feet in diameter mostly through solid granite. It was begun earlier than the other construction because it was estimated that it would take five years to complete. It was completed in the record time of forty months.

Mulholland and his engineers developed the following plan for design of the aqueduct: The water was to be taken from the Owens river thirty-five miles north of Owens lake. It was to be carried through an open canal for sixty miles to a large reservoir, the Haiwee, which had a capacity of 63,800-acre feet. It would then be carried another hundred and twenty-eight miles through combination conduits, tunnels and siphons to a reservoir at Fairmont in the Antelope Valley. This was on the northern side of the proposed Elizabeth Tunnel through the San Fernando Mountains. The tunnel is a pressure tunnel regulated by the reservoir at Fairmont. From the southern portal of the tunnel water would drop through the rapidly descending San Francisquito canyon, where big possibilities for power development existed. Then carried on by natural channels, tunnels, siphons and conduits, for a distance of fifteen miles to the San Fernando reservoir at the upper end of the San Fernando Valley. The total distance of the aqueduct from the intake to the San Fernando reservoir would be 233 miles, all of which would be by gravity flow, with no pumping required. At this time it would be the longest aqueduct in the Western Hemisphere.

This was the plan that took an army of five thousand men five years to complete, working under the difficulties of extreme desert heat in the summer and just as extreme cold mountain winter weather.

However, the pioneer farmers of Owens Valley had other thoughts about taking their water and transporting it to the city of Los Angeles. No better historical evidence can be available than that of an eye witness whom can say, "I was there." This is what Richard Coke Wood could say about what he called, "California's Little Civil War." His story was about the struggle that occurred in the 1920s between Owens Valley pioneer farmers and the great growing metropolis of Los Angeles. He tells the following in his book, The Owens Valley and the Los Angeles Water Controversy:

> It seems only yesterday, really it was August, 1918, that my sister and I rode the little "Slim Princess," narrow-gauge railroad into the station of Laws, five miles from Bishop, and took a hard rubber tire bus over to Bishop. I was only eleven years old and water problems had no meaning to me. However, I had been impressed by the blue and sparkling water of Owens Lake as we had come by it on our trip through the valley. I'm always glad that I have this memory as I drive by the dry and dusty lakebed today. Owens Valley was still a beautiful agricultural area at that time. As a high school boy at Bishop, I remember working during the summer vacations on the fine dairy ranches with their large

> fields of alfalfa. In my free time, I amused myself by spearing enormous carp in the large irrigation ditches that took the sparkling Sierra Nevada snow water from the Owens River and transported it to the arid lands of the Valley.

> It was during these years from 1919 to 1923 that I became conscious of the struggle between representatives of Los Angeles, the "city" men, and the farmers, supported by the bankers of Owens Valley, Wilfred and Mark Watterson. They were good men, fighting with their financial resources to sustain the farmers in their efforts, first to keep their ranches and, then after this became hopeless, to force the great city to pay a fair and honest price for the property.

> I remember the night a group of indignant farmers dramatically rushed into a restaurant in Bishop, threw a hangman's noose over the head of Lawyer Hall, who had "sold out" to the "city," transported him a few miles south of town and told him not to come back. He didn't!

> I remember the year of talk about arbitration and compromise and fair appraisal. I remember how real hatred developed for the leaders of the Department of Water and Power in Los Angeles, especially William Mulholland. To the residents of Los Angeles he was the great hero engineer who had built the impossible 233-mile aqueduct. To the farmers of Owens Valley he represented greed, arrogance and overwhelming financial power that finally brought resistance in the valley to a halt, with the failure of all the Watterson brothers' banks in the four towns of the valley.

> I remember the desperate acts taken by the farmers in an effort to gain publicity and support in their struggle for a "fair deal" with the city. The opening of the spillway gates at the Alabama Hills, turning the waters from the aqueduct back into Owens River and Owens Lake is a strong memory. I was first aware of what was happening when I read the sign on the flagpole on Main Street in Bishop saying, "If I'm not in my place of business, you'll find me at the Alabama Spillway."

> I remember the growing bitterness when promises to negotiate if the farmers would close the spillway were not kept and dynamiting of the aqueduct was resorted to in an effort to dramatize the farmer's cause. They never really intended to destroy the aqueduct. That would have been easy.

> I remember the morning in Mojave when I was held for three hours by the local deputy sheriff for investigation because I had just come down from Bishop on my way to Pasadena and a dynamite blast had blown up a section of the

siphon on the aqueduct. I could be a suspect even though my sister-in-law and two-year old boy were with me. Everyone coming out of the Valley was being stopped and investigated.

I remember hearing the "booms" of the explosions that would go off around Bishop for several years during the intense struggle and we would say, "There goes another city well." Finally, I remember the excitement of the little crowd around the closed door of the First National Bank of Bishop. I had just returned to work at 12 o'clock on August 4, 1927, I saw a crowd, ran across the street and read the sign, which said, "We find it necessary to close our banks in the Owens Valley. This result has been brought about by the past four years of destructive work carried on by the City of Los Angeles," signed by Wilfred and Mark Watterson. The state bank examiner had found irregularities and misrepresentation and the Wattersons were indicted on thirty-six counts for fraud and embezzlement and sent to San Quentin.

I remember the gloom and hopelessness that settled over not only the farmers but the businessmen of the towns after this financial collapse. For a few weeks we had difficulty getting enough money to carry on our businesses.

This crisis broke the resistance of the farmers but now the city, because of general public pressure and disapproval, agreed to buy all the property in Owens Valley. Farmers and businessmen in large numbers now began to sell out and leave this beautiful valley where they had been born and that they had loved so much and moved to other parts of California to start over again if they were not too old. A sign was erected on the highway on the north side of Bishop, which very simply told the story—"Los Angeles City Limits."

Before the work could commence on the aqueduct an enormous amount of preliminary work had to be done. A system of transporting freight north along the proposed route of the waterway had to be settled. There was no railroad into the valley from the south, although the Carson and Colorado narrow gauge came into the northern end of the valley continuing south to Lone Pine. Consequently they were faced with the problem of getting their equipment from the main railroad line at Mojave north through the Indian Wells Valley to Lone Pine. It was estimated that a total of 210,000 tons of aqueduct freight had to be transported from Los Angeles to the city of Lone Pine in Inyo County.

Typical desert construction camp; 3500 men were maintained in these camps during construction of the aqueduct

First, bids were taken on moving this large amount of freight with teams and wagons. The lowest bid that was submitted was 28 cents per ton-mile. In the area of the proposed aqueduct very little forage or water existed for the teams. Taking care of their needs would amount to 10 percent of the total tonnage hauled. It soon was evident that the only feasible plan was for a railroad to be built from Mojave north to the Owenyo Station at Lone Pine, a total of 125 miles. It was decided that it would be cheaper yet to have a railroad company build the line and they would charge for the freight. The city tried to obtain bids from several railroads to build the line, but the Southern Pacific was the only one interested. The city entered into a contract with the Southern Pacific in April of 1908 and the system, affectionately known as "The Jawbone," was completed in October of 1910. The "Jawbone" continued to operate for many years after the completion of the aqueduct. The section from Mojave to Searles Station, where it connects with the Trona Railroad is still in operation to this day.

A branch line needed to be constructed from the Cantil Siding up Red Rock Canyon to supply the north end of the Jawbone division and about fifteen miles of the Freeman division. Because this route was so sandy, it would have cost the city about 50 cents per ton-mile to build roads for teams. Using the Red Rock Railroad the cost was about eight cents per ton-mile. This spur railroad line was the most expensive part of the whole route. To complicate things this was also an area where numerous flash floods came down the canyon. To avoid these flash floods the main line turned eastward at Cantil and went around the El Paso Mountains, even though it added 18 miles to the total length of the railroad.

Regardless of the floods it was decided to build an 8.35-mile long spur up Red Rock Canyon that would terminate at Dove Springs Camp. In June 1908 the railroad reached Cantil which was 23 miles north of Mojave and the Red Rock Spur started here. The line was finished in May of 1909. A large amount of freight was hauled over this line, including four steam shovels to be used on the Freeman Division.

The Jawbone and Freeman divisions employed 400 workers, most of whom lived and worked out of the Dove Springs Camp. From the time the Red Rock Spur was started the City of Los Angeles viewed the maintenance of this section as, "A precarious proposition." They expressed the desire to make the time it would have to be maintained this section as short as possible. Their worst fear came true when a flash flood on August 31, 1909 roared down the canyon. It destroyed the local stage station and store owned by Rudolf Hagen, causing $15,000 worth of damage. In December 1910 the Red Rock Railroad was sold for salvage for approximately $40,000 and was dismantled.

In 1964 George Pipkin wrote an article for the Desert Sands entitled, "The Train That Was—The Slowest." Following are some excerpts from this article:

"The Sidewinder" passenger train No. 88 on the Jawbone Division of the Southern Pacific, pulled out of the Mojave yards at the break o' dawn on April 19, 1924, beginning its daily run. The Jawbone Division is unique in railroading circles, inasmuch as it was built by the City of Los Angeles Water Department to haul material and supplies needed in the construction of the aqueduct. The name Jawbone was derived from the finding of the jawbone of a saber tooth tiger by an aqueduct grading crew in a canyon north of Cantil. (This was also the name of the canyon.)

Around the first of the century the construction of the railroad started simultaneously with the construction of the aqueduct. The railroad and aqueduct paralleled each other and both progressed slowly northward together. In order to maintain gravity flow, the aqueduct skirted the lower reaches of the Sierra Nevada Mountains, while the railroad sought the level stretches in the valley below. At no time were the two more than a few miles apart. Tough, sweating, swearing, tobacco chewing long-line skinners hauled the material from the supply stations along the railroad up to the point of construction on the aqueduct.

When the Sidewinder, consisting of a combination mail and baggage car, a day passenger coach and a sleeping car pulled out of Mojave early on that April day, I was a passenger aboard the train. Twenty-one years of age at the time, I had been hired out of Los Angeles on the recommendation of Ralph Barnes, a buddy of mine from our hometown, Bauxite, Arkansas. Ralph had already been hired as a timekeeper for the newly formed Inyo Chemical Company at Cartago, which was located 20 miles south of Lone Pine on Owens Lake. The new company, backed by Michigan capital, was rejuvenating

Hauling with tractors on the Mojave Desert

the defunct California Alkali Company plant that was built during World War I, to produce soda ash from the brine of Owens Lake. I was hired to open and operate the company store, which was a necessity for small plants on the desert in those days. I was most anxious to get to my new job at Cartago and start what was to be my long desert career. There were times while aboard California's slowest train that I had my doubts about ever reaching my destination. In all fairness, let us say that the railroad was not entirely to blame for the slowness of the train, the County of Inyo also got into the act, as you will see.

On that Memorial Day, the train crew consisted of Pop Fuller, the engineer, who was nearing the age of retirement, conductor, Bill Lovejoy, was in charge of the train, Cecil was the fireman, and Old John who was the most accommodating and aggravating man I ever met, was the brakeman. As usual the pullman porter was named George. The advanced age of the train crew could be attributed to the fact that the Jawbone Division was, in railroading parlance, known as the "Rocking Chair Run" or the "Picnic Route." It took a lot of whiskers, seniority, to hold a job on the Division. The advantages were, the train crew lived in Mojave and could be home at night with their families. The run up to Owenyo and back was made in a day's time.

After the elapse of 40 years, why do I still remember the names of the train crew? I'll tell you why. During the course of the hundred miles to Cartago, I had ample time to make their acquaintance. The train was an hour late getting out of Mojave. When we reached Indian Wells Valley, the desert floor was carpeted with beautiful wildflowers. The train stopped miles from the nearest station and accommodating John invited the passengers to go flower picking, which we did. When the train arrived at Little Lake, seventy miles out of Mojave, it was an hour and a half late.

The fragrance of the wildflowers in our coach was out of this world. When we arrived at Little Lake, even though the train was behind schedule, we, the paying guests (7 cents per mile) were in a joyful state of bliss, for spring in the desert can be friendly, beautiful and adventurous. Then came the rude awakening. The hoof and mouth disease, which affected cattle, had invaded Southern California from Mexico. Cattle were dying and being destroyed by the thousands. Inyo County, which is a great cattle country, was determined at all cost, to keep the dread disease away from their door. Old '88' and its passengers must be dipped or fumigated. We could be, so said genial Tom Devine, an Inyo County deputy sheriff who was in charge of fumigating, a carrier of the disease. According to the law (local county ordinance) if we wished to enter Inyo County we would be subjected to a thorough fumigation. We were instructed to open our luggage and spread our

clothing over the seats. Soon the coach resembled a Chinese laundry on Monday, bloomers and all. After we alighted, containers of formaldehyde were placed in the coach and the windows and doors closed. Outside the train a crew of deputized cowpokes, the fumigators who were eager to have some fun with the dudes, met us. Large canvas bags about six feet in length were used for each individual. We were placed in the bags, a drawstring was pulled tightly around our neck and then a pan of formaldehyde was placed through a flap opening in the bottom of the bag between our feet. If by chance there was a skin abrasion on the body, the formaldehyde burned like the devil. One woman fainted. It was a slow process as there were only three bags and each victim had to remain in the bag ten minutes. Cecil, the fireman was fumigated first, as he had to get back to his boiler. George the pullman porter was last. Never, will I forget George's expression. His startled eyes reminded me of two large black grapes in a bowl of milk.

The windows of the coach were raised, the doors opened and the train was backed down the track for a mile and then came roaring back up to where we were standing. This was done, so they said, to air out the coaches, to blow the stinking fumes from the train. It didn't work, for when we got aboard we were coughing, sneezing, choking and crying. Trying to get fresh air,

our heads were stuck so far out of the car windows it's a wonder we didn't fall from the train. Gone was the fragrance of the wildflowers, replaced by the ill-smelling formaldehyde. Gone were our gentle tempers, replaced by a slow burn. Outraged we were, dipped like a lowly bunch of sheep. Let me say here, an everlasting credit to the Inyo County Fathers of the time, that the stringent methods employed to fumigate people and things worked, as it kept the hoof and mouth disease out of Inyo County.

The train was now four hours late, when a few miles out of Little Lake it came to a jarring stop. What now, we wondered. "Accommodating" John informed us that we had now reached Haiwee. Here the locomotive would take on water, assisted by the fireman, and during the delay, he and the rest of the crew were going fishing down to the reservoir, a distance of only a few hundred yards. Believe it or not, they did! Thirty minutes later, "aggravating" John came through the coach displaying a four-pound bass, which he had caught.

During my years at Cartago, I came to know and to respect the crew on the "Gravy Special" very well, as it was my duty to meet the train each day for the mail. Then came the day when Old "88," running several hours late as usual, plowed into a washout just south of Cottonwood Canyon. Pop Fuller rode his engine into the deep gully and was killed. Cecil, the fireman, jumped and was injured. Although the baggage car and the day coach fell into the wash on top of the locomotive, the pullman remained upright on the track at the brink of the washout. Fortunately the few passengers and the rest of the crew escaped serious injury.

It was said that George the porter, came to the door of the pullman, took one look at the chaos confronting him, went back and hid under a berth and it was half a day before he was found. It was also said that the Southern Pacific brought suit against the City of Los Angeles, claiming that the cloudburst alone would not have washed out the track, but that the water from the broken aqueduct did the damage. The City contended that it was an act of God, for which they were not responsible. The Railroad countered that the aqueduct was broken at 4:00 AM and the wreck occurred at 11:00 AM, and why were they not notified in time to hold up their train.

When she was 89 years old, Mrs. Ada Walker, mother of Jack Walker of Lone Pine, wrote an interesting and humorous account of her arrival in Brown via the railroad. Her paper is titled, "My First Impressions of America." Ada came directly from England on the Lusitania, cross-country by rail to Los Angeles, where her husband was waiting to bring her here where he was working on the aqueduct. In Mojave they transferred to the "Jawbone Line." She wrote, "The railroad was being built and all the equipment for it and for the aqueduct was on our train, consequently we were shuttled off on the sidings every dozen miles or so to unload material. I asked Alfie what the house was like? He looked pretty sly and said we had no house, we have a tent. A tent? I couldn't live in a tent. Traveling all night long didn't give me a chance to see the country until dawn, and then all I saw was miles and miles of sand and sagebrush. The porter announced that at the next town they would stop for breakfast. Glory Alleluia! At last we would get to see something. But I guess I had hoped for too much. It was just a siding with a closed-in shed like place where a table of bare boards set up with boiled meat and potatoes (with the eyes in yet), thick hunks of bread, butter and coffee, anything but appetizing, but I was hungry enough to eat anything."

They went a little farther to Narka Siding, just south of Little Lake, where they got off the train and went up the canyon to the Soda Hill camp by mules and a wagon. When they got to the camp, she looked around the inside of the tent and saw they only had boxes to sit on and not much more in the way of furnishings. But she said she survived. They settled in Lone Pine, where the golf course is now. Their son Jack was born there.

Intake at the Aqueduct. *Left to right:* engineers Lippincott, Mulholland and MacKay; and Edward Johnson of the Board of Public Works.

The railroad had a siding every 4-1/2 miles. The materials, as they came in on the train, were hauled from the sidings to the canyons on great flat-decked wagons supported by steel wheels with tires two feet wide. Mule teams pulled these wagons. The teamsters, as well as the railroad men, worked through the heat of the day with few rest breaks.

Fredrick "Fritz" Mills, who was later a resident of Ridgecrest, is the son of Captain Mills who was an engineer on the aqueduct and had his headquarters in Sand Canyon during 1909-1913. "Fritz" carried the mail in a horse drawn cart from Brown, where it was left by the train, to Sand Canyon, where it was sorted and sent on to other aqueduct offices by express wagon. Fritz earned $60 a month at this job. For a short time he drove a long line team earning $80 a month. Then he worked in the aqueduct office, again earning $60 a month. While working on the aqueduct, a miner earned $3.75 a day drilling holes, a mucker would earn $2.50 a day shoveling dirt into carts to be hauled out and a laborer would earn $2.00 a day setting track and cleaning up around camp. One dollar a day was spent for food and clean sheets. A new shirt cost 45 cents and trousers 65 cents.

For many miles across the Mojave Desert there was no water available for use in the construction. A pipeline virtually paralleling the aqueduct was laid from the intake to San Fernando.

Branch lines were laid up the canyons to camps for water supply, the total mileage of pipe laid was 260 miles at a cost of $229,000. Two power plants were constructed in Owens Valley, the Cottonwood and Division Creek No. 2, also 218 miles of transmission lines.

Telephone and telegraph lines had to be laid from the main offices in Los Angeles to the intake in Owens Valley, a distance of 240 miles. Also 218 miles of transmission lines had to be built. Roads into the valley were very inadequate, many of them being only trails. The Gray Ridge road into the Jawbone camps, a distance of about nine miles, cost $44,000 to construct. A total of five-hundred-five miles of roads and trails were constructed at the cost of $279,300. Fifty-seven camps with suitable housing had to be established.

Housing of the forces engaged in the construction of the aqueduct required lodgings, dwellings, offices, mess houses, hospitals, warehouses and miscellaneous structures, such as blacksmith and machine shops, tunnel plants, hay barns and stables.

The climate along the aqueduct varies from intense summer desert heat, when the thermometer reaches 110 degrees, to temperatures approaching zero in winter. Efforts were made to make the lodgings comfortable in both summer and winter. Bunkhouses for laborers were made to accommodate from one to eight men to a

Mess House Crew, 1908-1913. Each construction camp along the aqueduct had its own mess hall and cooks to serve the work force. Pictured is a typical mess crew and hall construction. *Tom Chapman. Courtesy High Desert Historical Society.*

Electric dipper dredge cutting diversion canal

room, and each room had an outside window. The cost of these buildings was about $25.00 for each man housed. Four-room dwellings were erected for the division engineers, who paid a monthly rent to the city sufficient to return the investment. These dwellings each cost from $600 to $900 depending upon location and cost of hauling material.

Many of the aqueduct buildings, such as offices, dwellings and bunk houses, were designed so that they could be taken down in sections, loaded on wagons and expeditiously erected again at some other point.

The total expenditure for buildings used in connection with the Aqueduct construction was $341,554.00. Losses due to fire amounted to $12,826.00. The salvage value of the buildings was $18,881.00, making the net cost of housing $322,672.00. Total revenue from rentals of these buildings was $27,776.00. Following is a statement of the number of buildings erected:

Bunk houses, cottages and engineer's residences	248
Machine shops	10
Compressor plants	23
Barns and hay sheds	33
Warehouses	36
Office buildings	25
Hospitals	8
Sawmills	7
Powder magazines	50
Garages	1
Tents	1,600
Shops, sheds, corrals	250
Total	2,291 Buildings Erected

Provisions had to be made for a vast quantity of cement needed for the lining of conduits and tunnels. For this purpose the city bought 1,250 acres of land in the Tehachapi Mountains covering the necessary deposits of limestone and clay. A cement mill costing $550,000 with a daily capacity of 1,200-barrels was built on the Cuddeback Ranch, five miles east of Tehachapi on the main line of the Southern Pacific railroad. This plant is known as the Monolith Cement Plant. The output of this mill for use in construction of the aqueduct was not adequate when work was going on at maximum speed. Hence, an additional 200,000 barrels were obtained from other sources. A total of over a million barrels of cement were used.

One-hundred-thirty-five-thousand acres of land had to be bought for protection of water rights and sites for reservoirs. This was not an easy task as is seen by the difficulties that developed in the Owens Valley over this matter. These were some of the gigantic preliminary problems, which had to be solved before permanent construction could begin in October 1908.

After preliminary work was completed there remained the actual work of constructing the aqueduct. This, briefly, was the task faced by the engineers. Tunnels required the greatest amount of time; there were 142 tunnels, totaling 53 miles in length. Twelve miles of steel siphon, from 7-1/2 to 11-1/2 feet in diameter and 1-1/8 to 1/4 inches in thickness, had to be laid; 34 miles of open unlined conduit had to be laid and 39 miles of open concrete-lined conduit had to be constructed. Ninety-seven miles of covered conduit at a cost of $10,000 a mile had to be completed. Three large reservoirs, Haiwee, Fairmont and San Fernando, had to be constructed. Tinemaha, a fourth reservoir, just south of Big Pine, was built after the original construction.

In the first eleven months, twenty-two miles of tunnel were driven, sixteen miles of concrete conduit completed and four miles of open canal in Owens Valley dug. At this rate of progress, water would have been brought into the San Fernando reservoir in the fall of 1912, had there been no delay in providing funds. However, in 1910, due to the lack of finances, construction work almost ceased for several months. At the time of the shutdown there were four thousand men at work and within a few weeks there were only one thousand employed. This gives an idea of how greatly the work was hampered.

The first head of water was turned into the aqueduct in May 1913. When they turned the water in they did not know that the siphon had sprung a leak in Sand Canyon. They used a different method there than they had used in any other canyon. Two underground tunnels were built down both sides of the canyon walls. These tunnels were connected with steel pipe across the canyon. The first leak was spilling water down the north side of the canyon. The steel

needed to repair the leak was rushed up from Los Angeles and the siphon repaired. When the water was turned back into the system another leak showed up on the south wall. As the flow was increased slowly till it reached 42 second feet and the entire covering of the south tunnel was lifted upward by the pressure, water shot up into the air and the whole south canyon wall crashed into the bottom of the canyon. After close inspection it was decided that both tunnels would be abandoned and a steel siphon would be used down one side, across the canyon at the bottom end, and up the other side.

The opening ceremonies had to be postponed until repairs could be made. On November 5, 1913, a crowd of thirty thousand people gathered at the outlet of the aqueduct in San Fernando to celebrate completion of the greatest of all municipal projects. When the gates were opened and water came rushing from the aqueduct, Chief Engineer Mulholland was asked to make an address. It consisted of five words: "There it is, take it."

After the Aqueduct opened in 1913 and on through the '20s, '30s and '40s, many families of aqueduct patrolmen lived and worked out of the many camps along the system. These men and their families entered into the activities in local communities. Their children attended schools in the Indian Wells Valley.

One of these aqueduct stations was in Sand Canyon. In 1930 Dave Shelton moved there as senior patrolman. I remember that I attended the Brown School in 1932 and Dave Shelton's daughter was in the 7th or 8th grade. She was one of the older students that helped children in the lower grades, much like teacher's aides do today. Using this method Tiny Standard, the teacher, had four or five students helping her with the others.

There were two families stationed at Sand Canyon. The senior patrolman's home was down the canyon, east of the aqueduct, and the house up stream was the home of the other patrolman.

In 1933 Jeff Ramsey was Sand Canyon's second patrolman. Although Dave Shelton was senior patrolman both Jeff and Dave had the same duties. They were both on duty 24 hours a day. The men had two horses apiece. Each day they patrolled a section of the aqueduct. One day Jeff would ride eight miles to the north, checking for leaks or for any attempt of sabotage and Dave would ride eleven miles south to Short Canyon. The next day they would switch duties. This had to be done seven days a week. They both had telephones connecting them with other stations along the line. They were expected to be ready for any call, no matter what time of the day or night it came.

The Ramsey family was comprised of Jeff, his wife Maynette, and children Lois and Bob. Both Lois and Bob had many happy memories of the five years their family lived in Sand Canyon. The house the city built for them was comfortable. The walls were made of cement, one foot thick, which helped it stay cool in summer and warm in winter. They had a wood stove for heat, an indoor toilet that had a tank on the wall and a chain that pulled to flush and a nice bathtub, but no running hot water. At night their only source of light was from a Coleman lantern. They had a desert cooler. This was a frame built with screen on the sides, a door on the front with a small

pipe, which ran around the edges of the top. Small holes were drilled in the pipe that let water drip continually over the sides, which were covered with burlap. There was usually a slight breeze blowing and the wind going through the wet burlap sides kept the inside cool. The station had a cow that was kept with the four horses. She furnished milk and butter for the two families.

Lois Ramsey Carr was born June 14, 1914, in Los Angeles. She wrote the following:

I had graduated in 1933 from the Antelope Valley high school before we came to Sand Canyon. We shopped at Ives store in Inyokern, and at Safeway in Mojave. We attended church in Inyokern, and at the Schuette's when the minister came there. Dad drove a 1927 Plymouth sedan. Bob and I drove a Model T Ford coupe to school.

My dad was a welder for the Los Angeles Department of Water and Power. He did repair work all along the aqueduct, and was given the

Opening the Aqueduct headgates, February 13, 1913

THE OWENS RIVER — LOS ANGELES AQUEDUCT

Sand Canyon aqueduct station along with Dave and Sally Shelton. Having come from Orange County, we found the adventure of country living very interesting.

I especially liked it because we made our own fun and really learned to appreciate one another. Dad "rode ditch" and had the usual run-ins with sidewinders and diamond back rattlesnakes. He sometimes found stray sheep. Some, we ate, and some he got back to the sheepherders. His reward was sheepherder bread and wine, and a leg of lamb or two. The wine was OK if you put lots of lemonade with it. Hunting and eating whatever nature had to offer certainly helped with the food bill. Dad planted a garden, and raised chickens and turkeys.

I married John Carr in 1935. Our marriage was blessed with four children, Jeanne Evalyn in 1936, Robert Warren in 1938, John Norman in 1943, and James Herbert in 1946. I have 12 grandchildren and three great grandchildren as this is written (1989).

Bob Ramsey, who was 16 when they moved to Sand Canyon, remembers some additional information. Although he was lonely when he first moved there it wasn't long before he found his own amusement and came to enjoy the quiet beauty of their canyon. One type of recreation he had was climbing one of the canyon walls and rolling rocks down the side. He would find a rock he thought he could dislodge and prying it with a hefty stick to get it into position. Then lying on his back and pushing with his feet, down the mountainside it would bounce. They enrolled in the school in Inyokern and there were four grades in one room: 7th, 8th and the first two years of high school. There were only twelve students in the room. After two years in Inyokern Bob transferred to North Hollywood where he lived with an aunt and finished high school.

Bob enrolled in a program to learn all the aspects of welding. He went to work for the Los Angeles Water and Power as an inspector on the southern end of the aqueduct. While Bob was serving his apprenticeship at Trona he met Elenore Potter, whose father John Potter worked for the county road department. They were married in 1940. In 1978 Bob and Elenore moved to Kernville. Elenore's uncle, Bert James, gave them a piece of property and they built their home. After 59 years of marriage Elenore passed away and in 2001 Bob was still living in their home.

Bob at this time is still making trips back to Sand Canyon when groups of school children are bussed there so he can tell them how life was for a boy of 16 living there 68 years ago.

In 1942 Oscar Crowell took over as patrolman of Sand Canyon. His Daughter Litha was ten years old and went to school in Brown where she was taught by Tiny Standard. The house, which was newly built for the patrolman, had a few advantages. There was a small generator run by waterpower from the aqueduct. It produced direct current. During the day an iron could be used, at night a few lights could be used, but you couldn't use the iron and lights at the same time. They also had a radio, which ran by direct current and they could receive several stations from Los Angeles and other areas.

Litha's father, Oscar, maintained a small swimming pool, which was built near the house. Water coming from the aqueduct was ice cold, but after a day it was just right. The pool had to be drained and cleaned every few days because the algae built up and there were no chemicals to use.

There were two cloudbursts in Sand Canyon; the first was in 1922 the second in 1945. Joe Lacy, an eyewitness of the 1922 flood, told the story with graphic descriptions to the Los Angeles Times as follows:

The day of August was hot and humid. Seeking to avoid heavy labor during the day I had engrossed myself in a volume of Bret Harte. Shortly after noon I heard thunder back in the mountains, and coming out to take a look at the weather, I noticed two thunderheads gathering. A tremendous storm was forming over the high divide above Sand Canyon. The second storm was moving back toward the mountains. Thunderstorms, however, are not unusual in this vicinity during the summer. I paid no attention and went on with my affairs. Later in the afternoon I noticed that the storm over the desert had moved back and merged with the one over the mountains.

About 9 o'clock that evening the thunder and lightning became unusually violent and I came out of the house to take a look at the storm. I could see the flashes of lightning, and when the flashes came I could see the great black clouds piled up like mountains over the top of Sand Canyon. The thunder was echoing clear out into the desert, but I could not see any rain because the lower part of the storm was cut off from my view behind the nearby hills. As I stood there watching the storm I heard a noise that sounded like a motor truck coming down the canyon. I couldn't account for it because there was no road up the canyon and I couldn't imagine how a motor truck could have gotten up there.

The noise began to sound like several motor trucks, then like 100 trucks, then like 1,000 freight trains. By this time the thought had dawned upon me that it was water coming down the canyon. For an instant I think I stood there with my hair on end. I don't suppose I stood there more than a second or two before I realized that I must act and be quick about it. I ran into the house and shouted to my wife and family to run for the hills. Then I grabbed the telephone, a direct private line that connects with the water department of the city, and got one of the engineers on the wire. I told him that Sand Canyon was about to be washed off the face of the earth; that the aqueduct would probably go out and they had better rush help.

Before the conversation was finished the wall of water that came down the canyon took down the line of poles where they crossed the wash, and the connection was severed. Then I ran for the hills. An instant later the torrent of water, brush, boulders and trees, thundered past, surging and tumbling the canyon as if the Amazon River had turned loose in it. I didn't care anything about my house being washed away, but I was greatly concerned about the aqueduct siphon. I knew if it went out the water supply would be cut off, and that the city would be at the mercy of fire.

The siphon was about fifteen feet above the floor of the canyon and the pipe is eleven feet in diameter, but when I made my way down out of the hills to see what was going on, the water was going clear over the top of the pipe. Logs, brush and boulders were battering against it, and I decided that if the pipe were not already broken, it would probably go out before the flood passed. When the water subsided about 4 o'clock in the morning and daylight began to dawn, myself and a party of engineers, who had arrived from Mojave about midnight, took a look at the pipe. We scarcely believed our eyes when we found it was still standing, even though it was badly battered, and the great concrete piers were rounded off on the corners. The only thing that saved the aqueduct was the width of the canyon at that point. It let the flood spread out, so as to reduce the force against the siphon.

The entire canyon presented a scene of wreckage and desolation impossible to describe.

Where great pine trees had stood and where deer and bear and all kinds of small game used to come down to the gentle trickle of water in Sand Canyon Creek, there was nothing but a bottomless deposit of thick black mud strewn with logs, brush and boulders. A jackrabbit couldn't find a living there now, much less a deer or a bear. From the marks of the flood on the canyon walls the water in places had reached unbelievable heights. The canyon is very tortuous, and where the flood hit the curves in its mad rush toward the desert, the walls of the gorge were gouged out as if all the combined placer mines of all time had worked upon them.

Mud and debris had been splashed high upon the walls. Here and there a giant tree dangled among the rock on the face of the cliffs. It was a silent reminder of a stately old monarch that had weathered the storms of untold decades far up on the high divide, only to go down to the irresistible force of the eight years of rainfall combined into a single deluge.

The completion of the aqueduct spelled prosperity for Los Angeles, but by 1934 it also meant that Los Angeles owned 85 percent of all the property in Owens Valley! When Will Rogers came to the valley in 1932 to make a picture, he informed the nation through one of his daily articles: "Ten years ago this was a wonderful valley, with one-quarter of a million acres of fruit and alfalfa. But Los Angeles had to have more water for its Chamber of Commerce to drink more toasts to its growth, more water to dilute its orange juice, and more water for its geraniums to delight the tourists, while all the giant cottonwoods here died. So now this valley is the valley of desolation."

Those who supported the policy of the city of Los Angeles argue that the greatest good for the greatest number had been achieved and that the property owners had been given a fair price for their property. The ranchers from the Owens Valley claimed that the engineers from Los Angeles had committed one of the biggest engineering blunders of all time. They claimed that the construction of the $25,000,000 aqueduct was without adequate storage above the intake. A number of surveys had been made showing that if floodwaters had been stored and conserved there would have been enough water to keep the aqueduct full and at the same time furnish water for irrigation in the Owens Valley.

The Owens Valley ranchers continued during the years 1925, 1926 and 1927 to try and get Los Angeles to pay a fair price for their land, which they felt they hadn't gotten. Though they knew they couldn't destroy the aqueduct many continued to be extremely unhappy and to cause problems.

During the months of May through July 1927 six different blasts broke the aqueduct wall. The first and probably the most serious dynamiting occurred on the morning of May 27, just after midnight at No Name Canyon, just south of Little Lake. This is where one of the large siphons carried the aqueduct across one of the mountain canyons. The force of the water along with the explosion carried away 457 feet of nine-foot pipe. Guards who were stationed at this point stated that ten men, who were unmasked not caring if they were recognized, seized the two guards and took them up the canyon while the dynamite was placed and exploded. When the guards attempted to report the situation they discovered the telephone lines had been cut in several places. The force of the water that was released in the canyon swept down across the highway and railroad tracks, which were a short distance below, causing considerable damage and delaying traffic.

Sheriff Hutchison went to the scene promptly and District Attorney Hession promised his support in prosecuting the offenders. Los Angeles officials sent armed men, detectives and aqueduct guards into the Indian Wells Valley and offered $10,000 reward for the conviction of the criminals.

On the same night that the aqueduct was blown up in No Name Canyon the penstock of the city powerhouse west of Big Pine was blown up, closing the plant for several days for repair.

One of the immediate effects of this lawlessness was the placing of armed guards all along the aqueduct, who with the aid of large searchlights stopped and investigated all the cars along the nearby highway. But even these precautions did not prevent the aqueduct from being dynamited five more times during June and July.

Ken Wortley in his book, *Adventures of the Misfits*, told what he knew about an incident in No Name Canyon which was just south of Nine Mile Canyon. "On a May afternoon in 1927, I was trailing a herd of pack stock southward from Inyo County along the old dirt road which is now Highway 395. Being in the vicinity of Grapevine Canyon at the time, I decided to drive my animals up that canyon where there was good grazing and spend the night with Indian Tom.

Arriving at Tom's old familiar abode, I was greeted by both Indian Tom and his guest, Casey Lloyd Davidson Jones. The latter seemed especially glad to see me. Moments later I discovered the reason. Never one to beat around the bush when it came to a business proposition, Casey explained that he had been advanced the fabulous sum of $1,000 by reliable Inyo County citizens, to blow up the aqueduct siphon in No Name Canyon. He further explained in rather uncomplimentary terms that Indian Tom had refused to participate and that since it would require two people to do the job properly, he would appreciate my help. When I thereupon sided with Tom and tried to persuade him to abandon the project, Casey, as usual, left in a huff avowing never again to do legitimate business with people with no guts.

The following day, the evening edition of most newspapers in the nation announced that a dynamite blast had carried away 350 feet of large and heavy steel siphon of the Los Angeles Aqueduct in a canyon near the southern Inyo County line. These papers also announced that a large reward had been offered for the arrest of the culprits responsible. Needless to say, neither Indian Tom nor I were interested in that reward.

Perhaps as notorious as Casey was in this area, he might have become a suspect in the incident had he not been the first to accept a well-paying job as one of several hundred guards hired by the City of Los Angeles to protect their aqueduct along a two-hundred mile front.

Sometime after the feud between the Inyoites and the City of Los Angeles had quieted down and his protective services were no longer needed, Casey was back in the moonshine business, and this time, being able to afford protection, was financially successful. In a few years he became one of the area's biggest operators, with at least three stills hidden in the hills.

THE SECOND LOS ANGELES AQUEDUCT

Soon after the first Los Angeles Aqueduct was finished in 1913, William Mulholland, Superintendent of the Los Angeles Water Department, who rightfully deserves the title of

Siphon crossing at No Name Canyon

"Father of the Los Angeles Aqueduct," started looking for an additional water source to supplement the water from the Owens Valley. He found these in the Mono Basin to the north of Owens Valley.

The City of Los Angeles started buying land and water rights in the Mono Basin. These purchases were made with the cooperation and assistance of the U.S. Bureau of Reclamation, with the primary purpose allegedly being to obtain additional water to increase agriculture in the Owens Valley.

The Mono Extension was under design and construction in the 1930s. The water was to come from Rush Creek, including its tributaries Walker and Parker Creeks and Leevining Creek. These creeks were diverted and collected in the newly constructed reservoir of Grant Lake, thence through the eleven mile tunnel under the Mono Craters to flow into the headwaters of the Owens River at the head of Long Valley.

The City of Los Angeles purchased 30,000 acres of land from the U.S. Government and the government also withdrew from entry many tens of thousands acres of federal land for the use and benefit of the city. The true purpose of Los Angeles was the development of electrical power potential in the Owens Gorge, downstream from Long Valley, and for increased water export for the aqueduct.

By 1940 the entire Mono Extension project was completed, including the building of a high dam to create the large reservoir of Crowley Lake. Although the Gorge hydroelectric plants were started by 1940 the interruption of World War II delayed completion until 1953.

In 1963 the Department of Water and Power decided to embark on the construction of the second barrel of the aqueduct, later known as the "Second Los Angeles Aqueduct." This was to run roughly parallel to the first and increase the delivery of water by one half.

The new aqueduct commencing at the Haiwee Reservoir would be 177 miles long. This second aqueduct was designed for a mean annual flow of 152,000 acre feet per year. Together with the delivery capacity of the first aqueduct of 330,000 acre feet, this meant a combined mean annual flow of 482,000 acre feet.

Construction commenced in 1965 and was completed in 1970. Water flows entirely by gravity, starting at an elevation of 3,760 feet at the Haiwee Reservoir to the elevation of 1,200 feet at the Van Norman Reservoir in San Fernando Valley. Fully one half of the line is pressurized pipe, with the majority of the balance consisting of covered reinforced concrete box conduit. At the southern most portion of the line common use is made of the first aqueduct, especially the Elizabeth Tunnel. Here water from both aqueducts flow together into one pipe which is sufficient to handle the combined flow.

The total cost of the second aqueduct project was $90 million. By 1970 the city was exporting an average of 100,000-acre feet of water annually from Mono Basin. In the several decades following, the level of Mono Lake had decreased significantly with ecological consequences. Legal challenges to the diversions were filed in 1977. After fifteen years of litigation the City of Los Angeles agreed to give up 40,000-acre feet of water annually to ensure that Mono Lake is maintained at the prescribed level of 6,390 feet.

Ground water pumping in the Owens Valley was an essential part (but not advertised) of the city's plan for the second aqueduct. Both Inyo County and the city failed to assess the negative impact the aqueduct would have on the environment. Concurrent with the construction period in the second half of the 1960s, the city increased the ground water pumping by large amounts. The impact on the valley's vegetation, springs, artesian wells and wetlands was immediate and severe.

In 1972 Inyo County brought suit under the 1970 California Environmental Quality Act, to limit the rate of ground water extraction by the city. Twenty-five years of litigation ensued. Final settlement containing a complex set of agreements among all parties was reached and approved by the supervising court in 1997. Not all were satisfied, but a mechanism for annual review of permissible rates of groundwater pumping by a joint oversight committee was established and is now in operation, together with a series of mitigation projects.

The first and second aqueducts provide 70 percent of the water utilized in the city of Los Angeles. The other 30 percent comes from wells in the San Fernando Valley and from the Colorado River and State Water Project.

Indian Wells Valley
Raymond Station–Brown–Inyokern–Ridgecrest
U.S. Naval Ordinance Test Station China Lake

Indian Wells Valley makes up the major part of California's Kern County Desert. On the north it takes in the southern portion of Inyo County and to the south, is a small slice from a corner of San Bernardino County. The valley is closed on all four sides; to the east, a portion of the Argus Mountains, the El Paso Range on the south; the Coso Mountains on the north; and on the west, the Sierra Nevada.

The name Indian Wells Valley originated from a spring on the edge of the upper Mojave Desert that still exists west of Highway 395. This spring is, in the year 2001, the site of Indian Wells Restaurant and Brewery. It is believed that the first white man to visit this spring was Joseph Rutherford Walker, a well–known trailblazer, who passed by here in 1834. In early January 1850 William Lewis Manly and John Rogers found water here as they attempted to bring aid to the families in Death Valley. The Bennett and Arcan families were stranded out of food and had very little water. On their way out to find help, Manly and Rogers found this sparkling spring already walled up with rock and also found a well–defined Indian trail leading south.

The first race that was definitely known to live in this area were Native American described as "Pinto," who lived here as far back as 5000 years ago. Members of the Southwest Museum excavated one of their village sites two miles north of Little Lake between 1948 and 1951. It is hard to imagine that this desert was green and lush at one time, but archaeological evidence shows that this village site was located in a grove of trees along the bank of a flowing river. About 1000 years later, tribes of Shoshonean Indians lived here. A.L. Kroeber, a noted historian on Native Americans, puts the total population of the Coso and Panamint tribes who lived in this area at not more than 1,500 in 1770. By 1910 they were reduced to about 500.

In the late 1850s and 60s prospectors worked through this valley. The 1860s also saw the beginning of the California Sheep Trail. This trail was one-half mile wide and extended from Bakersfield, through Tehachapi, and up the Mojave Desert to the town of Bodie, Nevada. The 1860s brought conflicts between the Indians and white settlers who invaded their home range. Before 1870 army troops stationed at Camp Independence decided they would solve these conflicts by taking all the Indians to the Fort Tejon reservation.

In the 1870s silver and lead was discovered northeast of Lone Pine at the Cerro Gordo mine. These were shipped in 80-pound bars by wagon train from Owens Valley to Los Angeles. This greatly increased the traffic through the Indian Wells Valley. By 1871 stages were traveling this route three times a week. In 1873 Remi Nadeau organized the Cerro Gordo Freight Company to haul the silver-lead 80-pound bars. Nadeau's wagons stopped at Little Lake, Nine Mile Canyon, Indian Wells and Coyote Holes (Raymond's Station) to rest or spend the night. At the peak of Nadeau's operation in 1874 his

Mr. & Mrs. Freeman S. Raymond at the Freeman Post Office

teams were hauling eighteen tons of silver a day through the valley with wagons pulled by 14 mules. The Cerro Gordo Mine quit producing silver in 1879, and by 1881, Nadeau's freight system was abandoned.

Many times the question has been asked of me, "Just where was the original Freeman Station and who was it named for?" The site of this stage station and post office was one and one-half miles due west of where Highway 178 meets Highway 14, where a lone cottonwood tree grows in the gulch 200 yards south of 178. It was named for Freeman S. Raymond who was the first Caucasian to settle in the Indian Wells Valley. Freeman Raymond was one of the original forty-niners. For 22 years he prospected for gold and for two years he drove stage in early Kern County. Late in 1873 he came to the Mojave Desert to start his stage station.

This area was first called Coyote Holes because of the coyotes that came from miles around to water at the spring. Raymond filed on 160 acres in 1873 and later purchased another 40 acres. He kept a station here for stages that traveled from Visalia, through the Kern River Valley, and over Walker Pass. Other stages traveled down from Lone Pine through Bishop and then on to Los Angeles. All these stages stopped at the junction of these two very important roads. This was the logical changing station for teams. Raymond built a comfortable frame building

that functioned as a residence and station house. A few yards west of the historic old water hole were stables and corrals. A few cottonwood trees added shade and beauty to this desert oasis. Raymond had a locked cover over the spring and charged 25 cents a drink for horses and cattle and five cents for goats or sheep. Men could drink for nothing.

One occasion that stands out happened at Raymond's Station on February 26, 1874. A young lad of seventeen by the name of Oliver Roberts concealed himself southwest of the stage station and witnessed the notorious Tiburcio Vasquez and his gang as they robbed the station and then robbed the stage coach passengers.

About a mile from the station site on a gradual slope leading to the mountains is a peculiar butte formation consisting of two rhyolite rocks conspicuous for their isolated detachment from the mountainous area to the west. The mass intrudes abruptly from the uniformly smooth slope of the desert floor and is visible for miles around. It was here that Vasquez and his band hid out while waiting for the right time to rob the station. From this lookout stages, freight wagons, or even a lone rider could be spotted for miles away as they crawled along the floor of the desert. These rocks also provided an excellent hideout and gave protection in the event of a possible attack.

It is not known how long the Vasquez gang hid out here. Raymond told a mining promoter, who came by the following day, "He surely spent several days in the rocks near which you just passed, because I went there this morning and found a quantity of empty sardine cans, crackers and about a quarter of a sack of flour." This mass of rocks has since been known as "Robber's Roost."

Eyewitness Oliver Roberts, in describing the Coyote Holes raid, said an amusing incident was when Mrs. Raymond came running out of the house with a partly filled buckskin sack in her hand. A shot was fired and she fell on her face in the deep dust of the road. She was ordered back into the house followed by all the bandits except the two guarding the teamsters and swampers. Shortly after this the Darwin stage came in and the robbers piled out of the house reminding him of "someone disturbing a nest of ants." Although the stage driver had seen the horses, Nadeau's freight wagons and their mule teams, he had naturally supposed they all had stopped at the station for some reason of their own. It did not occur to him that a robbery was in progress.

After relieving the passengers of their valuables, the bandits moved on their way swiftly. It was then that Roberts saw Mrs. Raymond walk briskly to the spot where she had fallen and retrieve her bag which contained her rings and other valuables which she had hidden in the dust when she fell.

Another person who arrived the day after the robbery was a Frenchman by the name of Edmond Leuba. Leuba said he was greeted by Raymond, "a large American of rather good figure," who told him of the experience of the day before and pointed out more than twenty bullet holes in the building. Leuba mentioned that the stationmaster was much perturbed over the fact that Vasquez managed to get away with $1,300.00 of his money. He said he had this bag of money, which he had planned for sometime to take to a bank in Bakersfield, but had kept putting off the trip.

In the course of the robbery, Vasquez demanded that he turn over the bag with the money. Mrs. Raymond protested and said that all they had in the house was $50.00. He continued to insist that the bag with $1,300.00 be turned over to him. It was. The unfortunate stationmaster could not understand how Vasquez had learned of the existence of his bag with $1,300.00 in it. I guess the answer to that question we will never know.

In 1906 when the Los Angeles Aqueduct was being built, the U. S. Post Office Department wanted a post office to be established at Raymond's Station. However, there was a post office by the name of Raymond in northern California so they decided to choose Ray-mond's first name of Freeman for the name of the post office at this site.

Above: Tiburcio Vasquez, outlaw and murderer

Below: Vasquez Rocks, south of Freeman Station

Today all that remains of the historic old station is a lone cottonwood tree along Freeman Gulch. A cloudburst took out the spring and building but left enough water to keep a tree growing. I always felt bad that the beautiful monument at the junctions of Highways 178 and 14 doesn't mention this grand old man of the Mojave and where the name Freeman Junction originated.

Raymond's wife died in 1884 so he hired Mrs. Andress to cook and keep house for him. Mrs. Andress' husband had recently died over on the South Fork of the Kern River. There is a book titled *Freeman's a Stage Stop on the Mojave* by E. I. Edwards that gives a lot of the history of Raymond and his stage station. Dick and George Retzer who were grandnephews of Mr. and Mrs. Raymond and lived with them during the late 1800s gave much of the information in the book.

The Retzer brothers related that, "Raymond always had six to eight dogs on his property. Big dogs! He wasn't particular what kind of dogs, just as long as they were big. He always also had a chained coyote as a special attraction, calculated to entertain the stage passengers."

The *Illustrated Weekly Magazine* of the *Los Angeles Times* told the following story about Raymond: "If you stayed overnight he would treat you to music by his 'band.' He assembled his six to eight great dogs, each of which sedately took his place sitting on his haunches in a circle around the watchful restless coyote. When all was ready, he began to blow on an old cornet, every dog lifted his nose and his voice, and the coyote multiplied herself as only a coyote can and the music of the band could be heard on a still night for miles around." When asked if the dogs ever tried to attack the coyote, Raymond replied, "Attack that coyote? The dogs had profound respect for her. They would have fought for that danged coyote."

In 1891 an incident happened at Coyote Holes (Raymond Freeman's Station) when an Indian, who was working on the Smith Ranch near Onyx broke a pitchfork handle. Tommy Smith, the rancher he was working for, felt he had broken it on purpose and told him the price of the handle would be taken out of his $1.00 per day salary. The Indian, Wampei Jiggens was from a tribe, which lived in Sage Canyon on the Mojave Desert. He resented having to pay for his deed and proceeded down the road to the Onyx Store

where he obtained some whiskey (which was illegal to sell to Indians at that time). After drinking almost a pint he started back to his camp on the desert. It was night by that time and as he passed the Smith Ranch with the haystacks looming high in the moonlight he decided he would get even by burning some stacks of hay, which he promptly did.

Johnny Powers was the local constable. He had come to the South Fork as a cowhand to work for Bill Landers before being appointed constable. All the Powers boys were accomplished horsemen, which was not surprising considering their father, John Washington Powers, was a stockman and his boys had been riding since childhood. But for Johnny, being a working cowhand was no small feat, as he had lost his left leg in a shotgun accident as a small boy. This meant he had to mount from the right side of a horse and the horses he rode were not the gentle kind you would find around a livery stable now days. Once aboard, he rode the roughest parts of the country after cattle as wild as deer, with his peg leg stuck jauntily through

Johnny Powers, 1891

the stirrup leathers. His dark hair, good looks, and pleasing personality made him a popular favorite among men and women alike.

Thursday, July 2, 1891, Powers left Onyx with a warrant for Wampei Jiggens. Sam Gann, constable from Kernville, accompanied him. They stopped for the night at Raymond's Station. Working at the station was the Widow Andress and with her were her four children: Jessie 13, Lottie 11, Ernie 9 and Charlie 7. Lottie Andress Pettypool recounted the following account. Her mother tried to persuade Powers to wait until he had more help. She feared two men were not enough to apprehend Jiggens in his own territory. Young, healthy and self-confident, Johnny laughed off her warnings. His attitude was casual and "all in a day's work," Lottie said he came in from washing up, and quipped to her mother, "Mrs. Andress, you said you wanted my picture; well you can have the one I left out back on the towel."

The two constables started out for the Indian camp early the next morning. On the way they came on the camp of some coyote trappers. Oliver McCoy, one of the trappers, said if they could wait until he finished breakfast he would ride with them. Before leaving, Powers deputized him and all three continued south.

At seven o'clock they rode into the rancheria where Jiggens was. Powers and Gann tied their horses up a short distance from the buildings, and McCoy rode right up to where Chief Kiowa had walked out to meet them. After some discussion, Kiowa said he would get his horse and help them look for Jiggens. But as he stepped back across a small ditch, and as if by some pre-arranged signal, one of the chief's sons stepped to the door of a shack and commenced firing upon the officers with a rifle. At this time Kiowa pulled a pistol from his shirt, and fired on the constables, who were caught completely off guard. Although the three officers killed the chief and two of his sons, after a short hot battle was over, Powers lay dead and McCoy critically wounded. Gann, running out of ammunition and seeing no hope but to run for his life, caught McCoy's horse close by. Laying on the horse's neck and riding at a dead run, he managed to escape. Jiggens' mother, through an interpreter, later told that upon finding McCoy still living Wampei set out to finish him off. When she tried to intervene, he told her to leave or he would also kill her. It is said that he slashed Powers' throat after he was dead and further mutilated his body.

Gann covered the ten to twelve miles back to the stage station in record time. Lottie Pettypool remembers seeing him come over the pass to the south on his hard ridden, heavily lathered horse. Raymond had a wagon load of wood he had gathered earlier, so hiding the horse in the barn, and Gann under a canvas that was over the load of wood he set out for the South Fork. Gann and Raymond were well on their way by the time five mounted Indian men appeared in the pass south of Raymond's Station, and after watching for some time, they rode warily down to the dwellings.

Mrs. Andress, with courage typical of women of her day, came to the door and asked them to come in and have something to eat, as she normally did. It was felt that her quick thinking probably saved her life and the lives of her little family. If she had shown fright or panic, they might have continued on their grisly massacre.

When they said they wanted Raymond she told them he had gone toward Walker's Pass to get wood and they rode off in that direction. Meeting the stationmaster on his return from delivering Gann to the valley, they gave him no trouble, since the load of wood seemed to back up his cook's story.

In the meantime, Gann's arrival in Onyx had the whole valley in an uproar. Though he didn't arrive until three in the afternoon, by four, eleven men were ready, and followed him back to the scene of the tragedy. At ten that night an additional twelve followed. In the posse were two local Indians who had relatives killed by Kiowa's band. One of these was Bill Chico. These two Indian men took the lead and they meant business.

The posse reached Sage Canyon just after daybreak and immediately surrounded the rancheria. A most grisly scene met them. Lying in front of the house were the mutilated bodies of Powers and McCoy, which had been lying in the desert heat almost a full twenty-four hours. Powers' eyes had been punched out with his peg leg.

It soon became apparent that the Indians had moved out lock, stock and barrel. Just in case they later decided to come back, the posse made it as uninhabitable as possible, which included burning the buildings. As Gann was almost certain that Chief Kiowa, and at least one of his sons, were critically wounded when he took his hurried departure, they checked the area and sure enough, found three graves. They proceeded to dig up the bodies and, although two wrongs never make a right, their remains were left exposed to the elements when the posse rode out on the trail of the Indian band.

These bones lay scattered among the sagebrush for many years. Some of the old time cowboys such as Willie Nicoll remembered seeing them through the years, until they finally disappeared.

The Indians, upon leaving their camp, split in two parties. One group, mostly of squaws and children, after turning west, went up on Scodie Mountain. They hid in the rocks and eluded the posse. The other half of the band turned north after taking to the mountains. A posse of twenty-three men, led by Deputy Sheriff Jim Powers, brother of the late Johnny Powers, was soon hot on their trail. Moving down on the west side of Walker's Pass, the Indians turned and went back out to the desert by way of the canyon east of Walker's Pass Lodge. Coming out in Indian Wells Canyon, they fled up the desert. By this time some of the posse had to return to their ranches. However, twenty men stayed with Powers for two weeks as they played their deadly game of hide and seek in the desert country to the north. The terrain became increasingly more rugged each day, until Wampei and a few of the remaining men, evaded the posse altogether.

The authorities around Lone Pine were also in on the hunt and, by keeping a sharp eye out for the offenders, arrested Wampei when he showed up in town some three months later, wearing Johnny Powers' constable badge pinned to his hat.

He was taken to Bakersfield, where he was tried in Superior Court, and on December 11, 1891, was sentenced to spend the rest of his life in San Quentin State Prison. Some of the South Fork residents were quite apprehensive of further outbreaks, but nothing more transpired.

One of the band who at that time was a young boy, later lived and worked on various South Fork ranches for many years. He had been crippled by a shot in the running battle with the Powers' posse. Known only as Pinon John, he seemed destined to live his life out in peace, but

one day in the 1940s he became involved in an argument with another Indian, and was clubbed to death with the butt of a pistol. An odd note is this: the other participant of this argument was Andy Chico, son of Bill Chico, the Indian who took a very active part in running down Kiowa's band.

In 1901 a terrible cloudburst came down Freeman Gulch. A wall of water poured down the wash and tore away the stables, corrals and destroyed a portion of the station house. Raymond was in the kitchen when it struck and was washed down with the flood for some distance and never fully recovered from his injuries. He died in August of 1901 at the age of 80 after living at Coyote Holes for thirty-six years. The Los Angeles Times reported his passing in these words: "Traveler's Friend Gone—Death Robs Desert of Human Landmark. Death has closed the career of Freeman S. Raymond, one of the best-known men of the deserts of California at the end of four score years. When a stroke of apoplexy carried him away last Saturday, hundreds of men lost a friend who had succored them in times of distress.

For thirty-six years Raymond had been part of the desert in the vicinity of Mojave. In that time he had not made one enemy, but endeared himself to all men who knew no law but the guns they carried. He was the lord and master of Freeman, California, better known to the old prospectors as Coyote Holes. He was founder, postmaster, and head of the sole family which comprised it."

BROWN

Fredrick Samuel Karl "Fritz" Mills was the son of Engineer Captain Mills who worked on the Owens Valley-Los Angeles Aqueduct and had his headquarters in Sand Canyon. Fritz carried mail from Brown, also known as Siding 18, when the mail came in on the train and transported it to Sand Canyon. Here it was sorted and sent on to other aqueduct offices. He could only travel three miles per hour, so it took him two hours to go from Brown to Sand Canyon in his horse drawn cart. When Fritz Mills first saw the bustling teamsters' community of Brown in 1910 at the age of 14, Mr. Haelsig ran the general store and post office. He lived in the back of the store. Oliver Smith owned the saloon, and nearby was an enormous warehouse where they stored building materials for the Los Angeles Aqueduct construction. There was a big corral, and a hotel built by George Brown. There was no ice, air conditioning or automobiles. There were two houses, which were living quarters for the aqueduct workers. Sometime in 1910 the aqueduct company made a rule that there could be no saloon within four miles of the teamsters' quarters, so they picked up the saloon and moved it four and one-half miles south of the town, to Leliter, the next railroad siding.

Homesteader George Brown, promoter of this small town, called Brown "his town," thus becoming known as "Mr. Brown of My Town." Although Brown explained to everyone that the town was named after him, Ethel Mary "Tiny" Standard, long time resident of Brown seemed to feel that it was named after a railroad official named Brown. Oliver Smith, the saloonkeeper had a brother who was Deputy Sheriff of the area. He was called "Peg Leg" because he had one leg missing. He had a peg hole in one stirrup for that leg on his saddle.

Brown was popular with the gamblers and wore a big hat, frock coat or double-breasted coat with a satin or velvet collar. He opened a restaurant in two boxcars and served terrible grub as Fritz Mills remembers it. When the train came at 5 o'clock there was no place else to eat, so everyone had to suffer through Brown's food.

In 1909 and 1910 the Custer mining excitement in the Argus Mountains, to the east of Brown, brought many prospectors with their pack burros through Brown. They all stopped here, which made the town a noisy, busy place. The postal address was Siding 18, Mojave, Owenyo Railroad via Mojave.

After Gus Haelsig, store owner and acting postmaster, passed on from pneumonia, his wife ran the business until about 1913 when it was taken over by a Mr. Fleming who later sold out to Howard Gill.

George Brown employed Mrs. Rachael Barsness as his cook at the hotel. Rachel came to Brown in the early days of its establishment. She and her husband had made the mine rushes of

The saloon at Brown, 1910

Nevada and Colorado and acquired a fortune of $200,000. After her husband's death this faded away through no fault of Rachel. It was one of those unhappy things of fate due to trust misplaced.

Left alone, she continued working at the "Maid of the Mist" mine. Her heart and soul were in mining. Rugged and undaunted, she pluckily ran her mines alone when necessary. She hauled her own supplies and water as long as she had money left and the mines supported the venture. Finally when times became too hard she quit mining and put her hands, not "to the plow," but into cooking the meals in Brown's hotel, in mining camps and on cattle ranches. One early settler told that, "Mrs. Rachel Barsness was an amazing person who managed the hotel and restaurant for Mr. Brown. I peddled farm products once a week to the hotel and many other customers. She terrified me, though she was never rough with me. Later she was converted by the Adventist Church people and became a good and lovable old woman and lived many years of her old age here. We helped to take care of her after she could no longer work, and she lived in a boxcar by the side of the railroad. I learned to love and admire her very much. Her earlier years were shaped by being a victim of being born into a rough and rather brutal mining family." Brown, who didn't have much of a family, later sold the hotel to the Diddens in 1920.

The railroad had a storage cellar in which to keep the supplies they furnished to employees at prices cheaper than they would pay in the store. Prices were pretty high in the town during this time. The railroad hauled water in tank cars. There was a telegraph station here before one was in Inyokern. Vernon Carr, a nearby homesteader, tells one story of a miner shipping his ore on the railroad and the freight charges were more than he was paid for the ore. After the aqueduct work was finished, the store, post office, school, railroad section crews living in boxcars and hotel remained. Today it is all gone except for empty lots and the foundation of the last school.

Callaway

The first family to settle in the area of Brown was the Callaways. James W. (called J.W.) and Ann Callaway moved to Inyo County from the Stockton area. They located at Hubbs Creek near Big Pine and had a daughter and three sons. The sons, John D., Will H. and Lester, all worked hauling wood and mining machinery to the Fish Lake Valley area gold fields. After that they started hauling machinery to Mountain Springs Canyon in the Argus Mountains, to and from the Coso mines. They then located in Ballarat where J.W. and Ann opened a boarding house. From there, J.W. and the boys hauled mining machinery to mines in the Panamints. John D. established a stage line in 1906 from the railhead station at Johannesburg to Skidoo.

J.W. took up a homestead in 1908 two miles northeast of Brown. His wife Ann had an adjoining homestead. There they built a house and dug a well by hand, put in a windmill and a small water tank. Two years later their house burned down and they had to build another. James had six draft horses, a milk cow, and a large buggy team. He did a lot of hauling and moving of well drilling rigs and cleared land for the early homesteaders to make a living.

One day J.W. took his wife Ann and grandson, Art, to catch the train to Los Angeles. They got on the train, as J.W. stood by his team and buckboard. The trainman blew the whistle and away went the team! J.W. was left standing there while the team headed home without him! Their grandson Art, the son of John and Estella Callaway, came to live with them in 1911 when he was seven years old. Within a few years John and Estella moved to the valley where Estella took up a homestead. (Will Callaway also took up a homestead, which then made four homesteads, each containing 160 acres. They were located together in one big section of land.) John bought a house from the Los Angeles Aqueduct, which had been built in Nine-Mile Canyon. He and his brother moved it to the homestead with eight teams, which consisted of sixteen horses. They had to have this many horses to move the house through Brown as it was so sandy and there were no roads to speak of.

John brought 100 head of brood cows from Independence when he came to the valley, taking five days to make the trip. Later he bought the Paxton's cattle and ranch. He ran cattle on the eastside of the valley, bringing his herd to 350. Grass was plentiful. Rain in the wintertime filled the dry lakes and the cattle ranged far and wide, watering from the remaining puddles until far into the spring. John also had water troughs at five locations in the valley. He sold his cattle to Harold Eaton at Big Pine. Later John became the first county road foreman and worked there until 1924. He then went to work for the state as road foreman, and his son, Art, took his job as the county road foreman.

Art recalls the first day of school at Leliter September 11, 1911. Leliter was a railroad siding between Brown and Inyokern. He said, "I lived with my grandparents on their homestead. After a year or two, the school was moved two miles northeast and called the Brown District School, it was four or five miles from Brown at Siebenthal Corner. It was one of four schools, which were; Brown, Orchard, Los Flores and Inyokern Districts. Later, I went to high school at the consolidated school in Inyokern. My teachers were Miss Lacy at the Brown School and Professor Beach in Inyokern. We went to church in Inyokern and to Dr. Denton at Randsburg." Art married Lucille Bramlette. He said he remembered the dances at Inyokern Hall, where a man and his wife from Lone Pine played piano and drums.

Schuette

One of the earliest settlers to the valley was Henry F. W. Schuette, who moved to the Brown area during the early 1900s. Henry discovered the Indian Wells Valley when he was working for the Department of Water and Power in Los Angeles. He worked for Bill Mulholland ditching the Los Angeles River.

Schuette, his wife Johanna Marie plus their children, George and Emily, came to live and homestead in the north end of Indian Wells Valley. He worked on the aqueduct in Sand Canyon. The family raised cattle for a living. The Schuette cattle ranch was sold to the Navy in 1943. When the aqueduct was finished Henry worked for the California Alkali Company at Cartago on Owens Lake to support the family ranch. The cattle-ranching business "was a hungry proposition," in those early years, according to Henry "Hank" Schuette, their son. Hank was born in Los Angeles, his mother traveling by train to Los Angeles to have her baby delivered. In later years his sister, Millie, and brother Fred joined the family and lived at the family homestead.

The homestead was four and one-half miles northeast of Brown on the old "Mining Road" which ran from Brown to Mountain Springs Canyon. The Schuette ranch house was later moved to Inyokern and is still standing across from the Inyokern Town Hall.

Henry F.W. "Dad" Schuette and Mr. Siebenthal built the "First School" at Leliter. For this they refurbished the old aqueduct building at nearby Para. When Hank was ten years old he drove the local children to school at Inyokern. "I

Left to right, Aunt Elizabeth Schuette holding Mildred Schuette, Johanna Marie and Henry Schuette in buggy, George and Emilie Schuette standing in front.

was one of the richest kids in the valley because I had a paying job," he said. When he left the valley to attend high school in Santa Monica his brother Fred got the job of driving the children to school. Fred was so small he could barely see over the dash. One day another driver stopped to see about the driverless car. But there was Fred perched behind the wheel and all was well. After graduating from high school, Hank returned to the valley and worked on the family ranch at China Lake. He met his future wife, Alby Lange, at the top of the Argus Mountains near Wild Horse Spring, where her father had a mine. They met in early July and were married in October 1932. After his marriage he went to work for American Potash and Chemical in Trona.

Hank Schuette brought his new wife, Alby, to a home on the Hansen homestead at Brown. Modern for its day, the house had a kerosene stove for cooking, a wood stove for heating and indoor plumbing. Hank said Alby's mother was not happy about her daughter leaving the city where she was a cosmetician, to marry a man who lived in the Mojave Desert. They were married for 32 years.

The Schuette brothers, George and Hank, helped Jim Crum build "Crumville" as the future Ridgecrest was called. They did this by stacking old vacant homesteader buildings around an old dairy. Schuette said his dad "dressed them up a bit" so they could be rented out to westend workers by Jim Crum.

In the early days when the Schuette family made their living raising cattle they had some good feed years and kept their cattle on the range year round. They drove their cattle up Wilson Canyon, east of Brown, and spread them out on top, taking part of their herd through Moscow Creek to Mountain Springs.

Ten acres of alfalfa was raised on their 550-acre China Lake Ranches. When the Navy came in 1943 the Schuettes were told to move off their land because it was going to become part of the Naval Ordnance Station. Hank said, "We figured we got about ten cents on the dollar for our land or about fourteen dollars per acre. Although the ranchers didn't like the arrangement at first because they had to sell so cheap, they later thought the Navy had done them a favor. Although there were some good years of rain, and ranchers prospered, this was followed in the '40s and '50s by a drought that could have caused real hardships."

Carr

Vernon Carr was born in Hawley, Minnesota, on October 22, 1885. He and his mother went to live with an aunt in Pasadena in 1900 so Vernon could regain his health. Vernon went to school in Pasadena to the eighth grade but had to quit school because of his illness. He moved to Glendale to raise bees. He lived for a while in Long Beach but the moist air was too much for him so he moved back to Sycamore Canyon in Glendale.

Anabel Carr, whose maiden name was Anabel Gaffney, was born in Harvard, Illinois, June 21, 1882. She lived on a farm in Iowa from the time she was eight years old, until she was 22. She then got a job teaching school in North Dakota, and took up a homestead. She kept up the homestead and taught school at the same time, living in a 10' x 12' cabin. The winter of 1905 was very cold. Snowed in, with insufficient fuel, she got an abscess on her lung and the doctor ordered her to go to California. She came west in 1907 and went to live with a cousin in Glendale where she met Vernon while he was working on the bee farm. They were married in April 1908. They both wanted to live on a farm close to nature, and to raise a family. Anabel's Uncle Bart, who was greatly interested in the Indian Wells Valley, was instrumental in their coming to the area. Her doctor told her, "She should live forever on the desert".

Vernon Carr, his wife Anabel and their small son were the second family to move into the valley. Vernon homesteaded a plot about seven miles north of Inyokern. He dug a well and put together a home in October 1909. It was the first permanent home in the valley, and they felt that the Indian Wells Valley was "Their Valley."

Women's Lib would probably seem humorous to Anabel Carr. When she came to the Indian Wells Valley to homestead, doing a "man's" work was a matter of survival. Between cooking, cleaning and raising a family, she plowed and planted their desert acres, shoveled sand into bags to pile around the well when it rained and even set her own broken bones. Annabel was full of energy despite her mere 96 pounds. Her favorite outfit was a workshirt, blue jeans and bare feet.

A firm Christian, she had strong ideas about

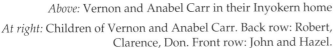

Above: Vernon and Anabel Carr in their Inyokern home

At right: Children of Vernon and Anabel Carr. Back row: Robert, Clarence, Don. Front row: John and Hazel.

eating healthy foods and avoiding sweets, tobacco and alcohol. Material things were sinful to collect, so she gave away anything she had two of. When wealthier relatives in Los Angeles sent her felt hats, she turned them into shoes for the children.

A new teakettle was a different story, however. When a fire broke out in the kitchen, first she gathered up the children and stationed them outside behind a hedge, and then she dashed back in through the flames to rescue her brand new teakettle. She hid it in some safe place in the yard and couldn't find it for a week.

The Carrs raised cattle, chickens, had an orchard and grew their own vegetables. Desert soil is thick with clay and short on water, but Vernon's watermelons and cantaloupes made him a star at church socials. Any fruit that wasn't eaten fresh was canned. In the mid '20s someone in the family would drive down to the Central Produce Market in Los Angeles and bring back vegetables to sell up and down the Valley, Trona and Westend.

Childcare was no problem for Anabel when she worked in her desert fields. She had her own system. She put her young children in large cardboard boxes set them under shade trees, and took away their shoes. The ground was too hot for them to walk on, so they stayed there.

Having babies was not a hardship for her, either. She had seven children, six who were born in the desert. When the labor began with one of her children, Vernon drove to the post office for help. While he was gone the baby was born. Anabel then washed and clothed the baby. Vernon hurried back from summoning help and asked what he could do for her. "Oh, I'd like a cup of tea," she replied calmly, showing him the new child.

Their fifth child was born in a tent near Big Pine during the middle of October. Vernon, who made a living with his horse team and wagon, was building a bridge over the Owens River. The family camped in a tent nearby until the bridge spanned both shores. It was too far to go for help, so the baby was born here. Then, at the end of November, the family rode home in an open buggy, new baby and all. She used to say, "if animals could give birth by themselves, why can't I?"

One afternoon she fell into the family well and broke her elbow. The bone was sticking out, but she finished her work for the day and put the children to bed before she sat down and set the bones herself, using freezer tape for dressing.

The seven Carr children were; Robert who was killed at the age of 18 in a construction accident, Clarence, Donald, John, Hazel, Helen and

Left to right, Robert and Clarence Carr.

Raymond who died at the age of 12. Clarence Carr has the distinction of being the first white child born in the Valley. His older brother, Robert was born in the Los Angeles area before the family relocated. Clarence is the senior living member of this "first family" of the valley and at this writing is 90 years old.

Clarence has remained in the Indian Wells Valley, except for three years away for school and three years in the army. He married the former Ellen Fertig from Kennedy Meadows and at the date of this writing they have celebrated their 64th wedding anniversary. They still live in his parent's relocated home on Carr Lane near Leliter. He has completely rebuilt the home. A true pioneer of Indian Wells Valley.

Ellen Fertig Carr came to Kennedy Meadows, on the South Fork of the Kern River, in 1920 with her parents, Joseph and Anna Fertig. She had asthma and the doctor told her she had to live some place other than Long Beach. Her father built a little log cabin just east of the South Fork River. She attended the Kennedy Meadows School until she was ready to go to high school in 1928.

Ellen's family moved to Paradise, California, and lived there for eight years. The family decided to spend a winter down on the desert in Indian Wells Valley and there she met Clarence Carr. They were married a year later in 1937.

Clarence attended the original Brown District School and has many memories. He remembers when Art Callaway dislocated his arm at the old

hand pump at the school. He said the kids came to school from all directions. The Hansen girls came by cart from the northeast. George and Emily Schuette came by horseback or by cart from the north, and kids from Brown and Leliter came from the northwest and the southwest. Transportation was by horse and buggy, horseback or simply two feet. He remembers Dr. Evans being the first doctor at Randsburg.

Helen Carr Cook Moore was the second daughter of Vernon and Annabel Carr. Helen's memories are the cold trips to school in the open-air bus and riding with Henry Schuette in the Willys Knight, which was a step up from the bus. Helen married Bill Cook. They had two children, but unfortunately, Bill passed away with a brain tumor. Helen married again, to Orville Moore.

In 1985, Hazel Carr Bramlette and her husband Tommy sent the following letter for the Early Timers reunion in Inyokern: Hazel wrote the following:

I was born in Big Pine, California, on October 3, 1917. I arrived home when I was three weeks old. We lived on the Carr Ranch, seven miles northeast of Inyokern. I went to the Inyokern School, where Mrs. Dixon was my teacher for three or four years. Mr. Coppock taught the seventh and eighth grades and the two years of high school that were offered.

I don't ever remember going to the doctor. We attended the Methodist Church in Inyokern. The first transportation that I remember is the

Model T Ford that we drove to Iowa in 1920. I also remember the open-air school bus that we rode to school in. I got frostbitten toes the first several years that I went to school. This was the bus in which Henry 'Hank' Schuette and I tied the driver, Mr. Gerhard, to his seat, resulting in my having to walk the seven miles to school the next day! That was my mother's idea. She really believed in discipline.

Both mother and father moved to the desert for their health, which certainly may have contributed to their longevity.

Hansen

The history of the Hansen family began in the Indian Wells Valley when Leslie Hansen's father-in-law traded one of his feed and grain mills for 160 acres north of Inyokern. There were few improvements on the place and Jennie and Leslie Hansen decided to try farming this piece of land. They brought with them their three girls, Ruth, Marion, and Esther. Vivian was born later. The ranch was located about five miles east of the town of Brown.

In preparing the place prior to moving the family onto it, a cement reservoir was poured in November and it froze and had to be poured again. This reservoir was the scene where kids gathered in the summertime, to swim and play, especially the Carr and Schuette kids. The ducks loved to join them when they were swimming.

The Hansen gardens were abundant and produced large vegetables including little yellow pear tomatoes and many grapes. They also had

Above: Ruth, Marion, Esther Hansen c. 1920

Right, above: Hansen Ranch about 1918

Right: The four Hansen girls in 1993. L.to R. Esther, Vivian, Marion, Ruth

alfalfa. The produce was hauled by wagon and later by truck to Randsburg, Red Mountain, Johannesburg and Trona. The citizens of these towns especially welcomed the watermelons in the hot summer months. When the melons were about ripe, Leslie would sleep in the melon patch with his ten-gauge shotgun to ward off coyotes.

Refrigeration was achieved by dripping water over burlap bags around a framework that had shelves inside. This "desert cooler" was located outside the house and you could always count on the blowing wind to keep the inside cool for milk, butter, eggs, and other perishables.

There were picnics with the Carr family in the canyons. In Jack Sweet's canyon the kids were warned not to pick or step on his strawberries. Trips to Grapevine Canyon were to pick wild grapes to make jelly. On the Fourth of July everyone would gather at the Carr Ranch and have potluck and at night the Carr boys would shoot off fireworks.

The big flood of 1922 was well remembered. They watched the large black cloud that hung in Sand Canyon for a day or more. About dark, a roar was heard and Leslie Hansen went out to look with his flashlight and saw water rushing past the ranch. The ranch was not damaged; however, a big detour had to be made in order to get to school for several days. One storm the girls remembered had their mother putting blankets against the windows so the heavy rain and hail would not break them. One huge sandstorm deposited so much sand in the house, you couldn't find the rug.

The Hansens attended the Inyokern Methodist Church after they got their Model T. Ford. They did their shopping at the Inyokern Store, and some at Brown, but raised most of their own meat and vegetables. Their mail came to the post office at Leliter, and the postmaster would signal with a mirror when anything perishable arrived. They raised goats for milk and cheese, finding that goats did better than cows on the ranch.

They moved to the desert in 1918 and moved back to Pasadena around 1926 so their girls would have more opportunities. After they moved back to Pasadena their fourth girl, Vivian was born. They leased the ranch to several people until the Navy bought their property for $3,250.00. At this time about 40 acres of the ranch was improved.

Schools

Henry S. " Hank" Schuette compiled a history of the early schools in the Indian Wells Valley. Some of the history comes from Hank's brother, George, who started school in 1912, a year after the Leliter school opened.

Hank's father, Henry F. W. Schuette, was one of the groups of settlers who organized the first school in the Brown District. Others included Eugene Siebenthal, John and Will Callaway, Loren Sterling Sr., Clete Paxton and Mr. Berry. The boundaries were indefinite. Children came from wherever they lived in the valley. The schoolhouse at Leliter, between Brown and Inyokern, was an existing Los Angeles aqueduct building, which had been used as a saloon at Leliter. It was fitted out with desks, blackboards and other necessities. Mr. Siebenthal the proprietor of most of Leliter donated the frame building. The school building was refurbished by Henry F. W. Schuette, Mr. Berry, John and Will Callaway, Loren Sterling and of course, Eugene Siebenthal. No flag was available but at the last minute some red, white and blue bunting was found and a section of this was run up the flagpole for the salute to the flag. When the railroad survey was run through in the early 1900s and the various sidings designated, Eugene Siebenthal saw opportunity and homesteaded a town site. Starting with feed barns, livery and blacksmith shops, he later became postmaster and storekeeper. There was also a railway building, which had been built some years earlier when Los Angeles aqueduct construction was approaching this point. During tunneling and siphon construction on the aqueduct in the Sierra canyons, Leliter was the principal off-loading siding in the valley.

School was held in this aqueduct building for two years, then a new school was built. The new site was chosen about five miles southeast of Brown. This put it in about the center of the school population at that time and still near the town of Leliter. A long hitching rack was built. Miss Tarr was the first teacher; Mrs. Kramess followed her. The third teacher was Miss McCartney. She married, but tragedy followed swiftly. Her husband's small child fell into the dangerous Kern River. She jumped in to save the child and the husband went in to save them both. They were all drowned.

Miss Mary Burke, Brown District teacher, wrote about the school in March 1913, "The building has not been repaired and during a storm the classroom was flooded. It was impossible to hold classes. The children's books were often damaged, from being wet. On warm days the children were unable to study because of lack of water. There is no place to keep library books, except in boxes. Mr. Schuette and Mr. Berry refurbished the building for the next year. Its basic construction was always questionable. It lacked studding and bracing, so it swayed in the wind, creaking loudly as the wind shifted. It was finally braced with a power pole against the East Side."

The teacher for the remaining years at Leliter was Miss Beulah Lacy from a ranching family at Olancha. Mildred Schuette relates how the boys built a "sweat house" out of greasewood and sagebrush, patterned after those of the Indians. They had a pool fed by a hand pump and a merry-go-round with seats around the periphery. The girls sat and the boys pushed! Oh the age of chivalry! The boys had a collection of captured horned toads, lizards, caterpillars and other "livestock." Trouble came when Miss Lacey found out that the boys were building a fire in the sweat house to get up a sweat before jumping in the pool. The only opening was a small crawl hole and the brush was tinder dry!

Mildred also related the incident when Art Callaway threw his elbow out of joint pumping water from the hand pump at the school well. Art was asked if he went to a doctor. He said, "No, we had a horse and buggy and my cousin Howard was driving. I'd say, 'Drive as fast as you can, and he'd hit a bump and I'd yell, slow down!' We knew my dad John Callaway, Gerald and John Lindsey and my Uncle Will Callaway were going to the cow camp (formerly the Paxton Ranch on China Lake) to move cattle. We were scared to death that they would be gone to the cow camp before we got there. We got there and they were just ready to leave, they put me in a chair and Gerald Lindsey got behind me and held my shoulders back, John got hold of my arm and pulled it back in place. I went around with my arm in a sling for a good long time!"

First school bus

In 1913 four school districts were established in the valley. They were the Brown, Orchard, Los Flores and Magnolia Districts. The Brown District School was three miles out in the valley along the Nadeau Road where Siebenthal had a homestead. Schuette and Berry constructed a new building, with help from various parents. It was moved to Inyokern in 1920 when the schools consolidated.

The Los Flores School was started about 1914. It was named after the Los Flores ranch, the first large alfalfa ranch in the valley. The school was located about twelve miles east of Inyokern, at the Rev. Early homestead. The parents assisted Rev. Early and Mr. Toombs with the building. Later it was also moved to Inyokern during the consolidation. After it was moved it became the classroom for the first six or seven grades. Both it and the Orchard building survived on the back of the school lot in Inyokern until the summer of 1983, when they were declared a fire hazard and burned. Rev. Early was the clerk of the School Board and Miss Clevanger the teacher. The Orchard and Magnolia Districts were formed soon afterward.

In the Magnolia School, classes were first held in the Community Church east of the tracks in Inyokern. Rev. Early and Thomas Toombs from the Los Flores area led in the construction of the church as a community project in 1913. The whole community took an active part. Fundraisers were held, such as box lunch socials.

The Orchard school was on the Ben B. Lindsey place, now a part of Armitage Field. This building was moved to Inyokern in 1920. It became known as the "Little Building."

Standard

When the four schools were consolidated and moved to Inyokern, another school was created in Brown, from a dwelling built out of railroad cross ties. This dwelling was unusual because all the ties were set on end. Tiny Standard was hired as teacher. The reason they called her "Tiny" was because she only weighed 80 pounds soaking wet.

Tiny was born in May 1887 as Ethel Mary Hibbard. She graduated from Pomona High School in 1907 at the age of 20. She then went to Manila returning to the United States in 1910. On her return she enrolled in Mills College in San Francisco and graduated in 1915 with a Bachelor of Science degree. While in college she held down a job as college librarian to meet expenses. In 1918 she married Earl Standard and moved to San Bernadino. In 1920 she and Earl moved to Indian Wells Valley for Earl's health. They homesteaded land northwest of the town of Brown and Earl took a job with the railroad as section foreman.

Tiny taught school at Brown for 31 years, from 1920 until 1951 and became widely known and admired. She never had a substitute. The few times that she was sick they cancelled school until she was able to teach again. Tiny was a lifetime member of several teaching societies. She was such an excellent teacher that teachers were sent from all over Bakersfield to observe her teaching technique. Her students, both Native American and Caucasian, numbered from seven to twelve until the Navy came to the desert in 1943. The enrollment shot up to 27 at which time they had to build a larger school. Some of her former students grew up, married and she taught their children. The Brown school graduates went to Inyokern for the first two years of high school.

As the author, I can't tell the story about the school at Brown without telling about my most memorable year in elementary school. The year was 1933 and I was in second grade. In fact it was my second year in the second grade. The first year while attending school in Weldon I just didn't apply myself to my studies so the teacher had held me back that year. The second year my mother had severe asthma where we lived in the South Fork Valley on the Kern River, so she and my dad decided to see if the desert climate might help her. They rented a house built by one of the homesteaders several miles south of Brown and my mother, my two brothers Marvin and Bill, and I moved there for the school year. My dad was cattle

Left: Brown School 1932. L. to R. Marvin Powers, Bob Powers. Bob was unhappy because he didn't have any feathers and Marvin was holding the hook rug he had made, boy to right unidentified.

Below: Brown School 1932. L. to R. Bob Powers, Marvin Powers.

Brown School in 1947. Front row: l. to r: Sandra Cooper, Bill Bramlet, Bill Standard, Arlene Bramlet, Gloria Sterling, Deedee Cooper, Pat Ball. Middle row: Tom Standard, Shay Shyaley Cooper. Back row, Stan Ball, Litha Crowell, Bill Bye, unknown, unknown, Virginia Cooper, unknown, Geraldine Cooper.

inspector for the state so he stayed on the ranch at Onyx.

That year being taught by Tiny Standard was truly a remarkable experience. I really started wanting to learn and we did such wonderful projects. I believe there were about 12 children attending there at that time. All eight grades were in that small one-room schoolhouse. I remember some of the older girls helping the younger students with their lessons. I progressed well in reading and math besides keeping up on all the other required subjects. What impressed me the most was how she stirred up my interest in so many other important subjects. We all joined the Audubon Society, started a stamp collection and learned the names of the local birds and flowers. We studied about many famous authors and artists and so much more. While doing all of these activities I also established a good foundation for the three R's. Every year Tiny put on a pageant and invited the children from the Inyokern School to attend. In the 1933-34 school year the pageant was based on the Native American culture. Her pageants were always very elaborate and colorful. The photo on this page shows one of the scenes from a pageant complete with teepee. My brother Marvin is on

the left, I am in the middle with one of the older Native American boys on the right. We all made hook rugs and Marvin is holding the one I made and still have. I remember I wasn't too happy, because I didn't have any feathers on my head and my brother was holding the hook rug I had made!

Thinking back 67 years, I can still see the aisle up the middle of the room with three rows of shining desks on either side. Tiny had everyone refinish the top of their desk and fasten a small block of pinewood on the upper part of the desk to doodle on, for those who desired to do so.

Henry "Hank" Schuette tells about a play that he attended ten years earlier, "In 1923 at the age of eight I attended the Inyokern School. We were bussed to Brown School to attend a pageant that Tiny Standard produced with her students, based on Greek Mythology. This was the fourth year of the worst drought in the Valley's history. The story was that the rain god had displeased the chief of the gods, and was banished in chains to a cave on Mt. Owens. We all joined in prayer at the end of the show. It did rain shortly afterwards! Actually I believe that was the first rain I remember. It started one night just as we were finishing supper. Big drops were hitting the tin roof of our kitchen lean-to. We all rushed outside and turned our faces to the sky and caught the drops in our hands. The next year was a good year for the cattle."

Tiny was a favorite among all the people of Indian Wells Valley. In later years, Tiny was widely known as "Chiquita," the Spanish for Tiny. She and her sister, Ruth Hibbard Powers, were an inseparable pair around the community. Approaching 90 years, Tiny was indeed impressively "tiny." She and Earl retired to the former Indian lands in Grapevine Canyon where they maintained a showplace of momentos and Indian artifacts.

Tiny Standard with the last students of Brown School, Gloria and Everet Sterling, the second generation of Sterling children to be taught by Tiny Standard, in 1950. Tiny was there for thirty years, watching one generation grow up, then finding herself teaching the three R's to the next.

ing he owns the historic Homestead Café just south of Indian Wells on Highway 14. It is one of the oldest continuously used establishments in the valley. It has been a restaurant since 1922. The first building burned and the present building was moved from Inyokern in 1926. Mrs. Gordon paid thirty-five dollars for the building and fifty dollars to have it moved to where it stands today.

When I think of the Homestead Café I remember a morning in 1941 when my dad, Marvin Powers, and I ate breakfast there. The day before a cattle truck had unloaded thirty head of three and four year old Mexican steers one quarter of a mile east of the café across highway 395. Some had been used as work oxen in Mexico and were shod and had holes drilled in their horns for lashing the ox yokes. There were several small corrals there, which had been built for sheep. After they were unloaded it looked like the corrals would hold the cattle. Our horses were in a separate small pen.

My dad had just bought a 1941 Chevrolet club coup and we had our beds loaded in the car. We would scatter our cattle up in the canyons in the morning, as it was too late to do it that day. As it got dark everything seemed peaceful. In the middle of the night the wind came up and it was really blowing a gale. No way could we sleep outside so we spent the rest of the night in the car. The wind blew the sand so hard that it pelted one side of my dad's new car. By morning it had calmed down and the steers were still in the corral so we rode off to get some breakfast. It was so comfortable in the café that we spent about two hours eating and talking. As we sat by the window looking out over the desert my dad said, "Look at that dust going out across the desert (in a southeast direction). Looks like a bunch of cattle." As we looked down at the corrals we realized that they were our steers. We jumped on our horses, and riding as fast as we could, finally headed them off and took them into Indian Wells Canyon, which was part of our winter and spring range. We had to watch them all the time after that to be sure they didn't try to head back to Mexico.

After about a year of discussion, in 1920 it was decided to consolidate the schools in one union. There was great difficulty choosing a site, as nearly everyone wanted the school located near them. Inyokern was chosen for the location of the school, which proved to be a fortunate choice. All three buildings, which were moved to Inyokern, were used as classrooms for the three teachers. A new building was erected in 1934.

Perhaps the main advantage that was gained was they would now have two years of a fully accredited high school. Also they now could hire experienced teachers who would stay. Before, they had to pay the minimum salary and the teachers usually taught only one term. With the consolidated school the three teachers divided the classes. The high school teacher also taught the seventh and eighth grades. Usually the high school boys would drive the busses.

Mrs. Vernon Carr wrote that between 1910 and 1917 when World War I started there were between 150 and 200 families living in the Indian Wells Valley. This included the families of the caretakers at the stations along the aqueduct and businesspeople along Highway 6 (now Highway 395).

Homestead— Dick Lewis

I believe the only person living today in the Indian Wells Valley that was an original resident of Brown is Dick Lewis. At the time of this writ-

Powers

One of the best known cattlemen in the Indian Wells Valley during the 20th century was John O. (Jack) Powers. Jack was born in Onyx on

Jack Powers, desert cattleman, with horses, and Don Powers at far right.

December 29, 1891. He ran cattle in Grapevine Canyon and furnished meat for the hotel at Little Lake. It was there that he met Minnie Corkhill. They were married in 1915. To this union were born Donald in 1916 and Mildred in 1920. Jack's home ranch was in Isabella, in the Kern River Valley. While living there Minnie drowned in the Kern. Later Jack lost his Isabella ranch in the depression in 1929. Valley life sometimes could be tough and unforgiving.

Don spent summers in his dad's cow camp in Grapevine Canyon and his winters with his aunt and uncle, Clara and Willie Nicoll in Weldon where he attended the South Fork School. He graduated in 1930 and attended high school in Bakersfield for two years but didn't return because of the cost of living away from home.

In the winters of 1932-33, when Don was just 16 and 17 years old, he took care of his dad's cattle and the cattle of Stanley Smith and Marvin Powers, while his dad worked for the W.P.A. on the roads out

of Randsburg. Don took his dad to the road camp early Monday morning, then rode the desert all week taking care of the cattle. He would then go back and pick up his dad on Friday evening. Both would go back to the cow camp until Monday morning.

In 1934 Don returned to high school in Escondido, where he boarded with his uncle, Jim Corkhill, who had a blacksmith shop. Don attended school from 8:00 a.m. until 2:00 p.m. and then helped in the shop.

At this time Jack had a cattle permit in the

Don and Mildred Powers, 1939.

Sequoia National Forest. The U.S. Forest Supervisor told him he could no longer hold his permit unless he had a ranch to qualify for the permit. So Jack and Don borrowed money on their cattle and bought the Calloway Ranch, five miles east of Leliter and were again assigned a permit.

Don met his wife, Mildred High, at the Sand Canyon aqueduct patrol station. Her brother was the relief patrolman for Jess Ramsey, while he was on vacation. Don and Mildred were married in June 1939. The two built a new house on the ranch in 1940. Not long after the war started, the Navy notified them that they would be purchasing their ranch for the China Lake Ordnance Test Station. They left the ranch in September 1942 and moved to Hawthorne. A short time later, Don was drafted into the Army.

After the war they bought a cattle ranch in Susanville, California. When a horse fell on Don and he could no longer ride they sold the ranch. They then moved to Escondido where they lived for eighteen years where Don worked as a shop forman in a blacksmith shop. 1974 brought them to Greenfield, California where they bought a blacksmith shop and farm hardware store. They now live in Hemet near their two daughters, Janice and Suzanne and their families.

Tom Spratt

Although Tom Spratt didn't live in the town of Brown, he did live in nearby Grapevine Canyon. The residents of Brown would go to his place for picnics in the summer and Fourth of July celebrations were held there. Don Powers wrote the following of his memories of Tom Spratt:

I started going with my Dad, Jack Powers, to the cow camps in 1925 when I was eight years old for all school holidays and summer vacations, as I had lost my mother when I was six. Our home ranch was at Onyx, but our winter range was on the Mojave Desert and the canyons of the Eastern Sierra.

Our main winter camp was at Tom Spratt's place. Tom was commonly known as 'Indian Tom'. At this time I was too young to follow the cowboys on their day rides so I was left with Tom. He had an adobe house that his father had built. It was small but he kept it warm and clean. I followed him around, ate beans, sourdough bread and venison. I guess now you would say he was my baby sitter, but the word

hadn't been invented yet. Tom worked for the City of Los Angeles when they built the aqueduct from Bishop to Los Angeles. It crossed Grapevine Canyon just a mile below his house. He was a very accomplished blacksmith and built himself a well-equipped shop. At the end of the aqueduct construction the city left a lot of material and equipment up and down the desert at their various campsites. A lot of the old time settlers acquired some of this material to improve their homesteads.

Tom's property was an Indian allotment as his mother was a full blood Indian. She was born in Grapevine Canyon, as was Tom. His father, Jack Spratt, was full blood Irish with flaming red hair and beard. He was reputedly a highwayman who quite often held up the stagecoaches of the area. A woman was traveling north on the stage from Mojave to Lone Pine when Jack held up the stage and robbed the passengers of their valuables. Several days later the stage was traveling south and the same lady was riding, when again Jack held it up. The lady exclaimed, "This isn't fair Mr. Spratt, you robbed me on my way up and now you are robbing me again." She recognized him by his bushy red beard that stuck out around his bandana.

Tom never had any formal education, but was quite a well-educated man by his own accomplishments. He could read and write well. He could read music and played both the organ and violin. He built two large sheet metal buildings. One had a wood stove, table and chair and two double beds. This was where we stayed when working cattle. The other one was for storage. We kept our saddles and pack equipment there.

These cabins attracted several of the area men who didn't have a home close. Most all of these men played some kind of instruments so they had quite a time when they all got together. Tom always made several barrels of wine every year from the wild grapes in Grapevine Canyon. This always livened up the party but also caused some problems. I remember well one night when my dad and I were sleeping in Tom's storage room off his kitchen.

Things were going well when we went to bed; lots of noise but the adobe walls insulated us from it pretty well. About 2:00 a.m. when Tom began to get drunk and surly he ran everybody out of the house firing his rifle through the roof. My dad sat up in bed and about that time Tom came looking for him. He had a kerosene lamp in one hand and his rifle in the other. He said, "Jack I'm going to kill you." My dad said, "Tom, calm down and give me that rifle." He had taken the barrel and moved it out of his stomach. Tom relaxed a little and my dad took the rifle as Tom released it. He then said, 'Now go to bed and get some sleep.' That is just what he did but I didn't sleep any more that night.

Tom had a large wood range in his kitchen that he had gotten from one of the aqueduct camps. He most always had a big pot of pink beans on and a pot of sourdough started behind it. He didn't bake his sourdough bread in the oven, always baking it in the back yard in a fire pit.

He had a Model T Ford and once a week he'd crank it up and make a trip to Indian Wells, to Bill Van Dyke's place. Tom would always fill up with gas, get his supplies and load them. Then he and several people would get up a poker game that would go on for several hours. It was prohibition but there was always sipping whiskey to go around. Whenever Tom's Indian Blood got enough Bootleg to make him ornery, Bill would tell him it was getting late, he'd better head for home before it got dark as his head lights didn't work.

Tom had a real nice small fruit orchard. In the spring I used to help him pick the plums, apricots and peaches. We would make jam and jelly and can fruit for a week or two. He had a small ditch from about a half-mile up the creek that brought water to his house. One year he ditched the water to a ten-foot bank behind his house and let it spill down over a water wheel he had made. He belted it to a 6-volt generator off a Dodge car through two batteries and to the two headlights off the same car into his house. This worked for that year but most years the creek didn't run all summer and in dry years it only ran in the wintertime.

He dug a 50-foot tunnel into the decomposed granite bank behind his house. He cemented it inside and put a six-inch vent pipe up through the mountain. He put a door in the entrance and this was a wonderful storage area as it stayed cool all summer and warm all winter. I used to sleep in there when it was real hot in the summertime.

I always had a deep admiration for Tom and his talents and feel that I learned a lot from my association with him.

McConnell

Dorothy Francis Potts was born on November 19, 1899 in Los Angeles, California. She came to Brown in March 1921 with her husband, Marvin McConnell, and their two children, Eleanor and Bob. They also brought Marvin's mother and father, Lillian and Sylvester and his two sisters, Dorene and Fern. Marvin was born August 11, 1897 in Indian Territory before it became Oklahoma.

Dorothy was postmaster at Brown in 1925 and 1926. They then went to Kennedy Meadows where they homesteaded 160 acres. There was no road into the area at that time and they rode horseback on an old Thelan 'trail,' from the railroad opposite the red hill above Little Lake. They stayed in the area of Kennedy Meadows (near Chimney Meadows, at the head of Nine-Mile Canyon) for 15 months, which meant they were there during one full winter.

After this they moved down to Grapevine Canyon to go to work for the Los Angeles Department of Water and Power. They moved to Mojave for 3-1/2 years and then to the Fairmont Station for four years where Marvin worked in defense plants during the war.

Returning to the area of Kennedy Meadows, they lived there for many years. Marvin had a heart attack in 1970. In 1973 they decided the winters were just too hard and they bought a house in Onyx.

INYOKERN

The history of the town of Inyokern dates back to late in the year of 1908. In March of 1909 William W. McElroy filed on the north one half of section 30. This section would become part of the town site for the town later named Inyokern.

At this time the spot along the Owenyo Railroad, named for the Owens Valley and the County of Inyo, was simply called Siding 16. This was the railroad siding where supplies and materials were unloaded for the Los Angeles to Owens Valley aqueduct construction camp in Short Canyon, and Indian Wells Canyon.

Thompson

In 1909 Robert Richardson Thompson and his wife Marybell arrived in the Indian Wells Valley. They had been married in Bloomington, Illinois and moved to the Los Angeles area in 1906. They brought with them their two children, Fannie and Robert. The parents homesteaded 350 acres in the valley. Thompson's claim was just north of Inyokern. From this location on the Owenyo Railroad he could supply the people who lived and visited Railroad Siding 16 with food, lodging and a general store.

Inyokern in its beginning

Later Thompson returned to Los Angeles and formed a partnership with David Shanks who also owned land, which included the town site of Inyokern. The two men threw their lot together and formed the Inyo-Kern Company. They started by building a twelve-room hotel, a restaurant and general store. The town was an immediate success with the influx of laborers and suppliers of material for building the aqueduct.

By 1910 the town had a post office named Inyokern and David Shanks was the postmaster. By 1912 the company had grown immensely and was incorporated. Thompson and Shanks brought in three more Los Angeles businessmen to invest in their corporation. These five formed the Inyokern Land and Water Company. They immediately drew a map and filed it with the Kern County Recorder, which established it as the official town of Inyokern in 1914. During this time two other early settlers, John and Gerald Lindsey, drilled about 300 wells for people in the area.

By 1917 the elder Thompson had brought his son, Robert Hurd Thompson, into the business as manager. When the elder Thompson died in

1920, Robert took over his position in the corporation along with his sister Frannie and their mother Marybelle. This gave the Thompson family a controlling interest in the corporation. By 1922 the corporation was heavily laden with debts and unable to expand. The stockholders voted to dissolve the corporation and liquidate the debts.

In the end the Thompson family wound up with 95 percent of the land and assets of the now defunct business. Although most of the property has been sold, in 1994 the family still held title to some of the original lands developed by the Inyokern Land and Water Company. In 2001 the grandson of the elder Thompson, Robert Hoskins Thompson, still lives on some of the family's original property in Inyokern.

In 1913 "the church people" the Toombs, the Earlys and some others decided they wanted a church. They had a meeting and decided to have a box social to raise money for a building. All the ladies prepared their boxes. By this time there were a lot of homesteaders in the valley and all were anxious to have some good home cooked food. John Lindsey, a bachelor in the area, was stuck on the schoolteacher at Leliter. The Leliter

School was between Brown and Inyokern. However, there was another fellow who was real excited about her too. Art Callaway, at that time just a boy, said he would go over and see the basket she was making and tell John Lindsey which one it was, so he would be able to bid on it. Art went over and she showed him her beautifully decorated basket. Immediately he returned and told John what it looked like.

That night when the bidding started for the first basket, one man said $1.00, someone else said $2.00, and then the bidding stopped. The auctioneer said, "Now listen, we're here for a good cause, and we're not going to sell any basket for under $10.00. So if anybody wants to eat tonight, they'll have to pay $10.00 or more for a basket."

So the bidding started again and when the teacher's basket came up for bids her "would be" boyfriend bid $10.00, John bid $12.00 and it just kept going up. At $18.00 John said, "Well I'll just put a stop to this bidding." And he said, "$25.00!" Well he got to eat with the teacher. The other guy couldn't figure out how John knew which was her basket. Nobody ever told him. The church was eventually built across the railroad tracks to the east and Rev. Early was the preacher. Later the church was moved into town, next to the town hall.

Lindsays

In 1920, John and Mabel Lindsay arrived in Inyokern from Long Beach, California. Their daughter Gladys was to play a big part in the history of the Indian Wells Valley. That same year Clarence Frederick Ives arrived in town. Gladys was born in Lamarr, Missouri, on August 22, 1899. Her parents brought her to the desert for her health. Her asthma was serious and her mother had read that the desert would help this condition. Gladys later wrote, "Clarence Ives and I met in 1920, when we were both homesteaders. I went with other boys and he went with other girls until 1923. We were married in my folk's home in Inyokern on June 17, 1923." Gladys and Clarence moved to Long Beach and in 1929 returned to live in Inyokern.

Clarence worked for John and Mabel Lindsay, who had purchased a store from the Lindsey brothers, John and Gerald. They had the same last name but it was spelled differently and they were not related.

Ives

Clarence Ives was born in Ogden, Utah, on December 12, 1899. He was the second oldest of five children. He had been a cowboy and fireman, but had no chosen trade. Clarence and Gladys bought the general merchandise store in Inyokern from John McNeil in 1929 when they returned from living in Long Beach.

In the same building, besides groceries, was a 4th class post office and a library. In 1930 they built a Shell Service Station and a small Shell dis-

John and Mabel Lindsay presented the community with a festive wedding in their Inyokern home with all of the trimmings. Clarence was to become a leader in the town, even if he did not dream it during this wedding. Gladys and Clarence became a good team. John and Mabel always helped to provide encouragement and money.

Clarence Ives had not graduated from high school, even if several of his sisters and brothers were university students. In Inyokern, he attended high school and drove a "school bus" from his homestead. The Hansen girls needed a ride. Over the years, he had more students and a bigger "bus."

Clarence met the train every morning at 4 o'clock and carried the mail and packages in this cart. Claudean and her dog enjoyed riding in it, also.

tribution center. The supplies for the store came both by truck and train. Valley people sold to the store what produce they raised. Meat came from Wilson's in Los Angeles by train. Trips to Lancaster by car also filled the grocery needs for the store. Ice came from Lone Pine in 300-pound blocks. The mail came from Mojave on the train. In those early days the only telephone in town was at the Ives' store. The telegraph was one mile east at the California Electric Sub station. Inyokern was growing.

Clarence and Gladys Ives made a commitment to invest their lives in this desert community and they did this in a manner that is hard to match. During his long career in private enterprise, Clarence was at one time the postmaster and freight agent for the railroad. He provided weather data for the United States meteorologist, brought in the Shell Oil Company wholesale bulk plant and was a grocery retailer for 32 years. He was the founder and owner of the town water system and owned the town hotel. He organized the Inyokern voluntary fire department and was its chief for many years. He

Top: John and Mabel Lindsay established a business in 1920, and hired Clarence to work in the store, when he was not attending high school. They sold out (1924) and returned to Long Beach.

Above: Clarence and Gladys returned from Long Beach and were given $11,000 to purchase this store from John McNeil in 1929. Business was so good that it only took them two years to pay back Gladys' parents. Lindsay is standing on the porch. Notice the gas hand pump.

Gladys changed little in ten years, but the town was growing and a new Shell station had been added to the corner. Gladys holds Norma in this photo. Norma grew up in a different atmosphere than Lindsay and Claudean. The big "Boomtown Days" were coming in fast and the Navy changed the family, as well as the town.

also organized a baseball team, which played in the valley league.

Clarence and Gladys had three children. In 1925, Lindsay was born. He went to elementary school in Inyokern, finished high school in Bakersfield and later graduated from the University of Southern California. He had two children by his first wife. After working for Aerojet General and Lockeed, he worked for the State of California as a safety engineer for 14 years before he retired.

Their second child was Claudean who was born in 1929 and attended elementary school in Inyokern. She rode the bus for two years to Trona High School until Burroughs High School was established in China Lake. She was a member of the first graduating class in 1946. She later graduated from the University of Southern California. She returned to Inyokern in 1951 to teach in the same classroom where she graduated from the eighth grade ten years earlier.

Claudean remembers walking across the tracks for about a quarter of a mile to the

Methodist Church for an afternoon meeting. Mrs. Carrie Ovall, the minister's wife and she were the only ones in attendance. She said Mrs. Ovall conducted the service for her just as if the church was full of people. Later the church was moved to its present location in the north section of Inyokern. Claudean taught Sunday School here. Claudean married Robert (Bud) McAlexander whom she met in college. They have five children.

The third child in the Ives family was Norma who was born in 1938. She went to all eight grades in Inyokern then to Burroughs High School and on to Fort Collins Colorado for college. Norma has three children by her first husband.

Claudean Ives wrote about her father, "Clarence loved baseball. We all played and were good at it. Lindsay was the pitcher; the rest of us were better catchers. We were all home run hitters. My father's cowboying days were helpful to our activities; we rode horses as we grew up. We had chickens, goats, lambs, dogs and

When Clarence and Gladys returned to Inyokern in 1929, this was Main Street. In the background is the Wasmuth's place of business.

Left to right, Claudean on her pony, 'Lucky', Lindsey on his horse 'Pat' riding with their father Clarence.

cats. I never remember my dad fixing a broken screen door or car motor; though I'm sure he knew how. It just wasn't his bag of tricks. He was a businessman and ran the business efficiently, but hired 'Mr. Fix Its' to do that type of work. This was okay because this provided jobs for other people. One of the best fixers was my mother's 'Papa.' He was a great 'right hand man' on any project. Papa came up to the valley from Long Beach to build a house for John and

Lois Carr, when they married. There were three houses in a row on that street which he built."

Claudean continued, "A prominent man in town said, 'Clarence Ives has given away more money than most people make in a lifetime.' From my perspective that would be a true statement. Clarence took charge of seeing that his customers were remembered. I recall boxes of bacon wrapped in Christmas trimmings being given to each and every family for Christmas

Clarence and Gladys Ives were proud of their three children. Lindsay was in the Coast Guard Academy, at 19 years old, and Claudean and Norma were having their first visit to New York City. The family had taken a train compartment across the U.S. to see Lindsay at Christmas.

morning's breakfast. If some family or a loner, didn't get to the store for this gift I was sent down the street to deliver it to their door. He must have had a list for he knew just who needed this, even on Christmas morning. He did not quibble; he gave extra effort to projects and encouraged others by leading. He was a trend-setter and a trailblazer and I marvel that he never said 'No' to me. I was always encouraged by him to go do it, even if I was a girl!"

Behind every great man is a great woman and Claudean went on to say about her mother, "Gladys was a top-notch business woman. She related to all of us, 'Clarence and I would sit down to the table and battle through a tough question. We would come to an agreement and get up from the table.' If anything went wrong, neither said, "I told you so," for the agreement was mutual and final. Our home was open and all arguments or discussions were allowed, but when we left those four walls and went into the community we should not repeat what had been said." Inyokern was a small town and stories were not to be repeated.

I remember my mother walking outside following a "Gypsy" lady. When she halted her, she said, "Your little girl did not pay for that loaf of bread." "What loaf of bread?" said the lady, in a long flowing skirt. "The one your daughter has under her skirt," said my mother. When the girl was asked to display what was

General "Hap" Arnold was a friend of Norman Ives, and helped arrange military maneuvers in Inyokern.
The Battle of Inyokern (1934). They used facilities in Inyokern, as well as the dirt field south of town.

under her skirt, the loaf of bread appeared, and it was quickly paid for by the parent. If the mother needed the bread and had asked for it she could have had it. Gladys didn't like sneaking. She was a disciplinarian, generous, but strict!

She was in church on Sundays playing the piano or singing a duet with Lois Carr, or chairperson for the Parent Teacher's Association or

filling the car with gas to drive to Bakersfield as a member of the Grand Jury. I can never remember her staying in bed or letting anyone take over her duties.

Never did a "hobo" get off of the train that she didn't offer a meal. Never did a relative, friend, or even a mere acquaintance, come by that she did not offer shelter and a meal, or credit. After our new house was built, about 1940, it was a

Claudean enjoys telling the story about graduating from the eight grade and playing in the band in this building. As she attended one of Norma's Christmas programs, she was invited to come and teach, so she came back, in 1951, to teach in the same building. She even relates that some of her children actually attended classes in the same building, about 1960. (These memories are dear to her. Inyokern is a special place.)

meeting place for the school orchestra, graduation parties, Sunday dinners and New Year's Celebrations. We then had a big house and it was always open to the community.

Clarence Ives died in 1984 and Patricia Farris of the *News Review* in Ridgecrest gave his obituary as follows:

His personality was a beautiful mixture of honesty, compassion for his fellow man, generosity to his community and an unforgettable sense of humor which was with him to the end.

He donated the land for, and saw the development of, the Kern County Park in Inyokern. In 1959 Clarence and Gladys moved to Bishop. Perhaps it could be said that Clarence never really retired as he loved keeping his hand in business and seeing various projects carried through to completion. A beautiful cabin on Bishop Creek, at Aspendell, provided the Ives and their friends with many happy memories.

His retirement years were happy years, living in an area he loved, traveling much of the world and sharing the fellowship of his many friends.

"Other achievements recorded are the construction of the Kern County building at the park that was built as the result of his prevailing upon the Kern County Supervisors to use money that was set aside for the World War II Veterans memorial building, to be built in Inyokern. He also negotiated with the United States Navy for the acquisition of a sewer system. The system was built for the original housing at Harvey Field (Inyokern Airport) to be administered by the County as the Inyokern Sanitation District. He was instrumental in obtaining the original Kern County airport and had it designated as a federal airways emergency landing strip. Ives maintained a weather station at the airport for the Weather Bureau. He paid the taxes and maintained the Town Hall often from his own funds.

Our remembrance of our good and faithful friend Clarence Ives was that above all he was a true city father, always looking out for the needs of those in the community, paving the way for their future growth and development. He was a gentle man, a quiet rather reserved man, and a caring man with the ability to set things in motion.

His wife Gladys died in 1990.

In the beginning: The first commercial flight was the $5 Inyokern-to-Burbank flight aboard "The City of Inyokern" DC-3. *Pictured L.to R.* Cmdr. Burks, Cmdr. McLaren, Francis Drew, Capt. Vieweg, Julie Abram, Col. Shepard, Mr. & Mrs. Ives, and Capt. Criddle, preparing to board on February 26, 1951.

Inyokern Airport

The earliest known local airport activity occurred in 1933 when Clarence Ives created a private dirt strip south of town. He built this so his brother, Norman, who was a pilot for the U.S. Army Air Corps, could fly in and visit the family. The start of activity at the present site of the Inyokern Airport followed a short time later. The Civil Air Authority checked the proposed route and determined that an emergency field was needed in the vicinity of Inyokern. The necessary land was purchased. The WPA graded and paved a runway in 1935 and the airport was formally dedicated in late 1935 as Kern County Airport No. 8.

The U.S Air Force discovered the Inyokern Airport, using it for a variety of activities, including student pilot cross-country flight training. The latter did not start off too well. Two of

the first flights of 40 planes, which left Fox Field in Lancaster, got lost along the way. The other 38 landed successfully only to taxi off the runway and get stuck in the soft sand along the edge. Inyokern old-timers remember with amusement helping pull out the airplanes from the sand.

The arrival of the Navy changed the fate of the Inyokern Airport. Private pilots went back to using the Ives dirt strip. The Navy needed more land and started to acquire it, but started construction even before all the real estate transactions were recorded. Three runways were paved and Quonset barracks, a large hangar, tower building, ammunition bunkers, fuel tanks and other structures were built. On May 10, 1944 Harvey Field was officially commissioned. It was named after Lieutenant Commander Warren W. Harvey, a Navy squadron leader who was lost during the war. Harvey was a friend and

Left: Clarence's youngest brother, Norman Ives, was in the Air Corps at March Field. He flew in to see the family on a special airfield south of Inyokern, which Clarence had built. The two brothers enjoyed each other. Clarence didn't learn to fly, but he was always a willing passenger.

Below: Early view of Inyokern

classmate of Captain Sherman E. Burroughs, the first commander of China Lake.

From the start, it was evident that the Navy needed more room to grow than was available at Inyokern. Construction work at China Lake began with the Navy's arrival in the valley. In May 1945 the Navy left Harvey Field and moved to the new Armitage Field, about nine miles west on the China Lake reservation. The airport was again available to private pilots who moved over from the Ives' strip.

As soon as the airport was returned to Kern County, the name was changed from Harvey Field back to Kern County Airport No. 8. On February 26, 1951, the first commercial flights began from Inyokern. A 30-passenger DC-3 named the "City of Inyokern", complete with a

stewardess, made flights to and from Burbank. The fare was $5 each way. There were two round trip flights daily. The first outgoing plane took off at 9 a.m., with two Inyokern pioneers, Mr. and Mrs. Clarence Ives, holding the number one and two tickets.

RIDGECREST

The early history of the town of Ridgecrest is best told in an article printed in the *Daily Independent* in 1975: "Miners and alfalfa farmers moved into the Indian Wells Valley. Many years after increasingly hot climates and a steadily shrinking supply of wild game forced the Shoshone Indians, who roamed the ranges and Coso Mountains, to move on.

First came the miners. Gus Erdman came in

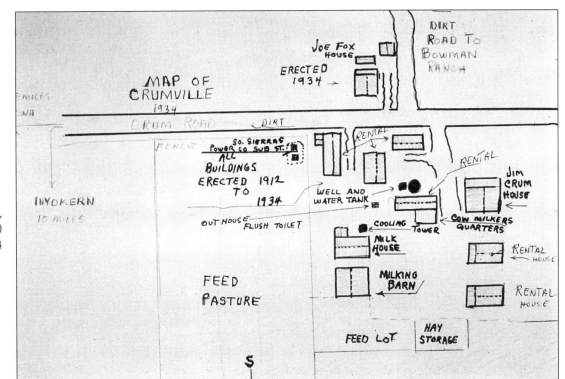

Dairy Complex, Crumville (Ridgecrest) in 1934

1903 to work on the White Star Mine just four miles west of the present Cerro Coso College. It was one of the first gold mines in Ridgecrest.

Erdman soon struck a pocket of gold and various sources estimated that between $5,000 and $25,000 worth of gold was eventually taken out of the White Star. Erdman hauled the gold ore by horse-drawn wagons to the Red-Dog Mine and Concentration Plant in Johannesburg, where mining was at a peak, for processing.

Erdman continued working the White Star until the federal mining moratorium of 1941, when apparently discouraged, he sold most of his equipment. Erdman told his son Frank there was probably more gold just to the west of the main shaft and left the mine to Frank when he died in 1945.

While the Erdmans worked their mine, other settlers moved into the valley. Some were miners, scratching holes in the hillside looking for the elusive wealth of the nearby Rand Mining District. Others like George and Bertha Robertson, homesteaded in the present Ridgecrest area, discovering that the dusty desert could yield well water to supply their 1912 ranch.

When Robertson became ill he sold his land to his brother-in-law, John McNeil, who operated a store in Inyokern. McNeil planted 40 acres of alfalfa and brought in 40 dairy cows. With these he had milk to send to Trona. West End Chemical Corporation and American Potash and Chemical Corporation were mining minerals less glamorous, but more prosperous than the gold others sought.

William Crum bought his employer's dairy from McNeil's widow when McNeil died. He provided the nearest homes for Trona families who were not permitted to live in the Searles Valley, where there were no schools. 'Crumville, U.S.A.' developed and housed ten families.

After William Crum died, his sons found the dairy impossible to operate without cool clear water, so they abandoned the farm. Joe Fox, who with his three sons had worked for Crum, bought the dairy and expanded the operation to include tending 7,000 chickens. Fox and the boys had already dug their own well on property Fox bought across from the Crum Dairy. He was able to sell lots with water piped to them to Trona and Westend workers for $25, on terms.

Grant Bowman moved his family to the Indian Wells Valley in 1913, settling south of town near the present Bowman Road. The Bowman Ranch was an outstanding success story in the valley in the 1920s and early thirties.

Located where Ridgecrest now stands, their 250-300 acres of alfalfa, two story veranda type ranch house and large family of handsome children were the pride and envy of the people of the valley.

Using incorrect Spanish, Bowman named his homestead Los Flores Ranch, a name that later applied to one of the area's schools. Mr. Bowman donated the land and built the Los Flores School. Rev. Early, Thomas Toombs, the Talbots and Lees helped him with this project.

By 1920 the ranch was shipping trainloads of alfalfa hay out of the valley to the Los Angeles markets. Grant Bowman organized a chapter of the Farm Bureau and was its first president. He led a fight to bring Owens River and Mono Basin water to the valley for irrigation. Los Angeles contested the filing and won. The decision was made in Washington that the water should go to the area that represented the most people.

William Bentham came to Ridgecrest in 1934 and bought the property where the present intersection of China Lake Boulevard and Ridgecrest Boulevard is. The town's first gas station at Bentham's Corners sold Red Lion gasoline. The station served its 96 residents of Crumville. Those residents shed the unappealing "Crumville" name in 1941 when a single vote favored the name Ridgecrest over Gilmore.

Recreation for the families in the area consisted mostly of dances at the Inyokern town hall, and at the White House in Randsburg, church activities, box socials, rabbit shooting, visits and cookouts at the ranch. The 4th of July was always a big event and held either in Grapevine Canyon or at Jack Sweet's place in Indian Wells Canyon.

Fox

In 1989 Lawrence J. (Larry) Fox wrote the following for the Early Timers celebration in Inyokern: "I was born February 6, 1920, in Dennison, Utah. I came with my parents to Hollywood in 1931. My father worked for his brother, a plumber, for several years.

In 1934, we came to the Indian Wells Valley to the Shangri La Ranch (formerly Bowman's). People were advertising for a foreman with diesel engine experience. In Hollywood we were neighbors of the Benthams. Mr. Bentham came here with us. He and my father decided that we should take the job.

During the first few months, it became clear that we were working for a rather shoddy management. When we asked for our pay, we were told that we had been on two months probation, so we wouldn't get paid! My father immediately got a job at West End. We loaded our belongings on our two trucks and moved to an area across the road from the Crum dairy.

We lived in tents until we could scrounge up enough material from old abandoned homesteads to build a house. In 1934 there were many homesteads but most had fallen down. We got permission from the County to salvage material and just keep a list in case anyone ever protested. Most of the land had gone back for taxes. My brothers and I did this while my father worked.

My father was Joe Fox. For some time my older brother Elliott, my younger brother Marion and I drove around the desert gathering up lumber. We built the house with this lumber that still stands at the corner of Norma Street and Ridgecrest Blvd. Elliott soon got work at

Bessie and Joe Fox by the egg cellar

Early view of Crumville, 1935

West End. That left my youngest brother, Bill, seven years younger and Burdette, a year and a half younger than myself, and me going to school in Inyokern.

After about a year we found out through the Bowmans the land that our house was on didn't belong to Crum. It really belonged to Bowman, and he sold it to my father. We were faced with a dilemma. If Mr. Crum found out what we had done, and the way things were, he would surely cut our water off.

We secretly dug a well behind the house, with a hand windlass. It took us about nine months. It was 3 feet across and 125 feet deep. We scattered the dirt from the well over the desert, so that no one would know what we were doing. We hit water and put a pump in.

By this time, I had been doing the milk bottling for Crum's dairy for about a year and a half. I thought sure that he would fire me when he found out, but he didn't . I guess he couldn't find anyone to do the work for the $18 a month that he was paying me.

Above: Elliot Fox held by Joe (?) on tractor. Larry Fox on mower—1935

Left: Joe and Bessie Fox and sons Bill and Larry, at home in 1935

INDIAN WELLS VALLEY   119

After awhile I quit school in Inyokern. I didn't graduate. In the meantime Mr. Crum had let his business deteriorate. He had a real bad drinking habit. His wife and nephew tried to keep the business going but after about two years they went broke. The dairy reverted back to the McNeil Estate.

McNeil had run the store in Inyokern and was a relative of the Robertsons who were the original homesteaders at Ridgecrest. After a while my father decided to buy the dairy. We bought out all the interest of the McNeil estate. In addition to the McNeil property and the Bowman property where we built our house my father bought the rest of the Bowman property. It extended from our house to China Lake Blvd. and south to Upjohn. We bought it from the Bowmans for $15 or $20 an acre. We paid something like $7,000 for the McNeil property.

We branched out into the chicken business, and farming. We raised feed for the chickens. It became evident that my father would have to quit his job or hire someone. As it turned out, he did both. When the war broke out, Trona and West End started hiring and people who worked there wanted to live in Ridgecrest because it was cooler and there was water so you could have grass. My father sold off much of the property along Ridgecrest Blvd. Of course, it was Crumville Blvd. then.

During the war I joined the Navy Seabees and was shipped to the Aleutian Islands for a year and a half. When we came back I was stationed at China Lake. I guess they thought that anybody crazy enough to live in the desert as long as I had would make a good sailor.

Going back, I had met my wife, Bette, prior to the war. She was the niece of Mrs. Parmelee who was the school principal at Trona. Her husband, Earl, was my boss in the powerhouse at Trona. I was interested in photography, and he was an expert. He was giving me instruction in camera and darkroom work. In visiting his

Facing page, top left: East on Ridgecrest Blvd.—1935

Facing page, top right: Sudie Bentham and Bessie Fox–looking North from old Fox home in Crumville. McNeal dairy barnes and rental buildings in view.

Facing page, lower right: The Fox and Bentham families, in a field of wild flowers, Crumville, Spring 1935

Right: Fox house, c. August 1979

home I became acquainted with Bette. We dated and became engaged, but nothing really developed until after the war. When I returned, we got acquainted all over again. We married July 25, 1944, in San Francisco. I had the distinction of being the only sailor that lived off the Base in a private home. I was a Navy aerial photographer, and I had permission to leave the base every day. Eventually we got a house, one that my brother built, and we lived there until the end of the war. Then I had to make a decision. I could either go into Civil Service and stay in photography, or go back and pick up my seniority in Trona. I really didn't think that the Navy would stay at China Lake, which was one of the greatest mistakes of my life. They tried to keep me but I said that I have a child and I have accumulated seniority. I know that I have a wage over there, so I went back to Trona where I worked until 1951. I then went to run the Fox water works for five years, until we sold out to the Ridgecrest Water District group. I worked for the family for another five years. Then I reestablished myself with West End, one of the chemical companies on Searles Lake. This time, I stayed for 21 years until I retired.

The Larry Foxes had two children, the oldest David Lawrence was the first child born at the Naval Ordnance Test Station dispensary. Their youngest was John Dale.

The Indian Wells Valley, which had been quietly removed from the modern advances of the 20th century, was changed dramatically with the arrival of the Navy in 1943 to develop and test the weapons needed for aerial combat in World War II.

The desert, which yielded little building material, saw an influx of workers using their "Yankee ingenuity" to construct an amazing assortment of desert dwellings. Schools, a theater, restaurants and cocktail lounges came with the influx of Navy employees. Some reports hold that some of the city's street names Peg, Norma, Vera, Jean and Florence honored popular barmaids employed at the early Village Supper Club.

Joe Fox subdivided property and donated land to many Ridgecrest churches and to the Veterans of Foreign Wars. He also donated the land for the USO Building, which later served as the Kern County Courthouse housing the Indian Wells Justice Court. The aging building now belongs to the City of Ridgecrest, which uses it for storage.

U.S. NAVAL ORDNANCE TEST STATION—CHINA LAKE

Nobody really knows how China Lake got its name. The most probable scenario being, the dry lake was originally noted for the presence of a few Chinese workers who harvested the surface borax during their brief sojourn there. The lake did claim the name in the 1870s. We know that Chinese labor was brought in to build railroads in California and to help develop the West. When the railroads were finished, the Chinese scattered out. Some re-worked the old mine dumps and became very well to do. Often the people who worked these dumps had been careless and left a lot of gold and silver in their eagerness to make a fast buck.

Many Chinese worked in the area around the Cerro Gordo Mine, when it was booming in the 1870s. It was at this location they made charcoal for the smelters. They later drifted down to China Lake, prospecting for placer gold. The Chinese had a camp on the east side of the lake. So it's quite probable it was referred to as China Lake in 1873.

The history of the U.S. Naval Ordnance Test Station, China Lake, is so extensive that even a book of over 80,000 words would not be able to contain it all. So in the space allotted, I will try to cover only a few of the important contributions to the national defense that were developed here.

Prior to 1943 this area was just a part of the Mojave Desert, shimmering under the glare of a relentless sun in summer, swept by desolating winds in winter. Only an occasional prospector would pass through and there were a few ranches on the outlying edges. It was off the beaten trail, the home of jackrabbit, coyote and sidewinder.

In the midst of World War II, adequate facilities were needed for testing and the evaluation of rockets for the Navy. California Institute of Technology (Caltech) worked on developing these. The Navy also needed a new proving ground for all aviation ordnance.

They needed to find an isolated area where people's lives would not be endangered by rocket firing. Security of the important work being done was also a factor in seeking out-of-the-way spots.

In the summer of 1943, while searching for the direly needed site, Dr. Charles Lauritsen, in a small plane flown by Cdr. Jack Renard spotted a two-way landing strip near Inyokern. It was in the middle of nowhere with nothing but empty desert for miles around, but not too far removed from Caltech's Pasadena base. Its remoteness and flat surfaces made it an ideal site for the experiments. The splendid flying weather afforded by the valley the greater portion of the year was an added inducement.

Settlers who lived on the property taken over by the government, entered into arrangements

Captain Sherman E. Burroughs, 1943

with the Navy for exchange of their lands for other property, or were paid in cash. Approximately one thousand mining claims were closed down on land now belonging to the Navy.

The base, first called the Naval Ordnance Test Station (NOTS), was established on November 8, 1943. Its mission was defined in a letter by the Secretary of the Navy as, "A station having for its primary function the research, development and testing of weapons, and having the additional function of furnishing primary training in the use of such weapons." Within a month of the Station's formation formal testing began.

One early drawback to the area was the shortage of badly needed labor and for administration as it progressed. Recruitment was carried on across the country and people rolled in to the valley in all types of cars, pulling trailers for living quarters. There was a considerable turnover in the first years for many did not like the desert and went elsewhere.

Quonset huts were used for living and administration quarters. To attract the necessary personnel the Navy created what is a veritable city on the desert. To house the military and civilian personnel houses were erected. The school system has grown from a few huts where children sat on boxes with their laps for desks to modern elementary, junior and senior high schools.

A food-mart, bank, library, fountain, ship's store, restaurant, pharmacy, barber and beauty shops, gas station, church facilities, numerous buildings for recreation, desert museum, and meeting halls are all phases of this city of the Navy. A part of the acreage was set-aside for picnics and dances. The Station covers an area of approximately one thousand square miles.

The outstanding single construction of this vast Station is the Michelson Laboratory. It was built at an approximate cost of eight million dollars. It is said to be the largest laboratory of its kind in the world, the laboratories within the main building are scientifically complete for the research being carried on. It is air-conditioned and earthquake resistant. The building is so large it is measured in terms of acres: seven and one-half acres of floor space. It is as long as a battleship.

The laboratory was named for Dr. Albert Abraham Michelson, American physicist, whose claim to fame lay in his work in the field of light and precision measurements. More than any other American he demonstrated that exact measurement is the basis on which exact science must always rest. Dr. Michelson was the first American to receive the Nobel Prize for Physics.

In the years following World War II, China Lake's projects included the development of the famed Sidewinder air-to-air missile, the world's first operational infrared-guided missile. It is still the most widely used air-to-air missile in the world. Sidewinder derived concepts went from undersea (Subwinder) to outer space (Spacewinder). The Sidewinder success story continues to this day, and the missile that China Lake invented, developed, tested, and evaluated is the world's most accurate, reliable, and successful dogfight missile. Also developed were the Shrike anti-radiation missile, the Zuni rocket, a series of aircraft rockets, an entire family of free fall weapons, torpedoes and the TV-guided Walleye glide bomb. China Lake tested the first submarine-launched ballistic missile motors.

In July 1967, NOTS China Lake and the Naval Ordnance Laboratory, Corona, California, combined to become the Naval Weapons Center. The Corona facilities were closed and their functions transferred to China Lake in 1971.

In January 1992, the Naval Weapons Center China Lake and the Pacific Missile Test Center Point Mugu were disestablished and joined with naval units at Albuquerque and White Sands, New Mexico, as a single command, the Naval Air Warfare Center Weapons Division (NAWCWD).

The physical plant at China Lake was then designated as the Naval Air Weapons Station (NAWS). Personnel at NAWCWD China Lake are involved in programs that range from the Tomahawk cruise missile to the new Joint Stand-Off Weapons System.

The China Lake community was planned from the start as a community where military and civilians would live and work side by side. Although most of the community has since moved to Ridgecrest, the traditions of military-civilian interaction and work-related socializing continue to this day.

From the installation's founding in 1943 until the mid 1950s, the Navy was practically the only provider of services in the surrounding Indian Wells Valley. Housing, schools, medical services, shopping and recreation were all provided for China Lake's civilians as well as for the military. Temporary housing, dirt roads, occasional floods and the frequent strong winds tested the mettle of early residents. However new housing, trees and lawns, extensive recreational facilities, community parties, clubs and social events, and a growing spirit of community rapidly improved the quality of life in the valley.

Conferring on a Sidewinder report are team leaders (from left) Cartwright, Wilcox, LaBerge, and Cdr. Wade Cone

Sidewinder as it went to the fleet in 1956. The F9F-8 aircraft carries two missiles.

Ridgecrest, the outside-the-gate community, little more than a cross-roads and general store in 1943, began to grow in the 1950s as residents there and at China Lake began to demand goods and services beyond what the Navy had to offer. During the 1950s a few more adventuresome employees bought houses "in town." Some more affluent residents bought a bit of land. However, most China Lakers didn't buy in Ridgecrest because widespread Federal Housing Authority financing was not available until the 1970s. Through the 1950s and into the 1960s Ridgecrest grew slowly, about three percent per year in population. Meanwhile, on the base, apartments, new housing, recreation facilities and a new All Faith Chapel were built, and new schools were finished. China Lake continued to be a thriving, self-contained military-civilian community.

The late 1960s were a transition period for China Lake. Ridgecrest was growing rapidly, and more quality housing was becoming available off base. When the Federal Housing Authority at last agreed that China Lake was a permanent presence in the valley and made widespread FHA

loans available, the exodus to Ridgecrest began. China Lake command mandated civilian relocation to Ridgecrest. The wartime civilian access to commissary and exchange privileges, as well as cheap housing with the Navy as landlord continued for many peacetime years. This was because of the successful argument that these amenities were necessary to attract and hold the high quality technical talent China Lake needed to create new weapons for the nation's defense. Ridgecrest merchants were of course not happy with that arrangement, and the authorities in Washington became less willing to maintain China Lake as a separate community as the amenities in Ridgecrest improved. The Station's role in the community evolved over 40 years from that of primary landlord and provider of services to that of being primarily a good neighbor. The City of Ridgecrest annexed the community area of China Lake in 1982. In the year 2002, the Navy remains the Indian Wells Valley's largest employer with more than 3,000 civilian and approximately 1,000 military employees. On any normal workday 10,000 people pass through the gates.

Desert Mining Towns
Coso Mines–Goler Canyon–The Millspaugh Colony–
Burro Schmidt–"23" Skidoo–Ballarat–Darwin–Panamint–
Owens Valley–Cerro Gordo

THE COSO MINES

The word Coso was an Indian word used for the hot springs and also for the Coso Mountains, which are now both inside the Naval Ordnance Test Station, China Lake. This area was used by the Shoshone and Pauite tribes, who considered the springs valuable for medicinal purposes. It was also of great importance because of its numerous obsidian outcroppings that furnished these Native Americans with material for arrow points and for its value as trading material when local tribes went over to the coast near Santa Barbara and Ventura.

Dr. Darwin French found the first rich ore ledges that were discovered at Coso in March of 1860. He and his party were searching for the lost Gunsite Mine. After failing to find the Lost Gunsite, on their way back through the Coso area they discovered ore rich in both gold and silver. They gathered samples and went back to the coast and formed both the Coso Mining Company and the Coso Gold and Silver Mining Company. In addition both of these companies were backed by an impressive amount of capital. The State Range Mining District was formed immediately and the Rough and Ready Mining Company was formed the following year.

Visalia was the closest town at this time, and a plan was submitted to the California Legislature in 1862 to build first a trail, then a wagon road over the Sierra. There were 28 applicants for the franchise, but nothing came of it. The Hocket Trail, (earlier known as the Coso Trail) and Jordan Trail were started from Visalia going toward the mines. The Jordan Trail was never finished.

Operators of the early mills for these companies did not manage their operations very well and the public lost confidence in both the State Range and Coso operations. Indian trouble added to their problems and the mines had to close during periods when the danger was extreme. During the time the operators were absent the Indians carried off or destroyed as much as possible. They burned the Searles Mill and also the Josephine Mill. The Josephine Mine was finally sold at a sheriff's sale for $30,667 and the great Coso boom ended.

Mines were worked later by Mexican miners during 1868 and the Coso Mines came to be known as the Spanish Mines. In the 1870s the Josephine Mine was filed on again and named the San Jose. A famous criminal lawyer, Pat Reddy, had an interest at Coso for awhile but nothing on a large scale ever happened.

In 1945 the U.S. Naval Ordnance Test Station, China Lake, withdrew both the Coso Mines and the hot springs near Coso from public entry as a restricted area. While the government made property settlements for those who had legitimate claims, many thought they didn't get enough. People who had used the hot springs for years were shocked at the withdrawal, especially a few aged Native Americans who were forbidden to enter the healing waters they had used to ease their aching bodies. At the time of

Left: 1914 Coso Hot Springs Stage. Henry Romaine driving his three-burro team, returning from Coso Hot Springs along the Midland trail. The Southern Pacific Railroad tracks are visible in the middle of the picture, and the east portion of the black lava cliffs are in the background. *Tom Chapman. Courtesy High Desert Historical Society.*

Below: 1920 Model T Ford. Henry Romaine's latest stage. Rommie, a lover of animals, always carried his dogs wherever he went. *Tom Chapman. Courtesy High Desert Historical Society.*

the withdrawal Coso was almost a ghost town with just a few rock cabins occupied.

The Coso Range contains an active geothermal system. True hot springs do not exist locally, yet fumaroles and boiling mud pots occur at Devil's Kitchen and Coso Hot Springs. Dry deposits of travertine and sinter indicate that hot springs were once present, perhaps during the Ice Ages.

The geothermal reservoir consists of a large volume of hot water contained within fractured basement rocks, heated by conductive radiation from a magma chamber that lies several miles below the surface. Temperatures as high as 640 degrees F. have been measured in geothermal

wells, while temperatures within the magma chamber are estimated to exceed 1,400 degrees F.

CalEnergy Company has developed the geothermal reservoir at Coso by drilling more than 140 wells to supply nine geothermal power plants. These plants produce a total of 250 megawatts of electricity, enough to supply the electrical needs of approximately 250,000 Californians. Actual resource ownership is divided between the U.S. Navy and the Bureau of Land Management, who are reimbursed by discounted electrical sales and/or royalties.

Steam and hot water flow from Coso's geothermal wells through pipelines and separators, which direct steam to turbines that spin electrical generators. Exiting steam is condensed and non-condensable gases are extracted. Hydrogen sulfide gas is processed into elemental sulfur and sold for agricultural use. Condensed steam and water from the separators are fed back into the margins of the reservoir thorough re-injection wells. Several large geothermal systems in California have been developed and are currently making a significant contribution to the state's overall electrical supply.

GOLER CANYON

In 1867, a German prospector named Goler on his way from Death Valley to Los Angeles, stopped at a spring in the El Paso country to have a drink of water and rest for awhile. While taking a drink from the spring he looked into the water and saw gold nuggets lying there. Because he was worried about the Indians he didn't stay long enough to investigate the area completely. He gathered up a few samples and continued on to Los Angeles. Goler tried to take a short cut and lost his way. When he realized he was lost he climbed to the top of a small hill and drew a map of the site to mark the location. To mark the location where he made the map he took his rifle and stuck the barrel in the ground and left it there so he might find it when he returned.

When Goler reached Los Angeles, he found many miners who had tried mining on the Kern River in the 1850s and '60s and left very discouraged. He could not find anyone who took him seriously. Then he met Grant Cuddeback, a former prospector turned rancher. Cuddeback helped Goler organize an outfit to go back and find the gold. With a group of men and Goler as their guide they crossed the mountains at Lake Elizabeth and went into Antelope Valley. There they stopped at Willow Springs where they prospected for awhile. Because they found no gold some of the party were quite put out and thought Goler had taken them on a "wild goose chase" and some even wanted to hang him.

Cuddeback took that group of prospectors back to Los Angeles, but feeling he had quit too soon, he organized another party. They ended up on Roger's Dry Lake, which was about forty miles from where Goler had left his gun. After finding no gold and no gun they returned again to Los Angeles. Not yet willing to give up finding the site of the spring where Goler found the rich gold samples they organized still another expedition. This time they found gold in Red Rock Canyon where they mined for several years. Goler still convinced he could find his gun and the spring left the group. He wasn't heard from again. In March 1893, twenty-six years after Goler left his rifle; the Goler Mining District was formed. A spring, which was a mile and a half up the canyon, is considered to be the spring Goler drank from when he found the gold nuggets.

In the fall of 1893 a stage line was put into operation from the Goler diggings to connect to the stage line that came from Owens Lake to Mojave. This stage line connected with the Mojave line at Red Rock Stage Station. When some men would reach this point they would leave their teams and wagons to follow the "gold fever."

In a canyon adjacent to Goler Canyon a man named Ramsey Cox found a gold nugget that was worth $1,900. Many other nuggets were found worth $10 to $50 each, which started a stampede of miners into the area. Immediately this canyon and surrounding canyons were filled with prospectors. They lived in tents, under rocks, in dugouts, shacks, under their wagon boxes, in lean-tos or any place else they could find where the winter rains would not destroy their lodgings.

Goler Canyon was one of the biggest strikes in the desert up until this time and miners started coming in from other mining districts. A community raised up over night. Charlie Koehn had filed on a homestead he named Kane Springs in 1892. Besides having a ranch operation when the miners started coming in he set up a tent store, which supplied the miners with food, supplies, and equipment. There was also a bar set up on a plank on top of two empty whiskey barrels. Koehn established a post office with each item of mail being delivered for 25 cents. The first year the post office was in business Koehn took in $50 and was definitely not making any money on the deal. After the Rand gold discovery in 1896, his post office moved to Garlock.

By the spring of 1893, approximately $50,000 worth of gold had been taken out of Goler Canyon and the surrounding canyons by a thousand or more men. Families soon came to join some of the miners. Water had to be hauled in and the charges would depend on how far it had to be hauled. By the end of 1893 there were 600 men, 14 women, 6 saloons, and 2 stores. Between $125,000 and $200,000 worth of gold had been taken from Goler Canyon according to an unofficial census. The Goler area produced about one million dollars before the miners left for other strikes.

But the camp didn't hold up, in spite of the gold and excitement. On the whole, the placers (surface gold) were spotty and the going was tough for most of the miners and greenhorns. All of the camps in the region were dry-wash diggings, which was a method of mining without water. Such camps had to be very rich to produce a steady or paying amount of gold by this unsatisfactory method of recovery. One frequently reads of the big times the miners had, the romance of the camps and their drama, sudden fortune, boom and excitement. What you don't hear of often are the inconveniences, down-to- earth every day hard labor, the hardships of camping and prospecting, and the monotony of pick-and-shovel work. That was the true miner's life.

Fifty years after Goler left his gun as a landmark, it was found on a cattle ranch about twenty miles north of Mojave, owned by Mrs. Rhoda Munsey and her son Will. Even after being left out in the elements for so many years, the words and dates on the gun left no doubt in anyone's mind that this was the old Spencer Repeating Rifle right where Goler had left it so that he might find his fortune again.

THE MILLSPAUGH COLONY

If you drive east from Junction Valley through Shepherd Pass and come to Shepherd Canyon you will find where the village of Millspaugh was. It was half way between Darwin and Ballarat. All that is left of Millspaugh today is a boiler and retaining rock wall for the road above the boiler.

About 1897 George Davis located a gold vein in the lower end of Shepherd Canyon and in 1899 he sold this claim, the Yellow Metal, to Almon N. Millspaugh. A mill was built to work the ore and it was hauled up the canyon. Near the mouth of the canyon was a boarding house, barn and corral. This was a family run business. Almon made a trip east and persuaded his brother-in-law, Oliver J. Bailey, to work the mine with him. Jessie Fowzer was the timekeeper and

cook. She was also related, but I'm not sure how. Her grown daughter, Elizabeth Fowzer Mecham, took care of the stock.

By 1902 Millspaugh had a store, post office, blacksmith shop and assay office. The estimated population ranged 50 to 200 people. They did alright for a decade. Then in 1909 a flash flood hit the head of Shepherd Canyon and washed out the road. The canyon has not been passable for a vehicle since then.

At this time Frank Howard had the mail contract. He made one attempt on horseback to get down the canyon, but it was impassable. He refused to continue the contract, saying, "If Uncle Sam sends me to the Atlanta Pen, alright. All I'll have to do there is read magazines." They had no mail deliveries for awhile. Quite a few miners and prospectors were around and would walk in to Millspaugh for mail and to visit.

Millspaugh got in touch with the Post Office Department in Washington, D.C. to see if they could get their mail delivered to Brown to be sent on by the railroad. In 1910 Elizabeth Fowzer Mecham started carrying the mail on horseback to Brown and back. She stated,

As miles were counted then, it was forty miles from Millspaugh to Brown, each way. One way of counting miles was to tie a rag on the wheel and count each time it came around to the top, and then figure it out! I was up at 5:00 a.m. to feed the horses. At 6:00 a.m. I left on my first trip down to Brown with the mail sack on my saddle. A good horse averaged four miles an hour. I picked up mail from the few boxes along the way and stopped at the mouth of Mt. Spring Canyon to water my horse.

Now on across Indian Wells Valley, arriving at Brown and delivering the mail pouch to Gus Haelzig. I cared for my horse and spent the evening. Aqueduct boys would come down from 9-mile Canyon and we would play the phonograph and talk. They liked to know about the country and not hang around the one and only saloon owned by Smith.

I was up at 5:00 a.m. to feed and care for my horse, left with the mail at 8:00 a.m. homeward bound. I did this six days a week, down Mondays and back on Tuesdays, then Wednesday and Thursday, then Friday and Saturday. Sunday was usually spent riding and hunting horses, or visiting at the Junction of Inyo-Coso Camp, which was then working. So the days lengthened and grew hot, 110 degrees at Brown, but cool at camp, 6,157 feet above sea level. The six months I carried the mail generally took eight to ten hours a day. Every two weeks I took the buckboard and team down for supplies, hay and grain, or a few times I had a passenger. Otherwise all trips were made on horseback."

Most everyone had left Millspaugh by 1910 except Millspaugh, Mrs. Fowzer and her daughters and a few others. The mill and blacksmith shop were sold by 1914 and everybody was gone. The boarding house was bought by Summers and Butler of Bishop, sawed in two and moved to Junction Ranch where the cattle grazers lived. It remained there until 1948.

Burro Schmidt's tunnel.

BURRO SCHMIDT

William H. (Burro) Schmidt was born January 30, 1871 in Rhode Island. His three brothers and three sisters all died of tuberculosis between the ages of 11 and 29 years. When Schmidt became sick in 1890 the doctors advised him to go to the desert for his health. He came to California but stayed only a year and when his health was better he returned to Rhode Island. His health began to deteriorate again so he came back to California in 1892. For five years he worked for the Kern County Land Company.

At this time the Rand mining area was booming and gold fever soon replaced consumptive fever. Schmidt located a number of gold claims on and around Black Mountain in the El Paso Range, which is northwest of Garlock. Although his claims were reported to be very rich he was in an isolated area and that was a problem.

Schmidt was on the north side of the mountain and the mining center and shipping rails were on the south side. To get his ore to a mill would necessitate building miles of steep road in the sandy and rocky desert soil to a shipping point on a railroad line. He came up with a plan. By driving a tunnel for 2,000 feet through solid rock, he could make a short haul to the main road (now Highway 14).

In 1906 he started drilling his tunnel, building a little shack near the spot where he intended to come out with his ore. During the first 26 years he worked on his tunnel only during the wintertime. Each summer he went to the South Fork of the Kern River and worked on ranches to finance his tunnel building operation. The only company he had during those winter were his two burros, Jenny and Jack. Jenny lived with him for 25 years, Jack for 19 years. Each spring Schmidt would turn his burros loose near his tunnel and each fall when he returned they would be there waiting for him.

He dug the tunnel, every inch by hand, with a four-pound Single-Jack hammer and drill and used 40 per cent dynamite. He would drill holes two to

Burro Schmidt on his way to Mojave

three feet deep in the tunnel face, load them and cutting the fuses short to save money, he would light them, and rush out to open air. After the blast he would go back in and haul the crushed rock out to the dump, first with a wheelbarrow then later in an ore car. He laid track as he progressed and would push the loaded ore car out by hand.

All his supplies had to be packed in. Not wanting to pay $10 a gallon for kerosene, he used candles to light his work. He bought three candles for five cents and a candle would last him for a day of drilling and rock hauling.

During the winter he lived on flapjacks, beans and baking soda biscuits. Sometimes he made what he called fish chowder, which was made with onions, rice and sardines. Once a month

Schmidt would hook Jack and Jenny to his buggy and go into Randsburg to get supplies.

While on the South Fork during the summer he worked mostly for the Smith Ranch where he irrigated the crops and helped put up hay to feed the Smith's cattle in the winter. The food they furnished for their hired hands put several pounds on Schmidt's lean frame. Because of his family's proneness to tuberculosis Burro never married, as he was afraid it might be passed on to his offspring.

With the tunnel half-excavated in 1910, the Southern Pacific rail line was completed through Indian Wells Valley, and the establishment of a good road to the Dutch Cleanser Mine made his tunnel useless. By now, however, it had become Burro's obsession. In 1938 he broke out into the

DESERT COUNTRY

sunlight on the southern side of the mountain, his slow journey at an end.

Burro's tunnel measures 2,087 feet from entrance to exit, and with side tunnels the total excavation is nearly a half-mile. Averaging seven feet high and five feet wide, the volume of rock removed by this man is estimated at 5,800 tons. The mountain itself was of such solid composition that no shoring was required, except for beams at each entrance.

Some thought it was only an obsession that drove Burro to complete the tunnel. Local legend has it that Burro Schmidt only stayed to protect a fabulous gold find, known as the "Crystal Room." When the tunnel was completed he dynamited this room shut to keep the wealth for himself, forever. No one has yet found the Crystal Room or knows if it is even true.

During the last four years of his life Burro had a partner, Mike E. Lee. Lee inherited the mining claims at Burro's death on January 27, 1954, just three days before his 83 birthday. Burro was cremated and his ashes buried alongside other hard rock miners in Johannesburg.

Mrs. Tonie Evelyn Ann Seger bought what was known as Mike E. Lee's Copper Basin Camp in 1966 (Burro Schmidt's original camp). In the year 2002, ninety-six years after Burro started his tunnel, it is still open to the public. You can locate it by driving south 7.4 miles south on Highway 14 from the junction of Highway 178 and Highway 14. On the east side of the highway you will find a sign which states, "Burro Schmidt's Tunnel." Traveling east on a dirt road some eight miles you will find his tunnel. Even without the gold, Burro Schmidt made himself a monument that might outlast the great pyramids of Cheops.

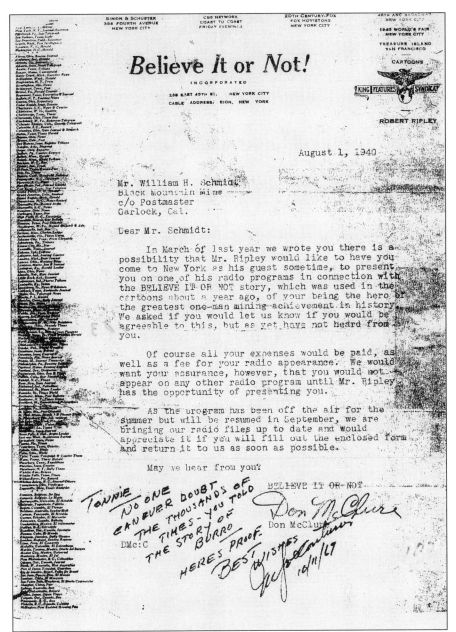

A letter to Burro Schmidt from Ripley's radio show.

Facing page, left top: Burro Schmidt's funeral in front of his tunnel

Facing page, right top: "Toni" Seger, 1964

Facing page, left bottom: "Toni" Seger, March 29, 1964

Facing page, right bottom: "Toni" Seger in her later years

Right: Burro Schmidt and Mike Lee

"23" SKIDOO

On a foggy night in 1906, Harry Ramsey and "One Eye" Thompson became lost on a trip from Furnace Creek to a new strike at Harrisburg. They bedded down for the night. In the morning they found promising ore bearing rocks within reach of their blankets.

This spot was high on the northern rim of the Panamints overlooking Stovepipe Wells. The elevation was over 5,600 feet. One of the main drawbacks of the new mining camp was the lack of a sufficient water supply. The miners addressed this problem by running a pipeline twenty-three miles from Telescope Peak. A major undertaking, but anything is possible when digging for gold!

Skidoo meant scram or vamoose and the twenty-three was said to refer to the twenty-three mile pipeline. This combination gave way to the slang expression of "Twenty-three Skidoo." By 1911 Skidoo was in its prime. The camp boasted a post office, a bank, a phone line that stretched across Death Valley to Rhyolite, a weekly newspaper known as the Skidoo News, general store, lumber yard, blacksmith shop, several saloons and a mill.

The most famous incident that happened in Skidoo was the hanging of a drunken saloon-keeper, Joe "Hooch" Simpson. It occurred in April 1908. L. Burr Belden of the Death Valley 49ers in his book, Mines of Death Valley, interviewed two men 50 years after the incident they had witnessed. The two men were George Cook of Lone Pine and Bill Keys of Joshua Tree. Their interviews were carried by loudspeakers to hundreds of campfire visitors. They hadn't seen each other for 50 years and their accounts of the events agreed totally. In the Inyo County Library of Independence, Belden also found a copy of the Skidoo news that reported the hanging and from these sources put together the following chain of events:

Simpson and a partner ran a tent saloon near the big store and bank. One morning business may have been a bit dull so Simpson took to drinking his wares. It was not uncommon, one surmises, for he was universally known as 'Hooch.' It was Sunday morning and Joe was not only drunk, he was drunk and armed. Jim Arnold was the town banker, at the Southern California Bank. Simpson weaved into the bank,

Joe Simpson who was hanged twice to oblige visiting journalists. Skidoo justice and hospitality at its best.

pointed his gun and demanded $20. Bystanders overpowered him and took his gun. Joe became abusive and Arnold threw him out.

Three hours later Joe recovered his gun from the stove where his partner had hidden it and went back to the bank. Confronting Arnold again he asked, "Have you got anything against me, Jim?" Arnold answered, "No, Joe, I have nothing against you." "Yes you have," Joe retorted, "prepare to die." With that he shot Arnold near the heart. Then he turned his gun on Joe Macdonald, also of the bank, and would have shot him had not his attention been diverted by a reeling drunk, Gordon McBain, who though unarmed attempted to arrest Joe. McBain accidentally got between Joe and a rifle aiming physician only 100 feet distant. Bystanders soon disarmed and handcuffed Joe. Arnold died that evening.

Simpson showed no remorse. In fact, he became boastful over his marksmanship. The poker parlor, Club Skidoo, was converted into a temporary guardhouse. The sheriff was not expected until Thursday; the miners determined that Simpson should pay with his life then and there. On Wednesday night the guard watching Simpson was overpowered by Skidoo vigilantes. The prisoner was taken outside and hanged to a telephone pole. The next day, Thursday, Judge Thisse conducted an inquest.

The Skidoo News remarked on how quietly the lynching had been conducted. A joker had told the drunken McBain that he was to be a second victim, McBain promptly left camp. The News editor remarked that McBain's running from imaginary pursuers made more noise than the hanging.

On Friday, 24 hours after Simpson had been interred on boot hill, a Los Angeles Herald reporter arrived. He came all the way from Lone Pine in a livery rig to get the story about the hanging. Skidoo folk were right proud of such notice and promptly set out to show their appreciation. They disinterred Simpson's corpse and hanged it a second time just so the reporter could take a picture. The second hanging was decorously staged with a tent frame, a far less public spot than the telephone pole. The coroner's inquest found Simpson died of strangulation at the hands of persons unknown.

In 1908, when the hanging took place, Bill Keys was mining in Skidoo and George Cook was hauling supplies back and forth to Rhyolite. At the Death Valley campfire November 10, 1960, Cook and Keys met each other for the first time in nearly 50 years. Around the fire Cook admitted he was one of the two men who went inside the guardhouse and hauled Simpson outside, turning him over to the vigilantes. Keys recalled that there was a crowd of 60 men surrounding the tent of Constable Sellers when Simpson had been moved.

The 23-mile pipeline in Skidoo was salvaged for metal in World War I. The mines were actively worked until 1917, spasmodically worked in the 1930s, and are now deserted and caved in. In 1966 there were a few old buildings and several old timers picking over the veins for high grade. About all that was left in 2001 were a few of the well-worn roads and trails to the mining scars of the days of old and the dreams of gold that went "Twenty-three Skidoo."

BALLARAT

The town of Ballarat, located in the Indian Wells Valley approximately 30 miles northeast from what is now the town of Trona, was organized in 1897 and was named after a gold mining center in Australia. It soon developed into a town of four to five hundred people. There were eight to ten saloons. The Calloway Hotel was there as well as a Wells Fargo Stage station, owned by Renaldi and Clark. In 1897 a post office was established and for a time it was the seat of government for southern Inyo County and even had its own justice of the peace. The

Inyo County Supervisors appointed Richard Deeker as justice of the peace and the first postmaster was John S. Statler, who was also a storekeeper. In 1899 a jail and a one-room schoolhouse were built. When Ballarat was booming there were three stores, two feed yards, a blacksmith shop, and an assayer. The buildings were a combination of wood, adobe and tents.

The first and only teacher in Ballarat was Mary Bigelow, who brought her three children from Bishop. The one-room school was only open during the school year of 1899-1900 and only had nine pupils. Mrs. Bigelow was paid $500 for the whole school year.

In 1898 when James Calloway built his hotel, the lumber had to be freighted from Johannesburg. The ground floor, which was made of adobe, housed the saloon, lobby, dining room, kitchen and living room, while the upper floor was made of lumber and contained twelve rooms. These rooms had an outdoor staircase. A veranda ran the length and breadth of the second floor of the building. "Ma" Calloway ran the hotel and boarding house while James Calloway ran a freighting business. At the Calloway Hotel burlap was hung from the eves and water dripped on it from pipes. As the breeze blew through the burlap it provided the hotel with its own air conditioner. Cooling was necessary, as the temperature at times stayed as high as 112 degrees even at 2:00 a.m. during the summer. In winter the wind brought the cold air from the snow capped peaks down through the town making the weather almost unbearable.

When mines developed in the Panamint Mountains, Ballarat was the supply center for both sides of the Indian Wells Valley. It was a convenient place to live for some of the 200 men working at the Ratcliff Mine, especially men that had families. There was a boarding house at the mine for single men who came into town mostly on weekends.

Sylvester Tappan, Mrs. Calloway's father, ran a feed yard in Ballarat under the trees of Post Office Spring. Post Office Spring was a quarter of a mile south of Ballarat where prospectors, and bad men from Pleasant Canyon, could leave letters in a box in the fork of a tree. These letters were picked up by the stage, and supplies brought back on the return trip. Post Office Spring and the tree were out in the open, safe from ambush. As the story goes, no one ever picked up supplies which belonged to someone else. The boarding house at the Ratcliff Mine had a standing order of two beef a week. There was no refrigeration so sheep and beef were slaughtered as they were ordered.

Dr. MacDonald, later of Randsburg, was in Ballarat in 1900. The doctor that followed him was Dr. A. A. Sanford and he stayed until 1903 leaving when the mines began to close down.

Buildings made of adobe will last forever if taken care of, but it they don't get a fresh coat of plaster from time to time the rain and wind gradually destroy them. No upkeep, wind and rain did just that to this old town. It doesn't rain often in Ballarat but sometimes a year's rainfall comes in a few hours. Today little is left of Ballarat, but ghosts and old roads.

It's hard to imagine what a busy, thriving community Ballarat once was, a gathering place for miners, prospectors and bad men from all over the Panamints, Death Valley, the Slate Range and the Argus Range to the west.

The regular resident population may not have been over three or four hundred people. But on a monthly payday at the mines there might be a thousand to 1,500 people in town for several days for recreation and supplies.

All the freight wagons hauling machinery and supplies from Barstow to the mining camps stopped at Ballarat, a place for rest and refreshments. Conversely, all the ore wagons and miners going out stopped at Ballarat.

Seldom Seen Slim

The last resident of Ballarat was Seldom Seen Slim. In an article by Sewell "Pop" Lofinck in his book, *Mojave Desert Ramblings*, published in 1966 by the Maturango Museum, he wrote: "Went over to Ballarat the other day and had quite an interesting chat with 'Seldom Seen Slim' Ferge. Hadn't been out there for almost a year, I guess. And you know Slim; he doesn't travel down here much, if at all.

"He is quite a character, a real desert rat. The last remaining resident of Ballarat. Some say he came there in 1905, some say 1910, some say 1917, and 'Slim' just isn't saying. Anyhow, Ballarat has been his residence or rather headquarters all these years when he wasn't out prospecting or mining or doing assaying work. I asked him, 'Slim, do you ever get lonesome living out here alone?' 'No,' he said, 'I talk to myself.' Some confirmed desert rats get that way."

He enjoys the wonderful desert solitude and he has his dreams of the past. Slim declined to say when he was born or where. He says he can't quite remember. He cuts his beard with scissors. He said, 'If I shaved, people might think I was a phony desert rat and hadn't spent my life prospecting in this desert.' He seems to be happy dreaming of the old days. I asked him if he would be over to the dedication of a historical marker (only three and one-half miles up to the main highway) on Monday, November 11th. He said, 'No, they can come down to see me'. He may sell you some rocks. 'Seldom Seen Slim' is photogenic, he doesn't mind having his picture taken, and in fact I think he enjoys it. You may have a chance to get your picture taken with a genuine desert rat."

DARWIN

An odd quirk of history is that so little has been printed about the Darwin area in comparison to the volumes that have been in print about Sierra Gordo and Panamint City. In spite of the fact that the Darwin District has produced vastly greater ore values and over a longer period than the above mentioned mining camps. Maybe one reason is that when Darwin burned down the records and pictures may have been destroyed in the fire.

Doctor Erasmus Darwin French was long gone by the time the town of Darwin was started and named. He made significant discoveries in the area. The town, Darwin Canyon and Darwin Falls, both northeast of the town, were named for him. Doctor Darwin had been in the area since the 1850s and was the man who named Furnace Creek in Death Valley.

In October 1870, William Egan, J.C. Watt and Paul W. Bennett discovered deposits of pure galena (lead & silver) near a spring close to what is now the town of Darwin. The same month they met James Brady near this discovery (Brady was the man who put the steamer Bessie Brady on Owens Lake) and they organized the Granite Mountain Mining Company. By 1874 there was a rush to the area and the town of Darwin was founded.

In November of 1874 brothers, Lafe (Lafayette) and William Gill, moved a building to the new mines to be used as a hotel and saloon. The town of Darwin had its start. The biggest mine in the area was the Promontorio. Raphael Cuero, a Mexican, had first located this rich silver ledge. However, two prospectors, the Brown brothers were given the credit.

On May 12, 1875, a post office was established at Darwin with Abner B. Elder as postmaster. Later that month a Wells Fargo office was opened. By 1875 Darwin had a newspaper called the *Coso Mining News*.

There were three big fires in Darwin over the years. The first fire in 1879 destroyed 15 buildings and the last fire was in 1918. By May of 1876 the *Inyo Independent Newspaper* stated that Darwin had become Inyo County's "most important mining district and largest town."

In 1879 the Caliente-Darwin stage was robbed seven miles north of Indian Wells of almost $400 in gold. The robber was named Jack Spratt who lived in Grapevine Canyon. He was recognized in this robbery and other robberies by his red beard that stuck out from behind the bandana covering his face. He was recognized but never arrested or jailed.

In 1877 Darwin reached its highest population of 3,500 people, but as fast as it became popular it rushed into decline. It seemed that Bodie was the place to be and even the *Coso Mining News* shut down. T. S. Harris loaded up his printing press and moved to Bodie as mining slowly died.

Darwin was a wild town in its earlier days and out of 124 deaths only two were listed as having died of natural causes. The rest were either shot or stabbed. It boasted 33 saloons.

Oliver Roberts, the same Roberts that gave the account of the robbery in 1874 at Coyote Holes (Freeman Station), came to Darwin in 1875 and recorded most of Darwin's history. Roberts was Deputy Constable of Darwin from 1878 to 1879, learning its history first hand.

A 1952 U.S. Geological Survey paper recorded that the total worth of minerals taken out of Darwin from 1875 to 1952 was about $37.5 million. Darwin never has become a ghost town. The climate is good, the elevation is about 4,500 feet and the only drawback is the water supply. In 2001 the residents had to purchase water from the China Lake Naval Ordnance Test Station which is two miles to the north. There are still about 50 residents.

Ruth Yarcho was the postmistress of Darwin from 1968 to 1988. She started working two hours per day, six days a week and worked up to four hours per day. She said that in those days you had to furnish your own building. She rented a building and eventually bought the one-room schoolhouse when the children started going to school in Lone Pine. Carrying on the family tradition Ruth's daughter, Carol Peterson, is the present postmistress and works four hours per day, six days per week.

PANAMINT

The mining town of Panamint, located approximately ten miles northeast of Ballarat, rose and fell in just three years. Its population never exceeded 2,000. In January 1873 three prospectors poking through the canyons struck silver in the Panamint Range. Rock samples showed astounding values ranging from $300 to $3,000 per ton. Before they could transform the ore into cash, three major problems had to be solved—lack of capital, transportation and remote location. Over a year was spent trying to arrange for the transportation and capital rather than digging for silver. In the spring of 1874 they found both. The Los Angeles Chamber of Commerce raised money and built a wagon road to Panamint Valley. Two Nevada Senators, John P. Jones and William M. Stewart provided the capital.

Stone shanties, log cabins built of pinon pines and even frame buildings made from lumber hauled in by mule team at $250 per thousand feet made up the rude town. Fifty structures lined the mile-long street. Six general stores and at least twelve saloons lined the main street. The Oriental had elegant furnishings and was advertised as "the finest saloon on the Coast outside of San Francisco." The town also boasted a bank, brewery, meat market (whose wagon also served as the town hearse), and newspaper. Cabins, tents and caves where the miners lived, dotted the sides of the canyon. When a blast was set off in the mines, showers of rock would rain down on the main street.

Law and order was unheard of in Panamint. Among the citizens was Ned Reddy, proprietor of the Independent Saloon, who had already killed two men in Owens Valley. Dave Neagel, owner of the Oriental Saloon arrived after a shooting scrape in Nevada. But the quickest gunman was Jim Bruce, a professional gambler, who killed two men right there in Panamint. One of them burst in on him in the boudoir of one of the camp's madams and was promptly filled with lead. Another prospector had a shooting argument with Bruce in front of the Bank of Panamint and came out second best.

Two stage robbers, John Small and John McDonald, sold Senator Stewart one of the biggest Panamint mines. On June 29, 1875, the twenty-stamp mill was fired up and began grinding the ore for the first silver bullion. Small and McDonald were on hand, armed with six-shooters and sheepish grins. But the crafty Stewart was ready for them. Out of his smelter rolled silver ingots weighing four to five hundred pounds each. The bandits abruptly lost their smiles.

"Do you think it's right to play that game on us?" one of them demanded. "And after we sold you the mine, too. Why, we can't haul away one of those boulders!" It was Stewart's turn to grin.

For months Small and McDonald had to suffer the torture of watching these silver bricks leaving Panamint regularly by mule teams. Before the cargo could reach Los Angeles and the steamboats, which would carry it to the San Francisco mint it had to travel 200 miles of lonely desert under no protection but its tremendous weight and an unarmed driver. The insult was so deflating that on April 20, 1876, Small and McDonald robbed a general store of $2,300 and left Panamint for good.

The most promising Panamint mines started running out of ore in the spring of 1876. The mill was shut down and miners headed out for more promising prospects. Merchants, stock promoters, saloon owners, and even the *Panamint News* editor with his hand press and type cases, started trudging down the canyon. Town lots that had sold as high as $1,000 could not be given away. By May 1877, the last mines were closed and Panamint was a dead camp. Today jackrabbit and ground squirrels take the place of the blasts from the mines, shouts from the saloon, and the creak of wagons down main street.

OWENS VALLEY

The Owens Valley—where did the name originate? In 1844-45 Frémont brought his expedition though this area and named the valley and lake after a member of his party, Richard Owens. For a time this area held no interest to the white man aside from the grandeur of the Sierra. Then in 1859 the rich "Comstock" silver discovery at Virginia City, Nevada, created a different attitude towards this desert area and prospectors started coming in.

At first the Native Americans who made the Owens Valley their home accepted the miners with a sullen indifference, but as the "white man" continued to come in greater numbers, they started taking over tribal lands and interrupting the Indian way of life. By 1861 open hostilities had begun. In 1862 Col. George Evans and 201 men from Companies I, D, and G, Second Calvary California Volunteers arrived in the Owens Valley to restore order. By June of 1862 Camp Independence had been established on Oak Creek and by the summer of the following year the worst of the fighting was over.

CERRO GORDO

Although the exact date is uncertain, sometime in 1865 Mexican miners started prospecting in the mountains east of Owens Lake. Rich silver and lead deposits were found at about the 8,500-foot level on Buena Vista Peak. The area was given the name Cerro Gordo, meaning "fat with silver." The names for these early discoveries were; Buena Vista Peak, San Lucas, San Ygnaces, San Francisco and San Felipe. These rich ore deposits soon caught the eye of Caucasian miners and in 1866 the Lone Pine Mining District was formed.

The first real effort to develop any of the

claims was in 1866 by José Ochoa. He extracted about one and one-half tons of ore every twelve hours and transported it in sacks by pack animals from the San Lucas Mine to the Silver Spout Mill, a few miles west of Fort Independence.

These shipments of ore yielded about $30.00 per ton and soon attracted the attention of Victor Beaudry, a successful merchant in Fort Independence. Victor was a French Canadian who had been a merchant in San Francisco. He had also been at Sutter's Fort with the First U.S. Infantry during the Civil War. Through old friendships with officers stationed at Fort Independence he came to the Owens Valley in 1865 to open a store. Beaudry was impressed by the quality of ore from the San Lucas so he opened a store at Cerro Gordo. In 1868 he got judgments against mine owners J. Almada and José Ochoa for overdue accounts at his store. He settled the accounts for an interest in both the San Lucas and Union mines, which were located close to the Cerro Gordo camp.

Beaudry then formed a partnership with Mortimer Belshaw and it was through this partnership that Cerro Gordo was transformed from an obscure mining camp to a roaring silver city.

Belshaw left his family in San Francisco and came to Cerro Gordo with a friend, A. B. Elder. Belshaw had spent two years in the silver mines of Sinaloa, Mexico, so he understood the silver mining trade. He knew how essential lead was in smelting silver ore and all three men agreed that whoever built a smelter would control the mines. They processed several tons of ore with the crude Mexican style furnace and took their first load of silver lead ingots into Los Angeles in June 1868. From there the precious cargo was shipped to San Francisco where Belshaw had financial connections.

One of these connections was Egbert Judson, president of the California Paper Company. Judson was active in mining activities throughout the Mother Lode country. He had the reputation of being a generous but shrewd operator. He was impressed with Belshaw's background, and the load of silver bullion brought to San Francisco could not be ignored.

It was agreed that Judson would provide the capital, Belshaw would control the operation with Elder acting as superintendent of the smelting works (I don't know what Beaudry's job was), The foursome formed the Union Mining Company, with Elder holding the smallest share.

The first obstacle to overcome was the rugged mountain terrain between Cerro Gordo's lofty perch in the Inyo Mountains and the floor of Owens Valley. At this point everything had to be brought in and out on pack animals. Before the machinery for the smelter could be brought in, a road had to be constructed up the treacherous slopes. Belshaw supervised the road project and by July 1868 the road was completed. Because most of the road was cut through a yellowish rock formation the road was called the Yellow Grade. Belshaw put a gate in the narrow canyon and charged a toll for everything and everyone arriving or departing from Cerro Gordo.

By December 1868 regular shipments of silver bullion were being shipped to Los Angeles. Each ingot was 18 inches long and weighed approximately 85 pounds. For the first time the Cerro Gordo was being hailed as another "Comstock." In the area around Cerro Gordo the sparse Piñon and Juniper forest east of Owens Lake were being consumed rapidly as the wood was being used to make charcoal for the blast furnaces. These furnaces at the smelters were using 350 bushels of charcoal per day. Today in most of this area the trees are gone because they were cut to make charcoal.

Recognizing the impending wood shortage, Colonel Sherman Stevens started a lumber mill that would furnish wood for the charcoal kilns of the Owens Valley. Stevens started the Inyo Lumber and Coal Company. His lumber camp was on Cottonwood Creek. Oxen were used to haul the felled trees to the mill. From the mill there was a drop of 5,680 feet down Cottonwood Creek to the valley floor. A flume twelve miles long was built in 15 feet sections and as it was being built each section was floated down the flume to be added on. Colonel Stevens' flume emerged from Cottonwood Canyon into Lone Pine by November 1873. From there, wagons hauled the lumber and cordwood the remaining three miles to the Owens Lake shore where two new charcoal kilns were located. These charcoal kilns have been preserved and can be seen east of Highway 395 south of Lone Pine.

Early in 1872 James Brady and D. H. Ferguson began building a steamboat that would transport Cerro Gordo's bullion to the southern end of Owens Lake. This saved three to five days travel

Left: Adobe charcoal kilns built in 1876–77 by Col. Stevens are the only remaining evidence of the Inyo Lumber & Coal Co. Already badly eroded in the 1920's, they also would have vanished if not for the effort of the Eastern California Museum, Henry Raub, Director. The kilns were sprayed with a preservative coating to prevent further erosion of the adobe walls.

Below: Down-canyon view of Cerro Gordo taken between 1871–1879. V. Beaudry's smelter is shown on right.

time and some forty to fifty miles of exceedingly bad road around the upper end of the lake. They called their boat the *Bessie Brady*, named after Brady's young daughter. This boat had an 85-foot keel and was 16 feet at the beam, with a keel depth of six feet. A twenty horsepower engine powered this shallow draft steamboat. The propeller was 52 inches in diameter and moved the craft seven to nine miles per hour. It was reported that the building cost was $10,000. The ship could haul 700 bars, or thirty tons, of silver bullion.

With a steady supply of charcoal now being transported to Cerro Gordo from the eastside of Owens Lake it brought to an end the charcoal burners in the Inyo Mountains. These charcoal kilns probably could not have survived much longer anyway because by 1874 the hills had almost been stripped of their Piñon and Juniper trees.

In 1869 Remi Nadeau was given a three-year freighting contract to haul Cerro Gordo's bullion to Los Angeles. In Los Angeles local farmers and businessmen found an ever-increasing market in Owens Valley for their surplus goods. By 1871 two stages a day were running from the town of Cerro Gordo to Owens Valley. By now Cerro Gordo was a well-established mining town. The

Remi Nadeau arrived in Los Angeles in 1861 and operated an extensive freighting business from 1868 to 1882.

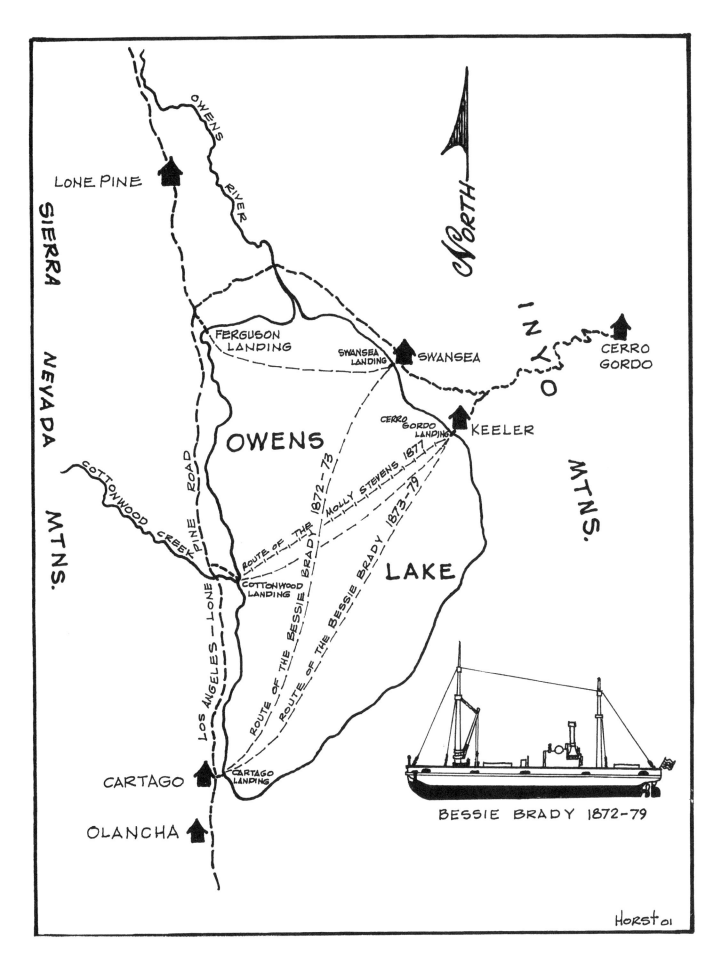

SIERRA NEVADA MTNS.

COTTONWOOD MTNS.

LONE PINE

OWENS RIVER

FERGUSON LANDING

SWANSEA LANDING

SWANSEA

North

INYO

CERRO GORDO

OWENS

CERRO GORDO LANDING

KEELER

MTNS.

COTTONWOOD CREEK

LONE PINE ROAD

ROUTE OF THE BESSIE BRADY 1872-73

MOLLY STEVENS 1877

ROUTE OF THE BESSIE BRADY 1873-79

COTTONWOOD LANDING

LOS ANGELES — LONE

LAKE

ROUTE OF THE BESSIE BRADY

CARTAGO

CARTAGO LANDING

OLANCHA

BESSIE BRADY 1872-79

Horst 01

DESERT MINING TOWNS   139

main street was lined with buildings as fast as lumber could be obtained. That year the two story American Hotel was completed. High false-fronted general stores, restaurants and saloons soon replaced the canvas shacks scattered throughout town. All of this was high in the mountains east of Owens Lake.

Cerro Gordo was classified as a "wide open town" with only a semblance of law and order. It was said that although law was available it was not respected by most of the town's inhabitants and the lawless element found Cerro Gordo's remote location a safe refuge.

County Judge John A. Hannah noted that crime seemed to be running rampant in several sections of Inyo County, especially there in Cerro Gordo. The editor of the *Inyo Independent* referred to Cerro Gordo as, "a prolific source of the man-for-breakfast order of items." The slightest dispute was apt to bring down the hammer on forty grains of black powder, pushing a bullet clean through a man.

Another drawback to the development of the Cerro Gordo mines was the scarcity of water in the higher elevations of the desert mountain range. At first burro pack trains were used to bring water into the region. The cost of getting water this way was staggering and this method could not keep up with the growing demand. Belshaw overcame this handicap in 1870 by installing a pipeline from Cerro Gordo Spring and several other springs north of camp. The water was pumped to storage tanks on the crest of the mountain and from there gravity flow carried it three miles into Cerro Gordo. Supplied with 1,300 gallons of water per day the water problem was suddenly dissolved. For three years Belshaw's water line met all the demands. However the frequent leaks, frozen sections of pipe during the winter and the spring's tendency to run less or even dry up during the long hot summer, cut down the water supply. Because of these disruptions, burro trains were packing 6,000 gallons a day from distance sources, again supplementing the water needs.

A Cerro Gordo mine owner, Stephen Boushey, with the financial support of a leading bank in Los Angeles, organized the Cerro Gordo Water and Mining Company. With a capital stock of $200,000, the enterprising Boushey planned to tap Miller Springs, ten miles north of Cerro Gordo and 1,860 feel below the crest of the

mountains on the Saline Valley side. The new system lifted the water over the backbone of the Inyo Mountains through three Hooker steam pumps placed 1,500 feet apart, each pumping station overcoming a vertical lift of 620 feet. The water system was completed in May 1874, at a reported cost of $74,000, and was capable of pumping 90,000 gallons of water per day. The citizens of Cerro Gordo were charged three cents per gallon, less than half of what it had cost them previously.

Delighted with the abundance of water, sanitary conditions began to improve. It was no longer considered sinful to scrub down floors or wash windows. Suddenly there was a large demand for wash tubs and soap. Clothing could be laundered more than once a week, and it no longer cost half a day's wages to bathe. Above all, the smelters could now consume as much water as necessary to maintain full production with no shortages.

If the inhabitants of Cerro Gordo were delighted with the abundance of water, the owners of the water works must have been overjoyed with the rate at which Cerro Gordo consumed it. The town's average daily consumption of 35,000 gallons was providing the company with an income of over one thousand dollars a day. At this rate, the Water Company would secure their investment within 90 days.

With abundant fuel and water for Belshaw and Beaudry's furnaces, wagons were transporting five thousand dollars worth of bullion down the Yellow Grade road every day. It is estimated the Cerro Gordo produced, and Remi Nadeau delivered, 5,290 tons of silver bullion worth $2,000,000 to Los Angeles in 1874 alone.

Los Angeles continued to benefit from Cerro Gordo's commerce and by 1874 the monthly freighting business had reached 700 tons. The Cerro Gordo Freighting Company's annual freight bill was more than $700,000, of which nearly half was spent over the counters in Los Angeles at a rate of almost $1,000 per day over the years. The teams of freighters alone consumed 2,500 tons of barley and 3,000 tons of hay while transporting an estimated 3,400 tons of supplies to Cerro Gordo, and 5,290 tons of bullion to Los Angeles. The total tonnage freighted to and from Cerro Gordo in 1874 was almost half as large as all the freight exported through San Pedro harbor in Los Angeles that same year. This

View of Cerro Gordo during the camp's revival between 1911 and 1919

becomes even more significant considering almost one-third of San Pedro's exports was Cerro Gordo bullion.

In comparison, 1875 must have been a depressing year for Cerro Gordo. The silver camps at Coso and Darwin, south of Owens Valley, were creating a scarcity of labor as miners left for the new diggings. By April, Beaudry was forced to temporarily close his furnace because of the water shortage. The Cerro Gordo Water Works was so efficient it pumped Miller Springs dry in August after being in service only fifteen months. Once again water had to be packed in by burros or transported by wagons until Belshaw's old water line could be reactivated.

To make matters worse, two bandits held up Belshaw's tollhouse, and adding insult to injury, two weeks later they robbed the "up stage" just a few miles below town. With everyone in Belshaw's employment armed and looking for blood, the outlaws decided it would be more to their advantage it they left the territory. And they did!

Although there were 700 claims around Cerro Gordo it soon became evident that three of these would be of the greatest importance. The three claims were Santa Maria, San Felipo, and the Union. Activities at Cerro Gordo started to decline in 1877. On top of that the Union Mine Works caught fire and burned to the ground along with the timbering in the shaft down to the 200-foot level. When the smoke cleared it was estimated that $40,000 in damage had been done.

The last stagecoach came down the Yellow Grade Road in April of 1878, and within a year, Cerro Gordo was almost a ghost town. Only Beaudry and a few selected men remained to protect the Union Mine's interest. Finally, in October 1879, the Union mine was abandoned. The next month Beaudry reluctantly shut down his furnace for the last time. Shortly after this one lone wagon descended the Yellow Grade Road. Its cargo contained several bars of lead, and one 420-pound ingot of pure silver. After transporting the wagon across the lake, the steamer *Bessie Brady* was beached at Ferguson's Landing, at Olancha and her machinery removed.

The ten years following Belshaw and Beaudry's departure from Cerro Gordo were extremely depressing. Still, there were those who refused to be discouraged. Thomas Boland, chairman of the county supervisors, thought it strange that Cerro Gordo was abandoned the way it was, without far more development work having been done. Boland owned a general store in Keeler, and invested a great deal of money and effort trying to prove Cerro Gordo's rich silver deposits were not depleted.

In September 1889, Archie Farrington took over the Union mine, and began re-timbering the Belshaw shaft. The 25 to 30 men employed by Farrington completed the job by the spring of 1890. Farrington also had the Omega tunnel connected to the underground workings of the Union mine from the 900 foot level. During this period, shipments of low-grade ore barely paid for the "dead time" spent re-timbering the Belshaw shaft and transportation rates charged by the railroad. Financially unable to keep up, the Union mine discontinued all operations in February 1892. Shortly after, Thomas Boland picked up the Union's lease again, but aside from keeping the mine in working order, little was accomplished in the years that followed.

The San Ygnacio, Belmont, and other mines that were formerly heavy producers were also idle. There was little, if any, ore being shipped. The State Mineralogist Report for the years 1894-96 probably summed up the situation best when it stated, "A number of mines, which were running when our last report went to press, have ceased operation. Until there is a revival in the silver market, it is useless to continue a record of them."

Today in Cerro Gordo most of the buildings are gone. The few left are a reminder of the town that once stood as one of the largest silver strikes in California.

Along Highway 395
Mojave–Homestead–Sterling's–Little Lake
Sam Lewis–Gill's Oasis

MOJAVE

On one of John Charles Frémont's expeditions he visited what is now the area of Barstow. Along the route of a stream that runs underground for approximately 100 miles he met Indians which were from Mojave country, near the Colorado River. Perhaps he liked the name or he believed this tribe was native to the region of this underground river. For whatever reason, he gave this river the name Mojave. However when he recorded the name in his report he spelled it Mohahve. Although the town of Mojave was quite a distance from the river, it wound up with the same name.

The town of Mojave was started in 1876 when the Southern Pacific Railroad laid its tracks from Tehachapi to this location. During the next ten years it continued to grow. First there were the wagons hauling silver and lead bars from the Cerro Gordo Mine above Owens Lake, then the 20 mule teams from Death Valley used Mojave as a terminus as they loaded their borax on railroad cars. During this time there were stagecoaches and freight wagons going both ways. In the years of the Rand mining boom Mojave was the central point from which miners left the railroad for the diggings. They purchased many of their provisions and tools here and also shipped ore from this point. It was a busy place.

One thing has never changed in Mojave and that is the wind. Folklore has it that the bodies of the inhabitants are bent to accommodate the heavy gusts that blow. This area has always been famous for its blowing wind. In an 1884 national journal they were called "Mojave Zephyrs"

Mary Austin, famous for her stories about Inyo and Kern counties, tells of her trips through the desert by stagecoach in her book *Land of Little Rain*. While stopping at Mojave she wrote, "If one happened not to know enough to engage in advance the seat beside the driver, the trip was rather a horror. Crowded into the stuffy interior between two 'old timers', liquor salesmen, mining experts and occasional stray girls from the local bawdy houses, or one of those distressfully 'lungers' (a person who had T.B.), whom you had to hope wouldn't die on your shoulder."

Mojave has its share of local mining history. In the 1890s gold was discovered nearby. For several years there was enough activity to cause the citizens to contemplate establishing another town at the base of Soledad Mountain, four miles from Mojave. But the settlement they would have named Goldtown did not materialize because the mines played out. However, there were left in the area the names of mines such as, Queen Esther, Exposed Treasure, Eagle, Karma and Gypsy. Once the mining boom ran its course Mojave again became primarily a railroad town.

In the early 1900s Mojave boomed again. This time because of the construction work on the Los Angeles Aqueduct, a project to bring the Owens River water to the metropolitan Los Angeles. Hundreds of men came to work on the venture. Others who came to get in on the fun and prosperity augmented the workers that go along with large camps. Dance halls, honkytonks, cafes, and saloons made the town lively. When the aqueduct work was finished the town once again went back to railroading.

Mojave had a later mining boom in the 1930s; George Hanes made another discovery of gold in the area. With his father and one or two associates the mine worked for a little less than two years before they were rewarded with a significant amount of gold.

Mojave had its "firsts," as is usual in a pioneer town. A man named Moon built the first store. Mrs. Morrissey opened the first hotel and Robert Charlton was the first postmaster. Another early name was W. C. Wilson who conducted a general merchandise business for some years and at one time was county auditor. Some of Mojave's past comes to light through old business directories. McKenney's Pacific Directory for 1883-84 lists the following: "Mojave, Kern County. A post, express and telegraph office on the Southern Pacific R.R., twenty miles southeast of Tehachapi Summit. Population 50." A few years later R. L. Polk and Company's *California State Gazetteer* gave further information about this desert town: "Mojave, located in Kern County at the junction of the Southern Pacific R.R. and the A & P, 382 miles southeast of San Francisco. The village contains a public school, several churches and 150 inhabitants."

Mojave was growing. In 1905 Suits-Shuman Company's *California Gazetteer and Business Directory* announced: "Mojave, Kern County, population 230. 382 miles from San Francisco. Southern Pacific fares $11.85. Has telegraph, express money order and post office. Bank at Tehachapi 20 miles." Some of Mojave's later growth stemmed from military activities in the surrounding areas. The Air Force installation at Edwards, formerly known as Muroc, has caused the town and adjoining communities of Rosamond and Lancaster to teem with business. A Naval air base at the outskirts of Mojave during World War II provided an added reason for Mojave's expansion. Today the base has been reactivated on a major scale. In the last few years airplane corporations have built plants at Palmdale, only 33 miles away. Mojave has naturally benefited from these activities.

When all is said and done, Mojave's railroad has sustained her as a permanent town through the last 124 years. With her unique and romantic Indian name this desert town has become widely known throughout the country.

HOMESTEAD— DICK LEWIS

Dick Lewis was fourteen in 1936 when he came to the Indian Wells Valley to live in Brown with Earl and Tiny Standard. He worked at everything from cowboying for Jack Powers and his son Don in the hay fields on the nearby Callaway Ranch to digging assessment holes for placer mining claims so people could file on their 160 acres of land. Dick received $10 for each hole he dug, which was a lot of money to a fourteen-year old boy. The holes had to be exactly four feet wide and ten feet long. The first four feet had to be four feet deep, then it had to graduate to eight feet and the last two feet dug to ten feet deep. It was hard work but he was a big boy and hard work didn't bother him, and the money was good.

Dick told about digging for water for Earl Standard in Grapevine Canyon. After digging about three feet he ran into some bones and later found a skull. Checking the bones he found there was an arrowhead that had broken off and was still imbedded in the right shoulder. He later found several other skeletons and decided they were all Indian burials. He later reburied the bones. This area finally became the Mount Owen cemetery.

When Earl Standard passed away several years later he wanted to be buried in Randsburg. At the time of his death the Randsburg cemetery had closed so it looked like Earl was going to have to be buried in Mojave. Earl's brother, Gordon, went to see a Mr. Turner. (I'm not sure what Mr. Turner's job was but he was in some way connected to the county.) Gordon said to Turner, "Tiny Standard has 160 acres in Grapevine Canyon. Wasn't there an Indian graveyard up there or something?" Turner looked puzzled and then said, "Yes Gordon, there is one up there." Gordon was thinking of the bones Dick had dug up in 1950. Mr. Turner said, "If you can establish that there are at least three graves I think we can work out something, if Tiny is willing to set aside a small parcel of land."

Tiny found a spot and they started to dig and found at least three Indian graves. About six inches below the surface they hit solid rock.

Going to Randsburg they brought back a powder monkey and drilled and blasted a hole four feet deep. That was where Earl was buried. In fact it is the Mount Owen Cemetery today. Dick said it is a beautiful spot and Earl's daughter is resting there also.

In 2001 Dick had been in the Indian Wells Valley for sixty-five years. The walls of his Homestead Restaurant on Highway 395 dining room are covered with several hundred early historical items. One display is a mailbag with the name Magnolia, which was the early name for Inyokern. He also displays a strong box that weighs 75 pounds that was found buried behind the present Bank of America building in Ridgecrest. The lock had been blown off with a .44 or similar type firearm. Besides the early day atmosphere, Dick serves some of the best steaks and seafood around. He has certainly carved his niche in history.

THE STERLING FAMILY

In 1910, Loren and Minnie Sterling came to the Indian Wells Valley. Loren went to work on the Los Angeles Aqueduct driving a team of mules, hauling construction material for the aqueduct. The Sterlings raised a family of six children. There were five boys, Delbert, Lowell,

Chuck Sterling - "His eyes have seen it all!"

Andy, Chuck and Ted, and a daughter, Mirth. After the aqueduct was finished, Loren was a guard at the Nine Mile Station.

The Sterlings built a store, café, garage and service station along Highway 395 on the southwest corner where the Kennedy Meadows road leaves the highway going up Nine-Mile Canyon. At that time this little spot was called Linnie. The Linnie railroad siding was where supplies were unloaded for Nine-Mile Canyon.

Loren passed away in 1944 and Minnie in 1949. At this time they had twelve grandchildren and 24 great-grandchildren. Sterling Road south of the Kennedy Meadows Road was named for Loren. There was an interesting fact about one of their children, Ted. Ted went to Brown School and was taught by Tiny Standard. Later two of his children were also taught by Tiny. His children were in the last class to attend the Brown School in 1950, after which the school was closed. Ted was married to Eva Honojosa. Another son, Chuck, worked for the aqueduct and lived in Short Canyon until his death.

Camp Linnie in 1938. Ninnie and Loren Sterling with their son Chuck.
Courtesy Tom Chapman and the High Desert Historical Society.

LITTLE LAKE

Bill Bramlette Sr. was the proprietor of the town, lake, post office, store, garage and other businesses in Little Lake at the south end of Owens Valley (called Rose Valley) on Highway 395 approximately ten miles north of the Kennedy Meadow turn off. Earlier, Little Lake had been a stage station on the stage line that ran up and down the Owens Valley. After buying the place lock, stock and barrel from Charles D. Whitlock in 1915, he rapidly developed it into a first class resort. It became the social gathering place for the area. On Saturday nights they held dances there. First, he threw a dam across a nearby stream creating a 200-acre lake. This tended to dry up the canyon below, and gave rise to some litigation. Bill immediately started building. He kept buying land in the area until he owned 1,200 acres. In later years Bill's son, Tom, took over the businesses. He moved the café into the hotel, planted bass in the lake and it became an excellent fishing spot with a campground.

Bill Bramlette was a contemporary of Death

W.W. "Bill" Bramlette established driving record between Los Angeles & Bishop in 1921; 293 miles in six hours and thirty-eight minutes. *Courtesy Tom Chapman and the High Desert Historical Society.*

Valley Scotty. While Scotty was building his "Castle" in Death Valley, Bill was building his resort hotel at Little Lake. He liked to engage in one-upmanship with Scotty. "How much do you

Bramlette's Service Station, Cafe and Hotel looking from east across Hwy. 395. In 1971 the Cafe was moved into the Hotel and nothing remained between the Station and Hotel.
Courtesy Tom Chapman and the High Desert Historical Society.

DESERT COUNTRY

pay your plasterers? I pay mine $28 a day," he would say. Of course, Scotty had to answer, "Oh! I pay mine $30." Scotty drove a Cadillac, but Bill owned and raced Lincoln cars. He competed with Barney Oldfield at his oval track in Corona, California. He held a widely acclaimed record of driving from Los Angeles to Bishop in six hours and thirty-eight minutes on the old wash board dirt roads of that day. He called his Lincoln car the Road Runner.

Bill and his sons gloried in trophy hunting and fishing. The lobby of the hotel was the epitome of a sportsman showplace. There were trophy-size heads of elk, deer, antelope, and prize fish mounted. There were a number of rattlesnake skins of six feet or more with eighteen or twenty rattles.

The Standard Service Station at Little Lake was the domain of "Buster" Bramlette who was Bill's son. An employee, George Schuette, worked there for four or five years. His standard shift was 12 hours on and 12 hours off, seven days a week, except by special arrangement. In 1934 Hank Schuette, George's brother, worked there for three weeks and was more or less in charge of the place while Buster was off on a vacation trip. Hank once said, "I would milk three cows every morning before going on duty at 8:00 am. Who needs 12 hours sleep?" His relief man was George Fogg. He didn't seem to mind being called "Fogg over Little Lake."

Buster Bramlette married Mabelle Porter from Kennedy Meadows. His brother, Tommy, married Hazel Carr. Tommy and George Schuette

Bass fishing was good on Little Lake in 1926. On the right is Grandpa Gurdy, father of Elvira Bramlette.

hunted and fished together. Tommy was the best off-hand rifle shot in the area, shooting birds out of the air with a rifle.

After the aqueduct was finished the population of Little Lake declined dramatically, but the business continued to operate. The highway department then moved Highway 395 to the east and even though there was an off ramp, not many travelers used it. Later the hotel burned and Little Lake became only part of the Rose Valley's early history. Today it is all gone with only a concrete slab to mark what is left of this fine old resort.

SAM LEWIS

Sam Lewis and his family have been friends of the author's family since the 1920s. His youngest son, Richard and his family, live just a few miles from where my wife and I live. My dad, Marvin Powers, packed horses for Sam in the 1920s from the Lewis' High Lonesome Ranch, northwest of Little Lake, into Kennedy Meadows.

Sam was well liked by all that knew him. He was a soft-spoken man of few words and a heart-warming smile. In his later days if a person had a question concerning the early history of Rose Valley they would say, "Ask Sam Lewis, he can tell you," and this was true.

Sam was born on July 31, 1893 in Bailsburg, Illinois to Charles and Estella Lewis. He had a sister, Isabelle and a brother Charles Jr. When Sam was two years old his folks moved to Carlsbad, New Mexico. As Sam grew to manhood he first went to Arizona and then in 1912 took the train to Los Angeles to live with his aunt, Eva T. Harris. There he worked for two years at the Harris Oil Company.

By July 1914 Sam was feeling the need for the wide-open spaces and left Los Angeles. He obtained a map and decided to make his destination the spot on the map called Little Lake. Riding his horse and leading a packhorse loaded with all his worldly possessions he headed north. His last night on the trail he stayed at Coyote Holes (Freeman Junction). To his great surprise he saw a car coming down the trail. He couldn't believe his eyes, out here where stage lines and horses was the mode of transportation, here was a car! After the shock had worn off he asked the driver if they had come from Little Lake. The driver said, "Yes. Does this lead to Los Angeles?" and drove off.

Above: Sam N. Lewis Sr., guide, philospher, and friend to all who knew him. He had the best pack horses in the business. Picture taken in 1940. *Courtesy Tom Chapman and the High Desert Historical Society.*

Right: Sam Lewis in front of his first home on the High Lonesome Ranch.

Below: Lewis Homestead, "Home Sweet Home."

On August 4th Sam arrived in Little Lake. At this time the only buildings were a hotel and a saloon. He needed a job and found work from Riley Hart breaking horses. Sam stayed at Little Lake until the fall of 1914 breaking 30 head of horses before leaving. He left Little Lake and moved five miles north to Rose Springs Valley. After working for a while drilling water wells for the Los Angeles Aqueduct he soon had his fill of working underground and went back to his horses and the wide-open spaces. He next moved a few miles south to work for J.D. Callaway who ran horses and cattle. The Callaway Ranch was sold to the Navy and is now part of the Naval Weapons Center, China Lake. While Sam was working for Bill Bramlette at Little Lake he homesteaded 160 acres at what was known as Portuguese Bench, an area eight miles north of Little Lake and two miles west of Highway 395. He called his place the High Lonesome Ranch. During the week Sam worked at Little Lake and on the weekend he would go to his homestead. In 1918 Sam married Olive Truax whose folks had a homestead south of Inyokern. At first Sam and Olive lived in a tent, but soon built a home, mostly of railroad ties. Sam planned to have a pack station and made several trips riding to Los Angeles, driving horses back. On one trip he returned with 20 head and said he had most of them broke to lead by the time he arrived home. These trips took at least five days one way. During World War I Sam served in the U.S. Navy. After he returned home he was able to start his pack station and his cattle business, but drought and the national depression put him out of the cattle business in the 1920s. He was

DESERT COUNTRY

Right: Sam N. Lewis and Family in 1937. Sam and his family at the homestead house on the High Lonesome Ranch. Left to right in back are: Sam Jr., Sam Sr., Olive, Lucille, Estella and Hellen. Two little ones in front are Barbara and Richard.

Below: Sam's last home on the High Lonesome Ranch.

Sam Lewis' pack station at Dutch Flats between the South Fork of the Kern River and Deer Mountain. *Courtesy Tom Chapman and the High Desert Historical Society.*

able to hold on to his packing business and with determination and hard work he built this business up. At times he had as many as fifty people scattered at his different camps, which were all over the high country. He had camps all through the Kern Plateau. He took people on horseback all the way north to Mt. Whitney and south to the Domeland on the Kern River. The fishing and hunting in those early days in this area was outstanding. The limit for trout was fifty and there was a two-buck limit for deer, which the hunters nearly always filled. Olive accompanied Sam on many trips and was "chief cook and bottle washer."

Sam and Olive raised six children. When they were small, some of them went into the moun-tains tucked into pack boxes on gentle horses that were led. The children from the oldest down, were Lucille, Estella, Sam Jr., Helen, Richard and Barbara.

After World War II the packing business began to decline drastically and that, along with Sam's age which was over 66 by now, made him decide to close the pack station in 1959.

Sam's wife died in the early 1960s and the

High Lonesome Ranch became lonesome once more. One of Sam's daughters introduced him to her friend's mother, Ruth Thuaxton. Sam surprised everyone by announcing on his Christmas cards that they were married on December 15, 1968. In June 1971 Ruth and Sam moved to Ruth's home in LaVerne, California. Many people in Kern and Inyo Counties really missed Sam. Both have since passed away. Sam is still remembered for who he was and the people he touched. A true pioneer.

Gill's Oasis

Gill's Oasis is located eight miles north of Little Lake on Highway 395 and has a long and interesting history. Marjorie L. Gill, wife of Ray Gill, wrote the following in 1940 for the dedication of the Caltrans Rest Area at Gill's Oasis:

A pioneer is defined as "an early settler, one who opens a way, to lead the way into many fields." In my mind, also, it is one who has dreams and visions of greater things. In every sense of the word, my husband, Ray Melon Gill, was a true pioneer. He had a deep love for the desert and like a sculptor, who gazes at a block of marble or granite, could see the potential beauty contained therein. He knew it would require hard work and determination, but of this he was not afraid. He had many disappointments and disasters, but after each experience, he would laugh and say, "Well, there went my first million, now I'll start on my next million." His determination was unquenchable and his attitude was "When the going gets tough, the tough get going." He lived neither in the past nor in the future, but let each day's work absorb his entire energies. As a result of his ingenuity and resourcefulness, he lived to see many of his dreams come true.

Ray was born March 13, 1906, in Warren, Pennsylvania. During his adolescent years his family made several moves, including Panama. As a young man he lived in Long Beach, California, where the Department of Water and Power employed him, as an electrician. At age 19 he received a promotion, and was assigned to Haiwee, a sub-station out of Little Lake to work on the installation of power and electrical gates for the Los Angeles Aqueduct being installed along the Sierra Nevada Mountains in the Mojave Desert. This was the last electrical panel wall he worked on. It was there he fell in love with the desert, and had a desire to develop his land and make it a desert oasis.

He met me, Marjorie Chance Lewis, in 1939. This association developed into love, and we were married. With three children, Edna Lee, George, and Marjorie Ann, we became a loving family unit. I also loved the desert and together we pioneered and built our dreams into a beautiful desert oasis.

In about 1928 he completed his homestead building and a year later he added an addition to the first building. He used railroad ties put together with lake mud, and this turned out to be the strongest part of the structure. Eventually this homestead did in reality become an oasis in the desert, and was known as "Gill's Oasis." This area was originally named Coso Junction because eleven miles off the highway, Coso Hot Springs were located.

He had a great love for trees, and planted many, about 125 in all. It was necessary to haul water in barrels to nourish their growth, and also to use for domestic purposes. In the early 1930s he began drilling his first well. It took over fifteen years to accomplish this, using hand tools. It was about 150 feet deep. He then constructed another railroad tie building to enclose his well.

He then built a service station, and his first pumps used Shell products, and were hand pumped. Radiator water came from barrels. Included in the station was a lunch counter. Next to the station he built rest rooms out of pumice blocks. Later Union Oil improved the pumps, so the station developed into a good business venture. An interest in mining led Ray to locate workable pumice claims in the area.

With the help of his father in 1940 he built a café. Our son, George, served customers standing on a soda pop box at age eight. The girls, Edna Lee and Marjorie Ann helped in the café and Mother in the service station. Gill's Oasis became a restful haven for travelers. Eating tables and benches were scattered among the shady trees. Also a trailer park became part of this charming oasis. The turtles and chipmunks were an entertaining attraction to everyone, young and old.

All this activity made it necessary to drill a second well. It is this second, larger well, that Caltrans now uses to obtain water for the new Gill's Oasis—Coso Junction rest area. Ray built a post office building from pumice mixed with sand, which made a good strong building. He served as postmaster and I as acting postmaster through the years.

He provided an emergency airport on the west-side of the highway, which was used by commercial flyers, gliders, private planes, and

The Highway Post Office Bus made its second stop in Rose Valley at the Coso Junction Post Office where Raymond Gill was Postmaster, and many people were out to welcome this first. Pictured from left to right, back row, John C. Livingston, General Superintendent; Lyle V. Lane, Service Supervisor; Raymong Gill, Coso Junction Postmaster; Osborne A. Pearson, Assistant Postmaster General; Warren McIntyre, Assistant Postmaster of Los Angeles. Front row left to right, Marji Gill 4 years; George Gill 8 years; Mrs. Marjorie Gill and Edna Lee Gill 14 years. *Courtesy Tom Chapman and the High Desert Historical Society.*

Edison helicopters. In 1969 forty-seven acres of Gill's Oasis was purchased by the State and developed into a modern rest area.

Ray was called by two nicknames. Some called him "Happy" because of his disposition, and sense of humor. Other desert friends called him "Windy" because of his knowledge of the desert, which brought forth many fascinating stories. The life of Ray Gill was an abundant one. Someone has said, "The abundant life does not simply consist of living longer or more years. It is a matter of height and attainment, rather than the mere length of life itself."

Ray and his family started developing the remaining property west of the highway, drilled another well and moved in. Ray lived a year and a half after he retired.

1872 EARTHQUAKE

The great earthquake of March 26, 1872, stands alone in its awe-inspiring magnitude as an item of Inyo County history. This earthquake was considered the most severe ever felt in California. The shake came at approximately 2:30 in the morning. The shock was reported by Camp Independence observers to have lasted three minutes. Its worst effects occurred in the first minute. The record noted 200 shocks or tremors from the hour of the big shake up to 5:00 the following afternoon. The courthouse at Independence was built of fired brick, and collapsed from the tremors. Rebuilding began promptly. The national government set aside $30,000 for reconstructing Camp Independence; most of it was used in putting up substantial frame buildings. Many frame buildings were racked, and all plastering was shattered.

A twelve-mile crack opened in Lone Pine where twenty-four persons were killed and about the same number escaped with significant injuries. (Only three people were killed in other parts of the valley.) The population of Lone Pine at this time was 200 to 300 persons. Ninety percent of Lone Pine's buildings had been constructed of adobe brick and mud mortar by Mexicans, well trained in adobe and stone construction. Nevertheless, these houses crumbled and went to earth like piles of sand, burying the occupants in the ruins. The property loss was never accurately determined, but was estimated at from $150,000 to $200,000, a considerable figure for this time.

At George's Creek water burst from the ground up into a floorless cabin in such volume it flooded out the occupants. Not far off a horse's hoof protruded from the ground, where a crack had opened and then closed. At Fish Springs a crack swallowed an ox, only his tail being left out in the air. Some cattle died from no apparent cause. Perhaps it was fear.

At Bishop, a stone chimney fell across a bed, which two young ladies would have been occupying had they not been away at a dance at the time. In another incident, Eva Lee Shepherd, who was nine years old when the earthquake struck, was spending the night with a little friend who lived in an adobe near her home on Shepherd Creek. She had slipped out unknown to her parents who thought she was asleep in the front room of their ranch house. The little girls were sleeping in a double bed with a high headboard so, although the adobe collapsed and the bed was covered with debris, the high headboard kept the roof from falling upon them. At the first jolt they pulled the covers over their heads and were dug out gasping for breath but unharmed. Carried out into the frosty night, they saw the moon swinging in a wide arc through the sky waving to and fro. "But," said Eva, "the moon was standing still and we were moving back and forth with the ground." Eva Lee wasn't even punished for running away. Her parents spent several anguished hours thinking she was buried in the ruins of their front room, the only adobe room in the house.

Dust hung over the Sierra for days after the earthquake. The rolling of stones and the sparks struck were vividly described by witnesses and people told of seeing streams of fire coming down the mountainside. From Lone Pine to Big Pine the Owens Valley landscape still bears the scars of the 1872 earthquake. In places the vertical displacement reached twenty-three feet and the horizontal movement was almost as great. One conspicuous fault scarp may be seen about a mile west of Lone Pine, an eastward-facing cliff twenty-three feet high. On the road between Independence and Mazourka Canyon there is a scarp three miles from town where the ground on the east side of the fissure fell fifteen feet while that on the west side was carried eighteen feet to the south.

Fifteen coffins, each properly inscribed and numbered containing sixteen bodies were deposited in one grave at the top of the earthquake fault just north of Lone Pine. The Rev. Mr. Orne administered the Protestant rites, and afterwards the Catholic service was read in Spanish. There is a large monument to mark the grave. Other bodies were buried singly or taken elsewhere by relatives.

On a lighter note, this earthquake formed Diaz Lake in Lone Pine. Today it is a park, lake and campground for visitors to the Owens Valley. Stocked with fish, it is a popular place to visit. As you camp in its serene atmosphere it is hard to believe that this lake and park was formed just a few years ago during this cataclysmic event.

Searles Valley—Trona

A miner leading his burro over the spongy surface of a dry lake in the Mojave Desert picked up some shimmering crystals and put them in his pack. The year was 1862 and the miner was John Wemple Searles. Searles was on his way to the Panamint Range along with hundreds of other roving prospectors in search of silver and gold in Death Valley. Searles, like most of his fellow searchers, had plenty of hardships but no great amount of gold or silver.

Ten years later in 1872, as Searles traveled through Teel's Marsh along the California-Nevada border he found Francis M. Smith reclaiming borax from the crystals he found on the floor of the marsh. An engineer, who camped with them, told Searles that his samples from Searles Lake contained borax. He realized the dry lake he crossed on the Mojave back in 1862 was worth more than all the gold that had eluded him.

John Searles and his brother, Dennis, filed on the northern end of Searles Lake in 1873. They built a plant on the northwest shore near where the town of Trona stands today. The two Searles brothers, J. D. Creigh and Edwin Schillings formed the San Bernardino Borax Mining Company. Searles had no way of knowing he had actually discovered the richest deposit of diversified chemicals in history. During the time they worked the lake they produced one million pounds of Borax estimated to be worth $200,000.

If the brothers thought they would have the dry lake to themselves, they were mistaken. Prospectors turned by the score from gold hunting to look for borax. Searles filed for much of the surface of his lake as a slime deposit. Now he learned that the land or marsh must be taken up as a placer claim limited to 20 acres. Together with his associates he was able to obtain 160 acres. This still left a vast amount of unclaimed surface for the lake was ten miles long and four miles wide.

Searles found that his competitors not only didn't bother him but actually helped. They realized that borax production would take capital and organization, things few of them had. They left even more rapidly than they arrived. Several had collected sizable dumps of crystals, which they either abandoned or sold to the Searles group at the latter's price. These supplies left by their competitors were part of the reason they were able to make such a big showing.

The closest pure water that anyone knew of at that time was twenty miles away in Indian Wells Valley. However, as John Searles searched the surrounding area he found sweet water just seven miles from his plant.

Searles found that 13 tons of crystals made one ton of borax. It was a simple operation to work the borax beds. The crystals would be raked into windrows and then hauled in carts two miles to the plant. Three or four years after an area was worked it would reproduce borax. At the plant the crystals were boiled in huge vats. Men were sent out on wagons to collect brush for the plant's boilers.

After the Searles Lake crystals were converted into marketable borax, transporting the refined product proved to be a major obstacle. The closest railroad was the Southern Pacific in Bakersfield. This system of transportation was not considered. Searles set up a mule drawn freight line all the way to San Pedro and later to Mojave after the Southern Pacific Railroad was built to this point.

To haul the borax to market two roads were used. In the winter months, when the desert

John Searles
Courtesy Searles Valley Historical Society

sands would pack down enough to supply firm footing, the wagons followed the route now spanned by the Trona Railroad. On the trip north from Mojave the wagons traveled to the present Cantil, then northeast up Garlock Canyon emerging near Searles Station. In summer time the sand on this route was too soft so teams went north from Cantil up Red Rock Canyon to the mouth of Walker Pass, then east to Searles Station. Searles Station had reliable wells and there they grew hay and built corrals.

The plant continued to produce 100 tons of refined borax a month until 1897. In this year John Searles died. After his death the operation was sold to Francis Marion Smith known as "Borax" Smith for $200,000 and became part of the Pacific Borax Company. Dennis Searles was killed in an automobile accident in 1890.

The operation at Searles Lake might have been abandoned if it had not been for a Baltic nobleman, Baron Alfred de Ropp. De Ropp became the president of the California Trona Company after his predecessors were unsuccessful in making soda and potash from Searles Lake brine. He

was confident that by using better methods, he would be able to turn failure into success and staked his reputation as an engineer on it. He was successful!

Baron de Ropp called in Charles P. Grimwood to make tests. Grimwood shipped an entire tank car full of brine to Grimwood's laboratory in New York. After several months of testing the brine, he discovered a process by which potash and other chemicals could be recovered at a low enough cost per unit to make it practical. Grimwood estimated it would cost one million dollars to build the first unit plus a second refinery.

Some of the California Trona Company directors talked of abandoning the project. Baron de Ropp put his weight of experience behind Grimwood and staked his reputation for the decision. He also would go after the needed capital. He felt that 100 million dollars in borax and potash in the Searles Lake brine was too great a prize to ignore, even though there were costly initial failures. Baron de Ropp obtained the needed capital. In 1913 the Searles Lake enterprise became the American Trona Corporation. The plant was completed in 1916.

The new process was based on pumping raw brine from the lower reaches of the salt beds and extracting the minerals; this novel approach was making the enterprise successful. With the new process the supply of fresh water Searles found seven miles away was no longer adequate. Water had to be piped over the mountains from Indian Wells Valley.

During World War I, de Ropp supervised the building of the town, the erection of a store, Trona Mercantile Company, and the planning of the plant which he alone had the vision would some day be a future giant.

De Ropp put in long hours in legal battles with groups who sought to jump the Searles Lake claims. He reigned as president of the American Trona Company until 1920. He was 62 years old and had spent the greater part of 40 years in mining camps and the last ten on the desert. At the time of his death in 1941 he lived in Coronado. Mrs. De Ropp survived him by eleven years. While he was in Coronado de Ropp became an American citizen.

In earlier years Searles Valley was covered by water supplied largely from the Owens River. Old shorelines still show several lake levels.

DESERT COUNTRY

Right: Handling Bulk Potash 1919.
Courtesy Searles Valley Historical Society

Below: Building the Trona Railroad

Bottom: The Trona Railroad

Heavy runoffs leached large quantities of minerals from the granites, volcanic debris and other rocks on the eastern flanks of the Sierra and other mountains draining into the Owens River. These minerals were carried into a chain of large lakes: Mono, Owens, China, Searles, Panamint, and Manly Lake in the present day Death Valley.

Searles Lake was the terminus of Owens River and the minerals carried by the river for thousands of years accumulated in the lake waters. Some of this water permeated downward through the mud covering the lake bottom. At around 300 feet below the present surface, this water encountered very permeable, soluble mineral beds. The saline minerals were subjected to leaching. The effect of this leaching was that the minerals in the saline beds 250 to 350 feet below the surface are still present today. Operations extracted much more than borax and potash from the chemically rich brine. Amazingly,

Unusually heavy rain during the winter of 1940–41 created this unusual sight of Searles (normally) dry lake.

formed below the surface in the layers of salt and brine are 98 of the 105 known naturally occurring chemical elements.

The principal products produced in this sediment includes muriate of potash, sulfate of potash, potassium chloride refined, soda ash, salt cake, desiccated sodium sulfate, borax, pyrobar (dehydrated borax), boric acid, bromine and lithium concentrates. From year to year the corporation's chemists have found additional products which could be produced if a commercial market developed.

In the early 1900s several companies tried to develop extraction methods based on treating the lake brines, but none were successful until American Trona Company developed a steam evaporation process in 1915, which recovered potash and borax. This company later became American Potash and Chemical Corporation, which was purchased by Kerr-McGee in 1967. Development of a second successful operation, Westend Chemical Company was begun in 1920. This was later sold, first to Stauffer Chemical in 1954, and then to Kerr-McGee in 1974.

In 1990 North American Chemical Company acquired all of Kerr-McGee's mining and manufacturing facilities in Searles Valley. In March of 1998, IMC Global acquired North American's holdings. Today IMC Chemicals, Inc. (IMCC)

operates three chemical manufacturing plants. The plants are Trona, Argus and Westend.

Vegetables, fruit, sugar, glass, nearly all paper products, charcoal, laundry detergent and many more household necessities are grown or produced using soda ash, sodium sulfate and boron products manufactured by IMC Chemicals Company of Trona. Almost two million tons of products are shipped from Searles Valley annually, enough to fill twenty-eight thousand trucks and eighteen thousand rail cars.

To provide for shipment of the output, an up-to-date equipped standard gauge railroad was built from the Trona plant to Searles station, thirty-two miles away, to the Southern Pacific railroad line. The Trona Railway brings in about one million tons of coal each year for steam and electric power. The Argus Utilities Plant supplies all the steam and electric power needs for the Argus and Trona plants. All steam is fed to turbine-generators. Even after supplying the electric power used by these two plants there is enough power left for sale to Southern California Edison to supply a town of more than 12,000 people. The Westend Plant generates its own steam and electric power, using a gas-turbine generator fired by natural gas.

IMCC facilities, representing a $400 million investment, were built between 1916 and 1978.

Austin Hall built in 1914, housed workers, had a dining room, mercantile store, open air movie theater, pool hall, offices, post office, drug store with soda fountain, market, Western Union, library and barber shop. It was demolished in 1965 to make way for a parking lot.

Aerial View of Trona 1936
Courtesy Searles Valley Historical Society.

Constant modernization has brought innovative technology to the site. Over 400 wells tap into the mineral-rich underground lakebed to a depth of over 300 feet. The extracted brine travels to one of three plants through 110 miles of pipeline. The plants then refine products through heating and cooling of the brine and through chemical reactions.

At the present time (2001) IMCC employs 714 persons plus hundreds of contractors and service providers, which support 784 additional jobs in the area. The company controls 70.6 square miles of Searles Lake. They use a total of 663 wells to pump the brine from three different levels of the lake. After the chemicals have been removed water is pumped back out to the lake and injected back into two underground levels or spread out onto the surface. This process requires 130 miles of pipeline, 189 miles of overhead electric power line and 135 miles of buried electrical cable. They pay $42.4 million annually in payroll and $3.9 million in property and sales taxes to the local economy; $3.5 million in royalties are paid to the Bureau of Land Management, with the Trona School District as the major recipient.

IMC Chemicals takes very seriously its role as a leading community benefactor. They give $30,000 each year to area schools, charities, organizations and special projects.

Discouraging waterfowl from landing on waters leaving the plant is an important part of their environmental program. The company employs biologists, environmental consultants, independent engineers and response specialists to help resolve conditions that may impact wildlife. Covering or piping water keeps wildlife from contacting brine waters, and construction of a waterfowl resting spot attracts birds to a safe area away from brine.

Trona, named for a mineral found in the area, is now and always has been a company town. Austin Hall, a city within a city, was built in 1914 and covered one square-city block. Within its walls was almost everything the populace needed for their daily lives. One trip to Austin Hall and you could visit the market, library, drug-store with soda fountain, post office, barber shop, dining room, pool hall, offices and outdoor movie theater in the center square. Trona had an ice plant at this same time, which furnished blocks of ice which were stored in a cold storage building. In this building they also kept meat for the market, and when needed, corpses were stored while waiting for the undertaker to arrive from Barstow or Mojave.

The population of Trona has fluctuated from a high of around 5,000 to today's low of 1,967. Even today, with its churches, lodges, clubs, and museums, you get the feeling of an old fashioned, close knit community — a place where people work together, take care of one another and call it home.

Index

Rough and Ready Mining Company: 125
Rush Creek: 83
Russell, Charlie (artist): 55

Sacramento: 61
Safeway (Mojave): 79
Sage Canyon: 64, 66, 88, 89
Sage Flat: 62
St. Elmo Hotel: 36
St. Louis World's Fair: 26
Saline: 59
Saline Valley: 140
Salt Lake City: 11, 21
San Bernadino: 29, 30, 33, 100
San Bernardino Borax Mining Company: 153
San Bernardino County: 85
San Diego: 67
San Felipo: 141
San Fernando: 76, 78, 121
San Fernando Mountains: 69, 70
San Fernando reservoir: 70
San Fernando Valley: 70, 84
San Francisco: 16, 21, 22, 26, 47, 61, 136, 137, 144
San Francisquito Canyon: 70
San Jose: 125
San Lucas Mine: 137
San Pedro: 141, 153
San Pedro harbor: 140
San Ygnacio: 142
Sand Canyon: 76, 78, 79, 80, 90, 93, 98, 104
Sand Canyon Creek: 81
Sanford, Dr. A.A.: 134
Santa Barbara: 125
Santa Fe line: 43
Santa Fe Mine: 47
Santa Maria: 141
Santa Monica: 94
Schillings, Edwin: 153
Schmidt, William H. "Burro": 129, 131
Schuette, Emily: 93, 96
Schuette, George: 93, 94, 96, 98, 147
Schuette, Hank: 147
Schuette, Henry F.W.: 96, 97, 98, 99; family photo of, 93
Schuette, Henry S. Hank: 93, 94, 98, 101
Schuette, Johanna Marie: 93
Schuette, Mildred: 99
Schuette, Tommy: 147
Scodie Mountains: 49, 56, 90
Searles, Dennis: 153, 154
Searles, John Wemple: 153; photo of, 154
Searles Lake: 34, 44, 121, 153, 154, 155, 157
Searles Lake Valley: 13, 19

Searles Mill: 125
Searles Station: 72, 154, 156
Searles Valley: 117, 156
Second Calvary California Volunteers: 136
Seger, Mrs. Tonie Evelyn Ann: 131
Selby: 47
Sellers, Constable: 133
Sequoia National Forest: 104
Seybert, Phil: 53
Shangri La Ranch: 118
Shanks, David: 106
Shell Service Station: 107; photo of, 110
Shelton, Dave & Sally: 78, 80
Shepherd Canyon: 128
Shepherd Creek: 152
Shepherd, Eva Lee: 152
Shepherd Pass: 128
Short Canyon: 79, 105, 145
Shoshonean Indians: 85, 116, 125
Sidewinder, The (jet): 123, 124
Sidewinder, The (train): 72
Siding: 91
Siebenthal, Eugene: 93, 98, 99
Siebenthal Corner: 93
Sierra Forest Reserve: 60
Sierra Gordo: 134
Sierra Nevada: 13, 60, 61, 62, 68, 70, 72, 85, 150
Sills, Ken: 47
Silva, Manuel: 60
Silver Grance Mine: 47
Silver King Mine: 47
Silver Spout Mill: 137
Simpson, Joe Hooch: 132, 133
Sinaloa (Mexico): 137
Singleton, John : 29, 40
Skidoo: 92
Skidoo News (newspaper): 132
Skillings, E.M.: 39
Slate Mountain Range: 44, 134
Small, John: 136
Smith, Aut: 33
Smith, Francis Marion: 21, 27, 153, 154
Smith, Oliver: 90
Smith Ranch: 88, 130
Smith, Stanley: 103
Smith, Thomas S.: 61
Smith, Tommy: 88
Soda Hill camp: 75
Soledad Mountain: 143
South Fork: 49, 50, 51, 61, 65, 88, 89, 90, 96, 130
South Fork Indian: 47
South Fork ranch: 49
South Fork River: 96
South Fork School District: 103
South Fork Valley: 49, 56, 61
Southern California Edison: 156
Southern Pacific Railroad: 72, 75, 77, 130, 143, 144, 153, 156

Spacewinder, The (outer space missile): 123
Spanish Mines: 125
Spratt, Jack: 135
Spratt, Tom: 104, 105
Standard, Earl: 100, 144
Standard, Ethel Mary Tiny: 80, 91, 100, 101, 144, 145
Standard Service Station: 147
State Range Mining District: 125
Statler, John S.: 133
Stauffer Chemical: 156
Steam Beer Saloon: 38
Sterling, Andy: 145
Sterling, Chuck: 145
Sterling, Delbert: 145
Sterling, Loren: 98, 145
Sterling, Lowell: 145
Sterling, Minnie: 145
Sterling, Mirth: 145
Sterling Road: 145
Sterling, Ted: 145
Stevens, Col. Sherman: 137
Stewart, Sen. William M.: 135, 136
Stovepipe Wells: 132
Stud Horse Canyon: 46, 47
Subwinder, The (undersea missile): 123
Summers, Charles: 61, 62
Summit Meadow: 62
Superstition Mountains: 56
Susanville: 104
Sutter's Fort: 137
Sycamore Canyon: 94

Tappan, Sylvester: 133
Tarr, Miss: 98
Taylor, Charley: 45
Teel's Marsh: 153
Tehachapi: 40, 42, 67. 77, 85, 143
Tehachapi Mountains: 56, 77, 144
Tejon: 17
Telescope Peak: 12, 132
Thisse, Judge: 132
Thompson, Frannie: 106
Thompson, Marybell: 105, 106
Thompson, One-Eye: 132
Thompson, Robert Hoskins: 106
Thompson, Robert Hurd: 106
Thompson, Robert Richardson: 105, 106
Thuaxton, Ruth: 150
Tinemaha Dam: 59
Tomahawk cruise missile: 123
Toombs, Thomas: 99, 106, 118
Tournament of Roses Parade: 26
"The Train That Was—The Slowest" (article): 72
Trona: 13, 48, 80, 94, 95, 98, 117, 120, 133, 153, 156, 158
Trona High School: 110

ABOUT THE AUTHOR

Bob Powers was born in "Old Kernville" and raised in the beautiful Kern River Valley in the eastern Sierras of California. His interest in the Valley and its people has been nurtured by the fact that his great-grandparents settled on the South Fork of the Kern River in 1862.

Bob has chronicled the history of the Kern River Valley and other communities in Kern, Tulare and Inyo Counties for the past thirty-five years.

Through Bob's nine books you can experience the fascinating history of the many places and people Bob writes about.

Other titles by Bob Powers

South Fork Country
North Fork Country
Hot Springs Country
Kern River Country
Indian Country
Cowboy Country
This Old House
High Country Communities

Make inquiries to:
Bob Powers
PO Box 204
Kernville, CA 93238
Phone (760-) 376-2329

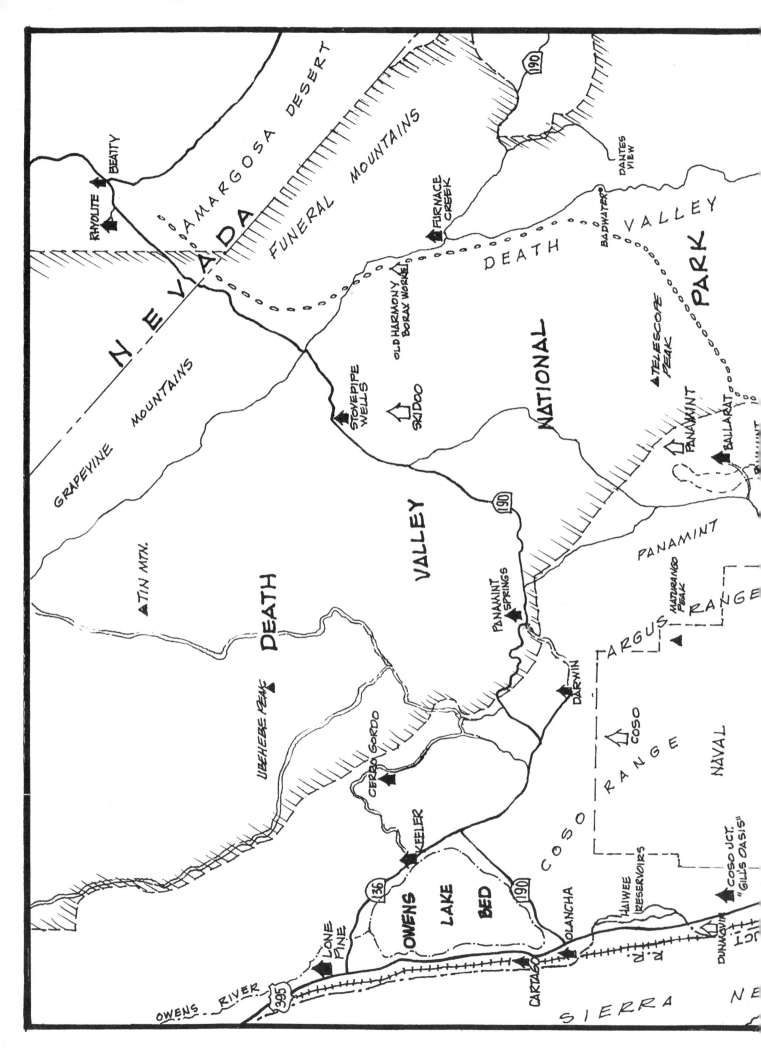